I'm That Girl

I'm That Girl

By Pearl Barrett & Serene Allison

I'm That Girl

©2021 by Pearl Barrett & Serene Allison

Published by Welby Street Press

Cover Design: Welby Street Press

Interior Layout Formatting: PerfecType, Nashville, TN

ISBN: 978-1-7923-7253-7

Unless otherwise noted, all scriptures are from the New King James Version. While we would have loved to put in more verses surrounding the scriptures chosen for context, there was limited space to do so. We recommend searching the scriptures for yourself and reading them in their full context.

To our Mom and Dad . . . for being the real deal, for being long lovers, for emulating joy grabbing, for loving the Word.

TABLE OF CONTENTS

Appetizers | 1

Main Course | 41

Sides | 227

Desserts | 269

Appetizers

Start Nibbling

CHAPTER ONE

Starter (Part I)

The You . . . You Never Knew

Every word you speak holds power.

Every thought you dwell on sets unseen things into motion.

Notice that was the ol' one line for each sentence, touch of drama, first chapter opener?

We're opening like that to reel you in because you've probably heard those sorts of statements before and maybe you're a bit . . . eye roll . . . yeah, yeah . . . about them.

That was us, too. But while we had heard them . . . we hadn't really **heard** heard them. They certainly hadn't taken root. Growing up as pastor's kids, we'd sat through thousands of sermons. You'd think it would have clicked. As adults, we'd read our plenteous share of both Christian and secular self-help type books . . . we even authored a couple best-selling, health-minded ones ourselves. Sounds a tad prideful, but just setting the scene here. Still, we hadn't grasped the enormity of the two very real consequences to words and thoughts. We were still living largely clueless to their life-changing freedom versus their life-binding chains.

Jesus said in Matthew 11:15 . . . "*He who has ears to hear . . . let him hear.*" Sometimes we can hear something over and over . . . nuthin' . . . but then the soil is right, the ears finally really do hear, and that is when incredible things happen.

So, get your ears tuned in. Incredible things are about to go down!

Our Dilemma

This is not a diet and health book.

We wanted to get that out of the way because unless this is the first book you've read from us; you know us as Trim Healthy Mamas . . . health and wellness authors. We've spent the last decade helping women become their trimmest and healthiest selves. It has been an incredible joy and privilege to watch hundreds of thousands transform their health. But . . . just going to be honest here. It has at times been sad and frustrating, too.

It took us most of that decade to realize diet and health advice helps . . . but only to a point. Cheering women on for their incredible progress . . . that's the fun part! Looking on powerless to help when they sometimes revert back to past harmful choices . . . that's the tough part. But it knocked this sense into us: an eating plan (even a Biblically-based one) is not the complete picture.

> An eating *plan* (even a Biblically-based one) is not the *complete* picture.

While the track record for people adopting the Trim Healthy Mama way of eating as a lifelong approach is thankfully much higher than the abysmal 2–3 percent average of diets that actually stick, we openly admit it is not the ultimate answer.

No "way of eating" is.

And yes, you did just read that right . . . diets on the whole have a 97–98 percent long term failure rate, almost everyone who goes on them regains everything they lost and then some within 3 years. Even though THM—as we call it, affords a lot more success than that, it's still hard to watch when people fall off track. Not trying to be narcissistic here, it is surely much harder for those actually going through the reality of falling off track. There's often shame, defeat, and other negative emotions to deal with . . . on top of the physically not feeling so great part in a tired, inflamed body.

But since this is not a diet book, let's stop talking about diets and ask the broader question . . . so why then? Why do so many of us just throw in the towel . . . revert back to old harmful ways? We're not just talking eating here. Relationships, habits, thought processes and actions . . . we've all struggled in some area. Why do we do well for a while then just lose the plot?

The longer we've helped women with their health, the more we've realized there's a bigger picture that is far beyond food plans and macronutrient details. The way we think . . . the way we talk . . . the condition of our spirit . . . these are much greater influencers on our health choices and other life decisions than any diet information in a book or any ten-step plan to "reclaiming your life."

We realized our help was capped. There was something more we were supposed to bring. This "something" is what you are about to read . . . birthed from our own struggles . . . our face plants . . . our miserable return after return to harmful thinking and behavior until God's truth emerged, entered and enlightened and we've never been the same.

But as we began writing this book, doubts crept in. We sometimes (nah . . . let's be honest . . . it was often) felt pangs of guilt that it was only taking us away from the obvious successful course of writing more cookbooks for our brand. This writing process for *I'm That Girl* has been slow going and at times all-consuming and we've had multiple moments of asking ourselves if we'd be better stewards of our time abandoning this and spending our time working on what we knew our readers were accustomed to and actually asking and waiting for . . . "More recipes and diet and health advice, please . . . yearly cookbooks, if possible!".

> There's a *bigger* picture that is far beyond food plans and macronutrient *details*.

Well, it's been over 4 years since our last cookbook (our awesome niece Rashida stepped in and wrote one for us). We've just been here in the background growing this big baby of a non-cookbook for you, not sure that you wanted it but sure that you needed it. It's been a long pregnancy you might say and the doubts just kept on coming as to whether we'd lost our minds for continuing. But we kept reminding ourselves of this . . . healthy recipes offer little help when identity is broken. If you're stuck in an "I'm that girl who eats her emotions" or an "I'm that girl who just can't seem to stick with it" mindset, no number of healthy recipes can dig you out.

There's no new diet that can dig you out. There's no old diet that can dig you out. There's no Quick-n-Easy version, Sugar-free March Challenge, Detox December, or No Cheat November that can dig you out. Meal planning tips, grocery lists, meal tracker apps, weekly menus and cooking videos are all great . . . but they're not best. Best is realizing who you truly are!

It's your identity that has to change.

So, no . . . this is not a "health" book. (But as cookbook authors we can't help but divide this book into metaphoric food categories . . . just for fun.) This is not a personal development book. This is not even a "positivity" book (it's for sure not a "toxic positivity" book as it's often labelled these days) although we expect you'll become more positive by default. This is an identity book. True identity . . . not just *hmmm . . . What should I make myself into? . . .* or *who, what, and where do I want to be in five years?* No, we're about to introduce you to the you, you never knew . . . just waiting to make her entrance.

> If you're *stuck* in an "I'm that girl who eats her emotions" or an "I'm that girl who just can't seem to *stick* with it" mindset, no number of healthy recipes can dig you out.

The message within these pages is the most important one we will ever pass along because understanding your true identity will impact your health in a way no amount of diet advice ever could. Sure, we'll keep coming out with more official cookbooks, more health advice and support tools in the future as we discover more truths and pass them along. But we have this burning feeling . . . this knowing deep down in our gut, that what will truly change your life is not the physical, and as much as you may think you want and need it . . . not the practical or organizational . . . it is the eternal . . . the stuff of your spirit.

Time to Work on Yourself?

Back to the personal development thing. We're simply not going there in this book. That's a big yay because it's a tiresome troubleshoot . . . that constantly trying to fix your old nature thing. It's not time to work on yourself . . . in fact, we urge you never to start on that! Got a feeling it will be as mind blowing for you as it was for us to realize we no longer have to work on all those areas of our lives that we're forever failing in. Instead, we only have to recognize who our *true* selves are, then walk in that understanding.

You're going to walk in the new, not work on the old.

Promise we're not being snake oil saleswomen here . . . this is not a "too good to be true" fib.

And get this . . . the true you is not how you've described yourself your whole life . . . the you with the issues and the problems and the areas that you thought needed a bunch of work, work, work. In fact, most of who and what you think you are right now is one big fat lie!

What the????

Yup.

You're not even who you were this morning. Your true you is a *"new creature"* who 2 Corinthians 5:17 speaks of. She's so jolly awesome, she has such a brilliant future, and you're about to get to know her well and good.

> You're going to *walk* in the new, not *work* on the old.

So, Just How "Woo-Woo" Is This Book?

What have you gotten yourself into by cracking open these pages? This whole "I'm That Girl" thing . . . is it some sort of personality typing? Nope, that load of fun is not even addressed throughout this book. What then? Girls have categories? This is not that either. Thankfully we're not about to label you as either a "Gazelle" or a "She-Wolf" or a "Mama Bear" depending upon your body type, birthstone, or eating preferences.

Simply put, this book is about your inner and outer messaging . . . your thoughts and your words. They can either be your rescue or your destruction (we're not even being purposefully dramatic this time . . . just the facts).

I'm That Girl . . . why this title?

I'm . . . that's short for "I AM" of course. "I AM" is actually another name for God. Unashamedly, we'll be speaking a lot about Him in this book. Whether you're a church goer or not . . . religious or not . . . the ancient scriptural wisdom we'll share in these pages can profoundly and positively impact your future. God is a great Believer in declaring Who He is. He describes Himself this "I AM" way over 300 times in the Bible starting in Genesis, weaving throughout the entirety of the Bible, then appearing a final time in Revelation.

> There *can* be no "I'm That Girl" without "I'm That *God*."

As God's children, encouraged to be imitators of Him frequently throughout the scriptures, we need to start declaring who we are in Him. Our true identity will only be known when we realize the complete image of who God wants to be in us. There can be no "I'm That Girl" without "I'm That God."

"Jesus spoke to them saying, "I Am the Light of the world, whoever follows me will not walk in darkness but will have the light of life." –John 8:12

So, I'm that girl who no longer walks in darkness but walks "IN" the light of the Word.

"I Am the God of your father, Abraham . . . Do not be afraid; for I am with you and will bless you. –Genesis 26:24

So, I'm that girl who's been set free from the chains of fear and whose God is with me and longs to bless me.

While on our own journeys of discovering who we are as daughters of the King of all Kings, we filled page after page with these scriptures where God reminds us of who He is so we in turn can know who we truly are. But, hey . . . no room in this Starter chapter for all those. (We put a bunch of them at the back of the book, page 368 for your later enjoyment.)

Hmmmm . . . (said with a concerned, skeptical look)

Err . . . *"Hold on,"* you might say. All this declaring and confession stuff. This better not be one of those holy-roller/fanatical/faith for a Lamborghini, positive confession type of books. Aren't we all so over that?

Yes . . . we are, so just stay with us and take a breath Dear Susser-outerer. We promise not to be kooks nor turn you into one. We get that the whole "name it and claim it, hyper-faith doctrine" leaves a bad taste in most of our mouths. We get that God has sometimes been made out to be some sort of Santa Claus and Christianity often twisted into a bunch of "gimmeee stuff" theology.

This is not that.

Buuuuut . . . those peeps (the "believe God for gold Rolexes" ones . . . follow us here) did uncover some undeniable Biblical truths. Those truths just got twisted and misused. They turned ugly in their mouths and hands. Due to that bit of nasti-ness, many of us so-called *normal* Christian types have only wanted to run far away from any teaching that encourages us to believe for and speak things over our lives and trust that they will come to pass. Many of us have seen and experienced hard things, have stood by others through immense pain and tragedy. All that hyper-faith mumbo jumbo seems out of touch . . . almost disrespectful in light of the suffering we as humans have to endure in our earth suits.

Familiar thoughts? We've wrestled with them too.

So, yup, faith theologies have certainly gotten a bad rap over the years. And sadly . . . some of this reputation . . . yikes . . . maybe even more than some of it is deserved. Those "name it and claim it" faith doctrines from the 80's and 90's are all too vivid in our minds. Ugghh . . . sorry to even bring up flashbacks of those decades with their preachers in white suits peddling for money on TV.

Shudder.

Yet, still . . .

Underneath all the yucky . . . all the deception . . . all the extremes and the damage to God's good name . . . was there something precious that far too many of us have buried because we don't want to align ourselves with shameful shenanigans?

Finding that out is going to be important.

Back to present day . . . you've probably noticed that Christians are still at bat with one another over the whole concept of faith and belief. Theological books differ with one another over the subject. That's okay . . . *"iron sharpens iron"* as Proverbs points out. We can all learn from another viewpoint. But where the debate really rages is social media and boy, does it ever get brutal! Modern faith enthusiasts (even if they have untucked shirts, hipster beards and look nothing like the scary TV folks from the '80s) are often viewed as dangerous, extremist stretchers of the scriptures.

Some scripture stricties (say that five times) want no part of these faith doctrines. "Let's just keep our eyes on Christ and have an attitude of brokenness." they insist. The "counter-hyper-faith-doctrine" mantra of our time goes a little something like this: "We should not presume to believe God for anything miraculous in our lives aside from forgiveness of sins. We are not here to grab and conquer, but to endure whatever God puts us through with a humble and grateful heart."

In the *Broken vs Victorious* chapters, we'll go into much greater depths digging for the truth on all this but for now let's begin to cross the great divide between both sides of this "declare and believe" debate. We all have so much more in common than social media would have us believe. And what we don't have in common . . . well there are still things we can learn from each other. None of us have yet to fully grasp all the fullness of God's Word.

> We can't throw parts of the *Bible* out or bury its treasures just because people mess up and put their *own* stink on things.

Hyper-faith skeptics are right . . . there are certain Biblical truths that have been mishandled. But here's the wonderful news . . . just because they've been abused, doesn't mean they should stay buried in the Bible and not be part of our lives as great and precious promises. The Bible is full of wonderful truths that have constantly been mucked up by people. Think of the countless wars throughout history that were started in God's name when they were really all about greed or hate or tyranny. It's appalling but we can't throw parts of the Bible out or bury its treasures just because people mess up and put their own stink on things.

If we have buried vital truths, too scared or ashamed to apply them to our lives because of the way they were misused in the past . . . this doesn't mean the truths themselves were wrong. Buried treasure . . . even if stolen by pirates is still treasure. And it only gets more valuable with time.

Time to dig it up, shine it up and deal with it correctly.

Simba's Comeback

Remember the Lion King movie . . . the scene where Simba is lying there broken, defeated and has lost his hope. His father's voice booms around him . . . "YOU HAVE FORGOTTEN WHO YOU ARE AND SO HAVE FORGOTTEN ME. LOOK INSIDE YOURSELF, SIMBA. YOU ARE MORE THAN WHAT YOU HAVE BECOME . . ."

Simba was heir to Pride Rock, but he was living like an outcast.

So, allow us to get a little Mufasa on you for a sec . . . YOU HAVE FORGOTTEN WHO YOU TRULY ARE!

Not just you . . . we had too. We were thinking, speaking, and living like broken little lion cubs, like we carried no authority, like we were not daughters of royalty. But this was a case of forgetfulness because the opposite is true!

Those who oppose Christianity getting watered down to a form that depicts God as some sort of Santa Claus figure . . . like a slot that you put prayers into and out comes material possessions . . . well, they have good reason. But there's just no denying . . . our Father's very nature is to give to His children. Santa has nothing on God's giving nature. Yes, Christ came meekly and humbly as a baby in a manger but that in itself was the greatest Gift of all . . . and we are in no uncertain terms told by God to receive this Gift, not ignore it. The entire Christian story is centered around a Gift. But not just One Gift . . . gifts galore!

> The *entire* Christian story is centered around a *Gift.* But not just One Gift . . . gifts galore!

The scriptures tell us He came to give us life . . . in fact . . . *"life more abundantly."* But He also came to give us joy and healing and power. It's not some made up faith doctrine. In fact, Christ said this very thing in Luke 10:19 (KJV) *"Behold, I give unto you power . . ."*

Our Father didn't create us to wear the identity of a broken failure because He is mighty and that same might that Jesus displayed lives in us! Matthew 7:29 tells us Jesus spoke as, *". . . one having authority."* He redeemed us to think, speak and act on His victory, His overcoming power and all the riches and promises that are wrapped up in His name. This translates not just to our spirits but also to our minds and our bodies. And you bet it translates to the way we eat! It is this gift of a new identity . . . this knowledge of our rightful inheritance that transforms our eating choices . . . our relationships . . . our health . . . every aspect of our lives!

> It is this gift of a *new* *identity* . . . this knowledge of our rightful inheritance that transforms our eating choices . . . our relationships . . . our health . . . every *aspect* of our lives!

So, yes . . . to be straight up and honest with you, right from the beginning, we are going to encourage you to make bold, "I'm That Girl" statements about the kind of girl you truly are. If you're living with a case of forgetfulness about your real identity, this book is about to remind you big time. But this won't even sniff slightly of woo-woo, looney bidness! You won't be standing in front of the mirror chanting scripted fake stuff about yourself ten times. Give us a little bit of non-woo-woo cred here.

Anyway . . . this is nothing new. You've already been doing it . . . no matter what side of the theology fence you are on.

What???!!! I haven't been part of any weirdo declaration cult doctrine . . . I have never spoken anything over my life expecting it to magically happen.

Oh, but you have! Your past is chock-full of self-declarations. Your future will continue with them. What we have to do now is make sure you think and speak God's truths rather than your own . . . which are full of bunk (yours, not God's . . . His are awesome). If you're not a Bible believer, science backs this all up as we'll show in the coming science chapters. We of course think the "God" part of all of this is the hugest but He made the science and it stands on its own.

Not trying to get off on the wrong foot using this "bunk" word we just pulled on you. It is a frequently used Down Under (where we grew up) word for baloney. Don't want to make you slam this book down so early in the read because we're being a tad mean, but hey . . . we're sisters here. If we're going to get through this book together and come out the other side transformed then we'll have to keep it real, tell it like it is in the way that only in your face yet caring and loving sisters talk to each other. In no way are we pointing fingers at just you, we used to say all sorts of bunky stuff about ourselves without realizing it. Took us years to figure out how very unawesome that was for our lives. You're going to thank us for the tough love at some point down the road . . . promise.

You . . . The Expert Declarer!

So, let's establish this . . . declaring what sort of girl you are is not something you will have to try to begin. It started not long after you were born. The difference is now you are finally going to get the things you are already thinking and saying on track because baby . . . by this stage you are a full-on expert at proclaiming things over your life!

You can hear two-year olds announce things like:

I a pwincess.

I bwewtifuwl.

Ise is pweshish and I wuv evwee body.

Have you also heard?

Ise mad and I don' wike ooo!

I don' wanna share!

I jus' wike ice cweam . . . I hate begetables!!!

Yeah . . . we all started early.

As time goes on, statements like the following begin to drip expertly from our female lips . . .

I'm a stress eater.

I just can't forgive him.

Feeling down today.

My marriage is barely hanging on.

I hate my thighs.

I have a terrible relationship with food.

My anxiety is so bad right now.

Feels like God's abandoned me.

I never got over that . . . scarred me for life.

I'm addicted to sugar.

I have, Hashimotos, PCOS, and six different food sensitivities.

I just can't win!

I'm no good at meal prepping.

If it's not one thing with me, it's the other.

No matter what I do, I can't lose this weight.

I hate drinking water.

I've never been able to quit soda.

I suffer from migraines.

My metabolism is broken.

Don't mind me . . . I'm PMS-ing.

I can't resist junk food.

I keep getting sick this winter.

I just can't seem to get myself back on track.

I can't shake this cold.

She and I don't get along.

I'm coming down with something.

Perimenopause makes me cranky.

I'm not much of a salad person.

I just can't deal with you right now.

I have so many bad habits.

We always fight.

I'm not a people person.

The stress is killing me.

My body hates me.

I'm a mess.

My husband is driving me crazy.

Wait till you hit menopause . . . it's the worst.

Those statements are all so common, nobody thinks it strange to hear them. Nobody secretly thinks . . . *Oh, my goodness . . . what a kook she is to tell me she can't get through the day without 3 Dr. Peppers! She must be part of a negativity cult!*

But to hear . . . "I'm free from sugar's bondage!" Now that sounds a bit kooky right? Might want to take a couple steps back from that person. Rarely do we hear ourselves or one of our girlfriends say, "I'm that girl who's her husband's best friend." or "I'm that girl who knows there is a promise to combat every problem." Or, "I'm that girl who loves to cook healthy meals for her family."

What if you just met someone and in the course of conversation, she said . . . "I love getting up in the morning and honoring my body by making a healthy breakfast." Would your Kook Alert radar start beeping? Is she from Planet Weirdo?

Those sorts of positive declarations feel "off" simply because we're so used to hearing it the other way around. It's not strange at all to meet someone who tells us in the first ten minutes of a "get-to-know you" discourse that she is awful about eating breakfast, hates all housework and has a husband who is basically her third kid. "I have three boys . . . well two, and one husband child." We barely blink at that. In fact, we might chuckle and think . . . *Now, this girl . . . she and I have lots in common. We should do coffee!*

The confessing of failings is *beautiful,* it is even scriptural . . . but only if it points to or seeks a *rescue.*

Perhaps you're thinking . . . *but hold on a minute . . . honest people are the relatable ones . . . those who confess their failings . . . who are transparent enough to not pretend their lives are perfect . . . they're so much more relatable and likeable than people who pretend they have it altogether.*

Agreed. We'll get into this more later . . . the confessing of failings is beautiful; it is even scriptural . . . but only if it points to or seeks a rescue. Blurting out all of our faults, screw-ups and mental and physical health issues for everybody to hear might be all hip these days but if it doesn't point to a way out, the words only cement defeat and prevent true transformation and victory in our lives.

But even more than words . . . our inner messaging. We're so going to be dealing with that as it has the greatest force. Chapter 5, *Journey into Your Secret Life* will take a deep dive into this subject because the stuff we say in our heads . . . oh, boy! We call ourselves . . .

fat

stupid

a failure

ugly

unloved

abandoned

sick

over the hill

all dried up

disgusting

broken

covered in cellulite

barren

stuck

allergic

addicted

offended

repulsive

defeated

fallen out of love

hurt

low libido

weak

a bad mother

a horrible wife

flawed

depressed

lazy

guilty

rushed

out of control

We think those words silently yet so frequently they actually become hard wired into our very anatomy. Eventually they become such a part of us we begin to say them out loud . . . over and over again . . . flippantly . . . like they're nothings.

But they're far from *"nothings"*.

You're going to come to see that they are really big somethings. They seep into our DNA and affect every cell in our bodies.

> We are all walking and talking *billboards* for the world around us to see, advertising who we are and *what* we are here for.

Have you ever announced to nobody in particular . . . just said it out loud because you messed up . . . "Gosh, why am I such an idiot?"

Yeah . . . that one is about to go in the word trash pile.

The truth is . . . you've declared yourself into who you are. We are all "that girl who . . ." just fill in the blank. We all make declarations and decisions every day to be "that kind of girl" no matter what side of theology fences we sit on. We are all walking and talking billboards for the world around us to see, advertising who we are and what we are here for.

Even if we haven't realized what kind of girl we are, those around us have usually figured it out. We send loud messages to people as we simply live, talk and move about our environments, from the stranger on the street to our close-knit circle of family and friends.

But those around us are not hit the hardest by these messages even though they are sometimes wounded by the collateral damage. We take the biggest hit since we are the ones opening our own personal mail all day long. We download messages about ourselves from our minds, from our speech, from our environment and from the spirit realm. These messages are constantly programmed into our ever-changing cells and we inevitably become "that girl".

It may feel foreign when you first begin this transformation you're about to undertake because you're so used to either downing yourself or being a "realist" about your life. But what you thought was real was simply a box. Only truth is real, and we only get that by looking at what the Word (scripture) says about us. Our attitudes and beliefs must be redesigned by the light of that Word.

As you begin to learn your true identity and think and "name" yourself appropriately, your very DNA will change (as we'll find out in the science chapters). You will be released from boxes made from prior phony declarations that literally suffocated the life out of you. Over time, the revelations of truth you'll discover about yourself within these pages will naturally start to spill out of your mouth like a cascade of life! These declarations will break you from tired old boxes you have put yourself in and smash down walls of mediocrity around you.

> Only *truth* is real, and we only get that by looking at what the *Word* (scripture) says about us.

CHAPTER TWO

Starter (Part II)

It's a Thing

Didn't know multi-chapter intros were a thing?
They are here. Smashing lots of needless boxes as we go along . . . single chapter book intros being one of them. We're still in "Appetizer-mode" though . . . the "Main Course" (or the meat as we like to call it on our podcast) starts in Chapter 4, but it's important to work through every stage of this full-course meal.

You've heard the term . . . "mind over matter". That term is often dissed . . . *Oh, that's just mind over matter nonsense*. But, not so fast. As you get further into this book you're going to find out through scripture and through science that absolutely your mind has massive impact on your matter! For now, let's begin laying out the case and bring to mind the scripture in Romans 12:2 that declares that you are ". . . ***transformed by the renewing of your mind.***"

Transformed . . . hmmm . . . we all know that means radically different. Simply put then, you are one way with one mindset, but another mindset completely changes you! This is why getting bogged down in the tedious task of "working" on ourselves is a trap. Working on our lack of discipline . . . our impatience . . . our bitterness . . . why keep trying to fix broken? It is a given . . . our old nature has issues! Thankfully we've been given a new one, as we'll **get** into in much more detail in the "-vs-" chapters.

Clearly, this walking in the new instead of working on the old doesn't line up with popular culture. Modern psychology has everyone working on themselves but it's just not scripturally accurate. Biblical wisdom tells us old things have become new. We get to open the beautiful gift of the new identity that was won for us by our Savior and actually replace the old, constantly needs fixing one with it. What an astounding gift! Yet, so many of us are leaving it wrapped and unused.

Here's the reality . . . your "old" or what you thought of as your natural self . . . perhaps that girl naturally lacking in self-control . . . naturally fearful . . . naturally anxious . . . she's not your true identity. Maybe you've spent your whole life thinking you were naturally the glass-half-full type . . . or the girl with the short fuse . . . or the girl with the follow through problem . . . you were just born that way. Well, it's just not accurate according to the Bible.

What an astounding *gift!* Yet, so many of us are *leaving* it wrapped and unused.

What is accurate is that you can walk in your rightful identity of patience rather than trying to fix your impatience . . . walk in forgiveness rather than trying to fix your bitterness . . . walk in kindness rather than trying to fix your anger. If you want to nutshell it . . . this whole book is one big "attagirl" to walk in the new! You . . . the new creature! At first, these new identity shoes . . . well of course we're all a bit wobbly in them but the more we wear them the more comfortable we get.

Back to this *"transformed"* scripture. What does walking with a new mindset actually look like?

In one mindset, you're that girl who is frequently hurt by others. With a new mindset, you're that girl who chooses happiness and forgiveness over hurt.

This whole book is one big *"attagirl"* to walk in the new!

You're that girl on the couch with the bag of potato chips, the sugar addiction and the inflamed and weary body. Renew your mindset and you're that girl rocking her body-honoring food choices and newfound energy.

You're that girl constantly self-sabotaging her goals. It's putting on a different mindset that allows you to become that girl who is growing, maturing, and off the self-sabotage merry-go-round.

You're that all or nothing girl, that one who makes one big mistake and throws in the towel in defeat. Switch your mindset and you're that girl who gives herself so much grace it's almost ridiculous, all the while walking into transformation.

You're that worried girl, that frequently anxious, glass-half-empty girl who goes to bed dwelling on the "what if's" and the "oh, no's." Change your mindset and you're that girl confident in whatever tomorrow brings. No matter what problem may arise, you choose peace knowing there will be a promise you can cling to that's big enough for any problem.

You're that girl with a *woe is me and my sin* attitude toward God. Renew your mindset and you're that girl who acknowledges her sin and repents then basks in the righteousness of Christ, not looking back into the ugly sin pit you used to wallow in but thanking Him for how much He's changing you.

But, please don't misunderstand us here. Renewing your mindset is not some sort of instantaneous, abracadabra-changearoonie, wave of a magic wand trick. This is you becoming that girl God destined you to be little by little and precept by precept. It is you messing up of course. Not even being close to perfect, but transforming over a life-time walk, with much practice and ever greater understanding of who you really are through the redemptive miracle of the cross.

Little Bit Deeper

We're going to really get into the meat of the why and the how of your new declarations in the Main Course chapters coming up. But

Switch your *mindset* and you're that girl who gives herself so much *grace* it's almost ridiculous, all the while walking into transformation.

This is you becoming *that girl* God destined you to be little by little and precept by precept.

since we're still in intro mode here, let's just start dipping our toes into the coming content.

Take a quick look at the example of you as the hurt girl versus you as the "let it go girl".

"I'm so hurt!" If you're like us, you've probably said that a time or two (or a hundred times or two—wink). We've all been that girl walking around wearing the hurt sweater. You know what we mean . . . feeling hurt . . . it's like wearing that ever so comfy, all stretched out, grey and gloomy sweater. It slips on easily and feels so right that it's hard to take off.

We say things like . . . "I'm working on not being so hurt . . . but it's hard because it goes so deep." And it takes us time to work through a hurt episode, right? We have to play all sorts of mental gymnastics in our heads to decide when or even if we can forgive. Even those of us who are Christians . . . we often still feel justified in showing the hurt for as long as necessary to be sure our offender knows they've wronged us.

It is simply adopting a different mindset . . . a *"renewed"* one that flips how we walk through situations of hurt. The mistreatment still may have happened but you, wearing your new mindset . . . wearing your new redeemed identity as a "let it go girl" . . . you don't even have to sit down and work it all out with your offender.

> **It is simply adopting a different** *mindset* . . . **a** *"renewed"* **one that** *flips* **how we walk through situations of hurt.**

It doesn't even matter if your husband didn't quite mean that insensitive statement as you took it, or whether he did. Doesn't matter if your friend's heart was in the right place but her words were a little harsh or whether she was jolly well harsh on purpose! Doesn't matter if your co-worker who said something behind your back seems really sorry for it or if they don't give a flying riff that they hurt you . . . or whether someone on social media who cruelly attacked your post was well meaning or a mean-spirited troll. You see, the beauty is . . . with a renewed mind, you get to drop it!

You **GET** to! You don't nurse hurts. What a notion!

I'm that girl who drops it? What is this crazy talk? Who does this? Isn't it natural to take offense? But think about that phrase for a minute . . . to *take* offense. It is not forced upon you. You actually have the choice . . . to take it or to drop it.

But what if I'm simply not ready to drop it, you ask? You shouldn't have to rush hurt . . . right? Isn't it natural to deeply feel it?

We've all been told over and over that it's okay to hurt. Countless books have told us that to hurt is to be human. Good friends and counselors tell us to just go ahead and hurt as they hold our hands or hug our necks after we share how somebody wronged us. They're there to simply listen as we express ourselves and imprint hurt ever more as part of our identity. I'm the hurt girl . . . that's me . . . deeper and deeper into our DNA it goes.

Don't mishear us here . . . we're not encouraging you to stuff your emotions and pretend things didn't happen when they did. We can certainly acknowledge when we've been wronged but that's totally different to wearing "WRONGED" as our identity. Your sister authors here admit to doing that for much of our past. It never dawned on us we actually had the choice to take it or to drop it. So, you betcha we took it! Taking offense had become so natural we assumed it was just what one does. We became offense taking experts, even between ourselves. Sister offenses are especially prickly; can we get an amen? Sisters . . . somehow, we know all the right ways to get under one another's skin and press the most painful hurt buttons.

> It is not forced upon you. You actually have *the choice* . . . to take it or to drop it.

Actually . . . if we more truthfully tell on our former selves, we should describe ourselves as Olympic Gold Medal Hurt Holding Winners. We snuggled our hurts like they were our "preciouses", had basically set up special guest rooms in our minds for good ol' familiar, come to stay again hurt. We knew how to make "her" (still talking about hurt here in this analogy fest in case you got lost) super comfortable with matching comforter and curtains and pictures on the guest room wall so she could really enjoy her stay and move in for as long as she needed.

That didn't do us any favors though. Giving ourselves permission to hold onto hurts is that bunk we were talking about earlier. It may be common advice . . . maybe even what is considered "sound advice," but it's bunk. So, to answer our own question from a few paragraphs ago . . . yes, it is natural to hold on to hurt. But Christ knew we were created for something far more amazing when he opened a new path for us that Hebrews calls *". . . a new and living way."*

> Christ knew we were *created* for something far more *amazing* when he opened a new path for us

We'll get much more involved with the science of all this in the upcoming *Promised You Some Science* chapters but regarding unforgiveness and hurt, medical science now backs up what the scriptures have already told us about them. The Bible calls hurt a broken spirit and lets us know in Proverbs 17:22 that it *". . . dries the bones."* Not surprisingly, the Bible is dead on. Holding onto hurt causes every cell in your body to respond negatively. Hurt contributes to a weakened immune system . . . study after study tells us this.

What's that? *Please cite the studies*, you ask? This is still the intro so we're keeping it uncluttered. For now, dear Skeptic-Cutie-Mama, (yeah that's you, you have a nickname, all our good friends get one) go Google or PubMed it for yourself. One or two cited studies squeezed in here won't give the vastness of the information available on this subject the justice it deserves. Type in . . . "hurt and bitterness effect on health". You'll be there for hours blown away by just how much the ancient scriptures got it right. (And just hang in there if we're bothering the heck out of you over this so early in the read. We'll grow on ya'!)

What about triggers? "That triggered me." Most of us have said that. Modern culture puts trigger warnings everywhere these days, all so we don't get our hurt buttons constantly pressed. But what if instead of going through life side stepping trigger mines, we simply put on the new mindset of that girl who isn't triggered . . . that girl who is stable? It's genius. But of course it is . . . God came up with it.

But back to mind over matter . . . it's finally time we all drop the notion that it's mumbo jumbo. You know that little pit in your stomach you feel when you're hurt

. . . when you're triggered? Some call it a ping. Whichever way you feel it, ping or pit—it is a signal of churning stress hormones. Cortisol is chief among them. Cortisol is a necessary hormone, but it needs to be kept in balance. When released too often and in too high amounts it raises inflammation, lowers your immune system, puts unhealthy weight on your belly and breaks down your body in countless negative ways.

As an "I'm That Girl Who Drops It," your cortisol does not have to spike or churn. You'll have much healthier, much less harmful amounts of cortisol as you learn to take off that hurt sweater. It needs to go in a give to Goodwill bag! On second thought, let's not pass it off to some other poor soul to wear . . . let's burn it! Thankfully you get to replace it with something far better.

> As an "I'm That Girl Who *Drops* It," your cortisol does not have to *spike* or churn.

After telling us what a broken spirit does to our bodies, Proverbs goes on to tell us what to replace it with. It says that the mindset of a *"merry heart"* is like medicine.

Can we nutshell this then?

Merry equals heal. Hurt equals harm.

The hurt girl . . . she's not merry so she's not healing. The merry girl? She's not hurt so she's not subjecting her immune system to defeat.

> Merry equals *heal.* Hurt equals *harm.*

Put on a merry mindset . . . walk in merriness and it literally rules OVER the matter of your body's cells and heals them! Thus . . . (nice sciencey word . . . thus) mind does change matter. Your identity influences your DNA!

Put Off, Put On

We did two podcasts called "*The Poddy of the Puts*"—Episode 162 and "*The Poddy of the Puts, Part 2*"—Episode 163. Check it out on our website where all our Poddies are archived, if you want. Stumbling upon this simple Biblical concept of putting off and putting on was huge lightbulb stuff for us and for those who listened to those episodes and let us know how it impacted their lives.

This whole "puts" thing comes from the scripture in Ephesians 4: 22–24 (NIV) which gives the splendid advice to *"**put off your old self**"* and *"... **put on your new self, created to be like God ...**"* It's your no guilt pass to ditch working on yourself. If scripture clearly says to put off (literally shove away) your old self, then trying to fix her makes no sense. Putting off your old way of thinking and speaking however ... it's brilliant! It makes room for you to put on new thoughts and words that you were actually God designed for! It is a simple put off, put on, swap, and waddaya-know ... it's life changing ... it's health changing ... it's relationship changing!

> It is a simple
> put off, put on
> *swap* and
> waddayaknow
> ... its life
> changing ...
> its *health*
> changing ...
> its relationship
> changing!

Once we started practicing these "puts" ... as we got better at "putting off" junk thoughts then hoisting a big "No Trespassing" sign to deny re-entry, our lives took on a flourish. Then looking back, we were able to realize something. We'd given ourselves too many choices ... allowed ourselves to think and say all sorts of things that were harmful. With fewer choices ... basically scribbling a big X over stinky thoughts and words ... we were far happier ... far healthier ... far better off in so many ways.

You can liken it to food choices if you want. There is a whole, huge smorgasbord of foods out there we *can* eat. But some of them ... no, in fact many of them are harmful to us. Sugary sodas, refined foods devoid of nutrition ... we can certainly eat them if we want ... look around ... almost everyone is ... but they don't do us any good. When we put a stop to them, many health issues clear up and our bodies start to flourish.

It is the same way with the smorgasbord of thoughts we get to choose from. Most of us are thinking "all the thoughts" but they're not doing us any good. Some thoughts are best left on the buffet and not put on our plates! Those of us who learn to choose our thoughts with discretion get to live far better . . . far healthier lives and you're that girl who's going to learn to do this very thing.

When you get to the core of it all, the answer is really this simple . . . put off the bunk words and thoughts and put on the truth words and thoughts . . . so simple it seems almost ridiculous but thank God it is not!

More about all this to come, but we need to pause and say . . . please don't feel we are being trite here. This book is not about urging you to become a pleasant little Pollyanna with your head buried in the sand pretending that dark hurts and wrongs of your past and present don't exist.

> Some *thoughts* are best left on the buffet and not put on our *plates!*

You're right, we don't know how your mother treated you all those years. We can't fathom the horrific things that perhaps your uncle or neighbor did to you or even what your husband said or did that seems impossible to forgive. Acknowledging that wrong things . . . cruel things . . . sometimes really-rotten-secret-things that may even need to be brought to justice actually happened is important. And while we're telling you to ditch the hurt sweater, we are not saying you don't have a voice and we're for sure not suggesting you stay with a spouse who is abusive, currently adulterous or involved in harmful addictions. If you are in such a situation, we urge you to reach out for help and support to make the life changes needed to ensure you and your children are safe and respected.

If you married a guy like our guys though, he's probably a good one . . . imperfect as heck of course (as you are and we are) but every bit worth keeping, loving and fighting for. We'll be fighting with you for a stronger, better marriage through this book journey. There are other books with focused help if you need to get out of a current dangerous one. This book has a different mission.

(If you're single . . . not trying to leave you out. There's so much God has for you here that we want to pass along. So, stay for the ride.)

It's time.

You didn't open this book by accident.

Get ready for *the best swap* you'll ever make . . . *putting* off your old and *putting* on *His new.*

Get ready for the best swap you'll ever make . . . *putting* off your old and *putting* on His new. Your exciting and hope fueled future is founded on turning your focus away from what has been done **TO** you and towards what Christ has done **FOR** you. It no longer matters what you have gone through but what He went through to give you your new "sweater" identity. It is not grey . . . not gloomy . . . it is vibrant . . . its value is priceless, and it suits you perfectly.

CHAPTER THREE

Starter (Part III)

The Wrap Up

There's something about your own voice. The tenth chapter of Romans tells us that faith comes by hearing and hearing by the Word of God. If you're a Christian, you've probably heard that verse many times before, but consider it again with fresh ears. Your mind needs to hear **you** declare some things over yourself for it to be renewed. Hearing other people tell you things is somewhat helpful, but you listen to yourself far more diligently. (More about that soon.)

(Admitted—before going on, we should probably recognize that there is a certain ridiculousness to the now 3-part intro you are embarking on, but we're definitely still in Starter territory. But you've passed the rustic bread dipped into herbed olive oil entrance to this full course meal and now you're finishing up the beet and goat cheese salad . . . if you don't like beets, think of your own favorite salad and insert. Look, this whole book is just going to mess with you a bit so best to just ride with it.)

Back in the '80s and '90s . . . those heydays of faith doctrines gone wrong: think big hair and far too much caked-on make-up (on second thought, don't think about that again 'cuz it's creepy). The delivery and the extremes of this faith message were indeed on the bizarre side. But we've already established that the true

Your *mind* needs to hear *you* declare some things over yourself for it to be *renewed.*

essence of the message is not so crazy at all. This is not about telling yourself you are going to grow a multi-billion-dollar business every day until you do, or telling yourself you'll be a size 2 by your birthday ten times every morning as you look in the mirror, expecting to slim down before hitting the breakfast drive-thru for sausage biscuits. It simply means you start declaring truth to replace the lies you've unknowingly and (rarely) knowingly told yourself.

> Start declaring *truth* to replace the lies you've unknowingly and (rarely) knowingly told *yourself.*

Once you start declaring truth . . . even truth you have not received yet, you hear yourself, your faith develops, and your mindset is truly changed. As your mindset changes your whole life (matter) changes with it.

So, how is your mind transformed?

The Bible tells us it is through truth. Nothing else will set us free.

How Do You Get Truth?

Jesus is Truth. But who actually is Jesus? He is the Word. We think of Him as a man who walked the earth, who said and did amazing things. Yes, He was and He did. But He's more. Modern Christianity says stuff like . . . "You need a relationship with Jesus." While that's true, we need to understand Who this relationship is really with. John 1 tells us He is the Word Who became flesh. Think about that more deeply for a second . . . the Word became flesh . . . woah! The Word took on matter . . . became a physical thing! That scripture has multiple layers of meaning, of course, but for most of our lives we somehow missed an obvious layer 101 truth to it . . . what begins as a word manifests as physical reality.

Jesus is still that Word today. He is the scriptures . . . Old Testament and New . . . that is our Christ. His words renew our minds and change our matter. You want to "have a relationship with Jesus" like this catchphrase of Christianity encourages? It can't be done without knowing His Word.

Know Him . . . know His Word. No other way around it.

Gonna get all preachy here for one ultra-long sentence . . . you can sing lots of worship songs . . . you can get all "feely" in a modern-style church service and sense His presence . . . you can pay tithes and volunteer for all sorts of church social services . . . but without diving into the depths of the truth of His Words . . . it's all in vain mate! (as we say Down Under). It's not the real deal.

Consider this book your truth-declaring handbook. Times up on the lies. We're waging full-on war on them here. You're that girl who's going to annihilate every lie you've spoken and believed over yourself and replace it with Jesus' truth . . . the Word!

As we mentioned in the first part of this intro trilogy, we realize we have lots of our readers here coming over from our health and wellness books—the *Trim Healthy Mama* series. We get that some of you are not professing Christians. People from all walks of life and from all religions or non-religions follow the Trim Healthy Mama lifestyle. We've never bashed you over the head with our faith in those books (and in our weekly Trim Healthy Podcasts) and we hope you won't feel overly Bible bashed here either. But we can't share any life transforming truths without sharing their source. The scriptures that we'll put on repeat throughout this book have breathed life into us, healed our minds and bodies, and transformed our lives.

Please feel free to hang here even if your belief system is different from ours. While we admit we'll be taking a deep dive into scriptures, don't give up on us because science comes into play in chapters 17–20 and we also hope that some good ol' common sense will shine through and rock your world. The final

> Consider this book your *truth-declaring* handbook. Times up on the *lies*.

> You're *that girl* who's going to annihilate every lie you've spoken and believed over *yourself*.

segment of this book *Desserts* is where the "I'm That Girl" declarations get a lot more down-to-earth and practical. We hope they'll resonate no matter your beliefs.

About Ready to Dive In?

You've noticed this is not a slim-size, finish on a short plane trip, or a few trips to the restroom sort of a book. It's fat for good reason. If you're not much of a reader and you've made it this far, but already feel exhausted, go get the audio book instead. Let us speak to you on your car rides or while you do dishes or while you're exercising or even in the shower. You need to get through every chapter . . . whether reading these words or listening to us speaking them. This is your mission . . . please complete it! Again . . . sister talk . . . being bossy, but for good reason.

We knew that if we wrote a quick little "tickle-the-ears" book about good things you can start saying about yourself, we'd only be wasting our time and yours. Why? Because this would be a tangent you might get into for a few weeks and then life would hit hard and drown any glimpse of lasting new identity away.

We *knew* that if we wrote a quick little "tickle-the-ears" book about good things you can start saying about yourself, we'd only be *wasting* our time and yours.

This whole "I'm That Girl" thing is not just some sort of method or dry formula. Saying stuff from a script or mental ascent only does nothing to release us from ourselves. We have to truly believe what we are thinking and saying. It has to burn within us and brand itself eternally on the substance of our hearts . . . not just our grey matter. Dribbling stuff from our mouths that has no roots wrapped around the very depths of our belief system is useless. You need to truly understand **why** you are that girl and **how** you become her through the life changing power of His Word.

So, we're not apologizing for being thorough here . . . and we don't mean thorough light . . . full fat thorough is what's going down. In this fast paced, give it to me instantly world, it is rare to take an in-depth probe into something, but sometimes that is exactly what is needed. Most of us have been conditioned for bullet points and highlights but it's important that we take our time here, labor point after point and scripture after scripture, delving into the breadth and depths of who we truly are in Christ. In turn, please take your time reading this. Get out your pen, underline or scribble notes if it helps you. If you're a skimmer (you know who you are) you're going to be tempted to jump over paragraphs and gloss over some of the real nitty gritty "splaining" we get into.

Don't.

No really . . . please don't. Okay, if you're not a professing Christian . . . we're not going to force every word on you but if you are . . . no skipping. We're not the boss of your life but can you let us be on just this one thing? Even if it takes you a year . . . even if you just read a couple of paragraphs a day . . . or heck . . . even if you put this thing in your restroom and just read a sentence or two when you're in there (we don't mind being your bathroom buddies) . . . or even if you only listen to us on your drive to work . . . and yes, EVEN if you find us annoyingly chatty . . . you can get through every paragraph on every page. We don't want you to miss something that God wants to build into you through His life-changing Word.

> Most of us have been *conditioned* for bullet points and highlights but it's *important* that we take our time here.

We figure there'll be some feedback and reviews about how this book is too long, too wordy and too bossy—fair enough on that last one but we've been through that before and lived to tell the tale. Our first book, *Trim Healthy Mama* was close to 700 pages. Before we self-published it, almost everybody told us it was far too long and way too chatty and couldn't possibly sell. But there was something inside us that knew women needed to understand the "why's" of how and what to eat if the truth was really going to sink down into their hearts and cause lasting change to their health and weight.

That book ended up selling well over half a million copies . . . literally printed one at a time or what is known as "on demand" in the self-publishing world. For that to happen without advertising or without knowing what the heck you're doing on social media or without a website or even without having the book properly edited (yeah . . . we somehow spelled piza . . . like that, with one z instead of two!!!) that is what is known in the world of publishing as a phenomenon. But really it wasn't . . . it was just truth connecting. Like this one, that book was birthed from our failures and our confusion. We'd listened to the wisdom of man for years as we'd flitted from diet to diet trying to find the truth. But that only left us hurting and broken. Once we found our way out, we knew we had to go deep and long to explain it. Later we wrote shorter books and quick start guides with major publishing companies and proper advertising budgets but to this day, hundreds of thousands of women have told us that way too long, homespun book is what changed their lives . . . and their waistlines!

So, we're back at it . . . endeavoring to leave no stone unturned. This might be a long read but it's an exciting one because truth and freedom greet you in every page. Every day you'll find more reasons to celebrate! Every day you can walk deeper into the confident path of your truthful identity. As you do, watch your relationships begin to change, your health transform and the entire way you look at your life take on a new picture. (Just also be that girl who gives us some grace for our long-windedness, our tendencies to repeat and our love for over hammering a point. If you find yourself wanting to roll your eyes at us sometimes during this book journey—no hard feelings . . . we shed our hurt sweaters a while back . . . but don't you dare quit the book!)

We want you to search into the matter of what sort of girl you truly are for yourself. We want you to open up God's Word and look into His beautiful mirror until your mind is reprogrammed with a fresh and true identity.

> Watch your relationships begin to *change,* your health transform and the entire way you look at your *life* take on a new picture.

You will have a new set of thoughts and words to plant. Proverbs 4:20-22 (NLT) says, *"My child, pay attention to what I say. Listen carefully to my words. Don't lose sight of them. Let them penetrate deep into your heart, for they bring life to those who find them, and healing to their whole body."* We'll be peppering that scripture throughout this book, unashamedly repeating it till it has set up shop inside you.

Big Fat, In Your Face Book

At the beginning of this writing process we had the grand idea to get this book done quickly enough so we could release it as a New Year's self-help read. In our fantasies . . . after an easy 3 to 6 month writing process, this thing would get swiftly and perfectly printed, you'd purchase it from Amazon with a quick press of a "buy now" button, then it would sit in your snazzy "Reading For My New Year" book pile . . . just waiting for your fresh and eager New Year's hyped up self to devour.

Well, after year two had passed and we were still barely halfway through, we of course changed our mind on all that. But it wasn't just because those fantasized, picture-perfect 3 months had long come and gone. It was because when we really thought through it, we realized people usually quit their New Year's resolutions by March. This information needs your attention for life. Better to release this book in a down month, a not very "sexy" one like late frozen February or the dog days of August or in the busyness of back to school Fall. This needs to resonate in the grind and in the valleys . . . not just the brief and easy mountain tops.

> This needs to *resonate* in the grind and in the valleys . . . not just the brief and easy *mountain tops.*

As for ourselves . . . your sister authors here . . . this journey to discover who we truly are through the power of the cross has turned into a love affair with our Redeemer and filled our days with intrinsic joy. But by no means have we discovered all truth yet. This book is your jumping off place . . . not your be-all and end-all. It's possible we'll get some stuff wrong here and a few of you may feel compelled to send us long emails explaining why we are theologically incorrect. That's okay. We're still on our own journeys of learning and growing . . . we're not your pastors . . . just your sisters . . . extending our own sister circle to you and just passing along what has transformed our own lives.

If you're new to us . . . we are blessed to raise our families here on a hilltop in the Tennessee woods with our other sister Vange, as neighbors and "in-your-face-style" best friends. While we were born and bred Down Under, we all came to the United States and ending up marrying American men. We moved out to "the sticks", as we call it, so our children could grow up together, running barefoot through the woods to one another's homes, more like brothers and sisters than cousins. Now we have grandchildren and this time of our lives couldn't be more fulfilling. Tough challenges and heartaches at times? Absolutely . . . but beyond precious still.

While the actual writing process of this book has taken a few years, the gaining of this knowledge took much longer. We three sisters spent years hashing these truths out together before the first word of this book was ever typed. There were countless long walks through the woods together and untold coffee and phone call and text "seshes" discussing our downloads from the truth of His Word as it slowly transformed our thoughts, our speech and our lives.

We even brought some of these downloads to our Trim Healthy weekly podcasts. But we saved most of what we wanted to say on this subject for this book. We knew there needed to be a big, fat, in your face book that you can really take your time with. Our other sister Vange came on our podcast a couple of times and shared her life changing insights but she is way too much of a wild mother of 10 (out kayaking down our creek or homesteading or fishing or hiking or doing a hundred other never boring things) to be tamed enough to sit down and write a book with us.

Vange may not have written these words but her journey to greater and greater freedom has inspired us as we walked our own journeys. She has her own book, "Wild Mothering", which one day we hope she'll finish. She just needs to get off her kayak and be a little duller for a few hours every day to get it done. When, and if, that book is ever completed, mothers' hearts are going to be set free and inspired like never before . . . so keep your eyes out for it. In the meantime, if you see a 6-foot tall, crazy, redhead maneuvering her kayak down some wild creek or river near you, tell her to get home and back to her laptop to finish a page or two more of her book, would ya'?

Before we say a goodbye to the triple whammy intro and hello to the first main course, can we be totally honest? Even as authors of this book and livers of this journey out of bondage and into freedom (not livers as in chicken livers, but "livers" as in . . . oh, forget it . . . you know what we mean) you bet we occasionally forget who God says we truly are and blurt out some old, bunky stuff. We are not even close to perfect, but thank God, we are **SO** not who we were! This journey brings to mind the scripture in Proverbs 4:18, *"The path of the righteous is like the morning sun, shining brighter till the full light of day."*

Each new day, with the identity of being redeemed is brighter and better than the day before. We might stumble here and there but we can say with full confidence, "I'm That Girl Who Doesn't Turn Back" . . . and neither will you!

> We are not even *close* to perfect, but thank God, we are *SO* not who we were!

Main Course

Start Chewing
on the Meat

CHAPTER FOUR

Words (Part I)

Let's Check 'Em

Words are the most powerful thing in the universe. God used them to speak everything that is into being. As His children, created in His image, our words also set things into action.

Not sure this is true? Think of what occurs in a relationship when the words, "I love you" are spoken for the first time. They change the entire course of things. If reciprocated, a whole different future unfolds, one where two single lives are thrown off their tracks; they merge into one, and a completely new family unit begins. Countless songs, poems, books, movies and plays have been written about the power of those three words.

> Words are *never* just *words.*

What about, "I want a divorce." Life altering. Four words that cause a massive change of events to unfold. A family's life is never the same.

Perhaps it is time to stop considering words as *"just"* words. Words are never *just* words. God created all matter with words. It is an interesting observation throughout the Bible that God does nothing without saying it first. God didn't *just* will things into being even though He could. He spoke *"Let there be light,"* and light appeared. This is further established in Numbers 23:19 (BSB), *"**God is not a man, that He should lie, or a son of man, that He should change His mind. Does He speak** and not act? Does He promise and not fulfill?"* In Jeremiah 1:12 (NIV), God declares, *"I watch over my **word** to accomplish it."*

Heads up . . . we're about to dig deeply into scriptures now and for the rest of this main course as we discover just how much of a big deal this focus on words is in the Bible. Jesus, like His Father God, didn't just will miracles in His mind. He spoke them. In Luke 7:14 (NIV), Jesus said to the dead son of the widow, *"I say to you . . . get up!"* Then the boy got up. Jesus said, *"Lazarus come forth"* . . . and Lazarus arose. To the paralyzed man He said . . . *"Take your mat and go home"*, and the man did. Jesus said to the leper in Mark 1:41-42, *". . . be cleansed . . ."* and the sickness left him.

John 1:1-3 (NIV), lets us know in no uncertain fashion that not a thing in this world could exist without first His Word creating it. *"In the beginning was the Word, and the Word was with God, and the Word was God He was in the beginning with God. All things were made through Him, and without Him nothing was made that was made."*

The law of *words* having actual power is every bit as real as the law *of gravity*

You see, this speaking and declaring "thing" is the way God set this whole life business up. The law of words having actual power is every bit as real as the law of gravity (more about this in *Promised You Some Science* chapters). But gravity is physical only. Words are both physical and spiritual. God, the Creator, made us to be both physical and spiritual beings and words penetrate both realms. Proverbs 18:21 (ESV) says it this way, *"Death and life are in the power of the tongue, And those who love it will eat its fruits."* Good News Bible translation makes it crystal clear, *"What you say can preserve life or destroy it; so, you must accept the consequences of your words."*

A Strange Case of Mix Up

When Jesus (the Word Himself) walked the earth, He spoke either blessings or curses to whatever the situation called for. He spoke to the storm . . . to the wind and to the sea, basically telling them to behave. He spoke to a fig tree and told it to dry up. He told demons to flee and Satan to get behind Him. In all those cases, He put an end to things that were out of order, setting them all straight with the power and authority of His words.

Regarding words of life, they spilled continually from His tongue. Jesus spoke healing to the sick, life to the dead, words of living water to the thirsty woman at the well, and life-sustaining words to the hungry and pressing crowds all around him. His words of life changed the course of all who interacted with Him.

Clearly, Jesus got it right. Here's the problem though—according to Ephesians 5:1 we are supposed to "*. . . be imitators of God as dear children.*" Somehow, we've gotten this imitating part way wrong. Most of us have our death and life speech completely mixed up. Not understanding the natural law of the power of our words, we flippantly speak death to our health, our relationships, our families, our minds, and our bodies when words of life are what they require.

> Most of us have our death and life *speech* completely *mixed* up.

If that wasn't bad enough, instead of putting Satan (who is known as the accuser in the Bible) in his place as Jesus did, we speak life to his plans and to his lies. We go around saying . . .

"I'm sick with worry."

or

"This is killing me."

Announcing we are sick with worry is a declaration of total agreement with the accuser. 1 Peter 5:8 tells us that Satan, "*. . . walks about like a roaring lion, seeking whom he may devour.*" So, you better believe he wants you sick with worry. Whenever we say this sort of thing, we're surrendering to his cause, basically joining his team. And sure . . . most of us are half-joking with "this is killing me," sort of statements, but the law of words still exists. Joking doesn't negate the fundamental premise on how this universe was established . . . by words! Proverbs 6:2 (NIV) says, "*You have been trapped by what you said, ensnared by the words of your mouth.*"

No more living like our words don't matter!

Ain't No Harm . . . Hhmm

Maybe you are thinking we are taking this whole "careful what you say" thing a little too seriously. Surely there's nothing wrong with a little careless speech? If pretty much everybody is doing it, how harmful can it be? Proverbs 14:12 (BSB) has this to say, *"There is a way that seems right to a man, But its end is the way of death."*

Hopefully, we're not coming across as never-crack-a-smile Bible thumpers who want to rip any sense of humor from you. We all need to laugh and should do it a lot as it is one of the best medicines out there. But you can be lighthearted and funny without causing harm with your words.

And please do not think we have come up with this "get more careful with your words" notion on our own. Let's look again to the Word which should be the rock on which we base our entire belief system. Matthew 12:36-37 puts it this way, *"But I say to you that for every idle word men may speak, they will give account of it in the day of judgment. For by your words you will be justified, and by your words you will be condemned."*

King David understood the danger of a loose tongue when he shows us what to pray in Psalm 141:3, *"Set a guard, O Lord, over my mouth; Keep watch over the door of my lips"*

The Tongue Corrupts the Whole Body

It is not so much other people's *words* and names about us that are the most destructive. It is our *own.*

When our words are subject to the authority of God's Word and we take on His words of LIFE, we have the power to begin to tame the tongue, which the Bible says can birth a world of evil. James 3:3-6 (NIV) describes this with crystal clarity, *"When we put bits into the mouths of horses to make them obey us, we can turn the whole animal. Or take ships as an example. Although they are so large and are driven by strong winds, they are steered by a very small rudder wherever the pilot wants to go. Likewise, the tongue is a small part of the body, but it makes great boasts. Consider what a great forest is set on fire by a small spark. The tongue also is a fire, a world of evil among the parts of the body. It corrupts the whole body, sets the whole course of one's life on fire . . .".*

Remember the old saying, "sticks and stones can break my bones but words will never hurt me" . . . WRONGO!!! But it is not so much other people's words and names about us that are the most destructive. It is our own. Seemingly harmless dribble such as:

"I'm a nervous wreck."

or

"I always get the short end of the stick."

or

"I bet I'll come down with a rotten cold right before our family vacay like I always do."

Those are all destructive sparks that can set the whole course of one's life on fire, as James described.

Proverbs 15:4 (ESV) shares this wisdom with us; *"A gentle tongue is a tree of life, but perverseness in it breaks the spirit."* Most of us do a knee-jerk translation of this verse in our minds. We automatically think of a perverse tongue as one that spews filthy curse words or cracks dirty jokes. If we rarely do either of those, we're in the clear . . . phew! But what if

The *accuser* wants to pervert our tongue from being an instrument designed to produce *life* into an instrument of destruction.

the truth is that a perverse tongue is simply one that, instead of speaking truth and life through the lens of God's Word, speaks lies fed by the accuser? The definition of perversion is simply when something created is used for an improper purpose. The accuser wants to pervert our tongue from being an instrument designed to produce life into an instrument of destruction.

Peeling the Deceit Onion

If you're honest with yourself for a minute (like we had to be) is a lot of what you say these *"idle"* words we learned about in Matthew 12:36? We realized we were unknowingly, but very frequently, uttering the sort of careless dribble this verse tells us we are going to have to give an account for.

As we kept sharing these scriptures between ourselves during our sister-hash-seshes on our Hilltop walks or over countless cups of tea or coffee, it finally dawned on us. We realized much of our speech was actually perverted. No, we didn't curse like sailors, but we had allowed our tongues to become instruments of destruction when they were designed to be something else entirely . . . instruments for life! It was a humbling realization. Here we were, so-called best-selling Christian authors yet we had perverted mouths. Ouch!

1 Peter 3:10 (ESV) was a huge wake-up call for us. Take a lookie if you're ready to adjust your mindset: *"Whoever desires to love life and see good days, let him keep his tongue from evil and his lips from speaking deceit."* We all want to see good days. Bring 'em on! But if God wants His words in our mouths but instead, we are constantly spouting the opposite to His truth, then . . . hmmm. Maybe . . . well, no, not maybe . . . definitely! (We realized it was a BIG definitely.) We'd definitely been filled with deceitful speech! How could we expect the blessings of good days when we were blurting deceit around the clock?

Just like the word "perverseness", meaning something created for a certain purpose but distorted into fulfilling another, the full meaning of the word "deceit" struck us in a similar way. Deceit on your lips is not just saying . . . "No, I didn't take the cookie" when you really did when you were six years old and staying at Grandma's. It's not just lying to your boss about a sick day or putting in a not entirely true weight on your driver's license. Deceit is even more deceitful.

Christ calls us beautiful in Song of Songs 2:10, (ESV) *"My beloved speaks and says to me: "Arise, my love, my beautiful one, and come away . . .".* If He is calling us that girl who is His beautiful love and we are like, *"No, I'm that girl who is unlovely and dirty from things that happened in my past, and I hate giving my body to my husband."* . . . then sadly, our lips are speaking deceit.

If we replace the truth of Ephesians 2:10 (NLT) where we are that girl who is told she is *". . . God's masterpiece"* and that God has *". . . created us anew in Christ Jesus, so we can do the good things he planned for us long ago."* with "Nah . . . I'm that girl who is trapped in my old habits and can't break my addictions. Might as well go eat a pint of Hagen Daz." . . . then we have deceitful lips.

If we ignore the truth of 1 Peter 1:16 (NLT) which calls us that girl who was chosen to be *". . . holy and without fault in his eyes."* and instead we're all . . . "I'm more of that girl who struggles in my Christian journey and lets God down day after day, and just can't get my temper under control." . . . then we are letting deceit spill from our mouths and that deceit literally shapes our future.

Even if we *do* struggle, even if we *do* feel like we let God down when we fall, let's repent and move on. First of all, God never gets down. Secondly, He certainly never intends for us to go down and stay down, believing we just can't ever get it right, letting ourselves and everyone else know over and over again what a failure we are. Not when He achieved such incredible work for us on the cross! Not when He longs for us to get up and walk forward as the new girl rather than the old.

> He longs for us to *get up* and walk forward as the new girl *rather* than the old.

We can't let struggle and sin be our identity. This new girl we've been talking about . . . she's us even if we don't feel remotely like her yet, even if we're not measuring up to her in our own eyes. Romans 4:17 encourages us to look at things the way God sees them . . . *"God, who gives life to the dead and calls those things which do not exist as though they did."*

Notice that? **CALLS** . . . He **calls** them differently! As imitators of God we need to call ourselves overcomers not undercomers! We are told in Romans 6:11(NIV) to *". . . count yourselves dead to sin but alive to God in Christ Jesus."* Let's count ourselves in that group . . . let's call it as He tells us to, not as we see it but as He sees it!

> As *imitators* of God we need to call ourselves overcomers not undercomers!

Hopefully, some lightbulbs are going off in your head like they were for us when these scriptures smacked us upside the head (lovingly, of course). Psalm 34:13 is another scripture that urges us to: *"Keep your tongue from evil and your lips from speaking deceit."* How had we seen these scriptures so many times, yet the full truth of them had never sunk in? Our speech had to change!

But, how?

CHAPTER FIVE

Words (Part II)

Teach Your Mouth

Proverbs 16:23 has this important instruction for us; *"The heart of the wise teaches his mouth, and adds learning to his lips."* Notice that root word *teach*? Our mouths obviously don't know how to spout the right things on their own. They require training. So, if we are wise, we have to teach our mouths, which involves stopping them from being lazy blurters of *"idle"* (that which opposes God's Word) speech.

To get the *"idle"* out, we have to get the truth in. What we said in Chapter 1 bears repeating . . . the only place for full truth is the Word. We have to teach our mouths the truth of the Word otherwise; on their own, they'll just keep dribbling all sorts of destructive nonsense.

The Word tells us what our speech should be like in Psalm 107:2 (NLT), *"Has the LORD redeemed you? Then speak out! Tell others He has redeemed you from your enemies."*

Notice Psalm 107 was not all like:

"If you feel like it, go ahead and say some stuff about how you've been redeemed."

Or

"Those who are ENTJ or Type 7 personalities on the Enneagram, feel free to speak out about how you've been redeemed. The rest of you shouldn't feel like you have to."

Nope, it was a command . . . *"Speak out!"* We all need to proclaim the goodness of the Lord in our lives. God knows it is imperative for our own ears to hear these things from our own lips. As our Creator, He knows what is best for us. Again, let's be reminded of Isaiah 55:8-9, which tells us His thoughts and ways are higher than our own. God knows how the cells in our bodies respond to words of life, how these words build our faith, how they cause spiritual enemies to run, and how people we live with or come in contact with need to hear us speak them too.

Psalm 89:1 teaches our mouths what to say, *"With my mouth will I make known your faithfulness to all generations."* Have you made known God's faithfulness today in front of your children? Not yet? Okay, you get a pass for now. We're only in Chapter 5. You'll hardly recognize your own mouth by the last chapter of this book.

If you allow your mouth to say that you're broken, abandoned and full of fear, you haven't yet instructed your lips or persuaded them in the truth. In short . . . you ain't taught your mouth properly!

> If you *allow* your mouth to say that you're broken, abandoned and full of fear, you haven't yet *instructed* your lips.

Here's the simple swap remedy to having a wayward mouth . . . put the Word in it! The Word will take up the room of all that other bunky stuff you were tempted to say. Look at Psalm 119:172, *"My tongue shall speak of your word."* While it is not absolutely certain the author of Psalm 119 was King David, the acrostic nature of Psalm 119 was David's specialty and it leads many Biblical scholars to believe he was the likely author. But whether he wrote this particular Psalm or not, it is evident throughout the entirety of the Psalms that he was a wonderful example of someone who practiced this truth-speaking thing. Sure, he spoke some doldrum stuff too sometimes . . . but he didn't stay down in doldrum land. He practiced encouraging himself with positive words of truth. In chapter 66 of that same book, verse 16 he says . . . *"I will declare what He has done for my soul."*

Jesus himself taught this same thing in John 15:7, *"If you abide in Me, and My words abide in you, you will ask what you desire, and it shall be done for you."* His words rather than our own, girls! This *"abiding"* basically means to set up house inside us and take over. This is such a fantastic thing as Christ's words are correct, powerful, victorious and will never, ever steer us down a wrong life path. Psalm 19:7

puts it this way, *". . . The testimony of the Lord is sure, making wise the simple;"* We can fully rely upon His words as they are *sure"*. When we give testimony to them, i.e. . . . speak them out, there is no uncertainty that we're saying the wrong thing. His words are always right, correct, spot on truth. They transform our speech from foolish to wise.

His words are *always* right, correct, spot on *truth*.

Let's look at some Word-based truth subs that can replace idle words and make known God's faithfulness in our lives.

Instead of allowing the "sick with worry" phrase out of your mouth, how about . . .

I'm that girl who has *"not been given a spirit of fear but of love, power and a sound mind."*

(you're speaking 2 Timothy 1:7)

or

I'm that girl whom God has told, *"Fear not, for I have redeemed you; I have called you by your name; You are mine."*

(you're speaking Isaiah 43:1)

Feel like everything and everyone is against you? If you're all . . . "Man, feels like I just can't win lately," your mouth needs some teaching. How about . . .

I'm that girl who is *"redeemed from the hand of the enemy."*

(you're speaking Psalm 107:2)

or

I'm that girl who *". . . is born of God . . . and the wicked one does not touch"* me. (you're speaking 1 John 5:18). This is such good stuff, right? If you're alone right now . . . or just with your children, try saying it aloud right now. You don't have to yell it . . . just let your lips utter these incredible words. "I'm that girl who is born of God and the evil one does not touch me!" We can sense their incredible power even as we're typing them.

Christ's words are *correct*, powerful, victorious and will never, ever steer us down a wrong *life path*.

Perhaps your future feels uncertain . . . you have some health issues looming over your life and they're sucking away your joy. If you're going around saying: "I'm sick and tired of being sick and tired" and "I'm not sure how I'm going to get through this," your mouth needs some teaching.

How about . . .

"I'm that girl who remains confident of this; *"I will see the goodness of the LORD in the land of the living."*

(you're speaking Psalm 27:13)

or

I'm that girl who *"by his stripes I am healed!"*

(you're speaking Isaiah 53:5)

> Wouldn't it make *sense* that continuing to confess these good things . . . *"the Good News"* about who we are in Him be the next logical part of our *Christian* walk?

Continue the Confession

Christianity is actually called the "Great Confession". Romans 10:10 tells us, *"For with the heart one believes unto righteousness, and with the mouth confession is made unto salvation."* We have to confess our belief in Jesus and what he has done on our behalf in order to become a Christian. If confession and speaking from our lips is the beginning of our new birth in Christ Jesus, then wouldn't it make sense that continuing to confess these good things . . . *"the Good News"* about who we are in Him be the next logical part of our Christian walk?

Hebrews 10:23 (KJV) strengthens this idea, *"Let us **hold fast the profession** of our faith without wavering; (for He is faithful that promised;)"* The root word profess literally means to declare. Positive profession (or confession) is therefore not an extreme . . . far too woo woo, uber super spiritual tangent. Rather, it is a foundational weapon that ensures victory over the accuser's lies.

This Christ-following life is clearly a life of professing His Word that needs to be knit within us. It is not a one-time confession then done . . . it is a natural continuance in our lives.

We're guessing you've heard Matthew 16:19 before but let's have a little reminder sesh of what Jesus said, *"I will give you the keys of the kingdom of heaven; whatever you bind on earth will be bound in heaven, and whatever you loose on earth will be loosed in heaven."* Again, in Matthew 18:18 Jesus repeats this binding and loosing stuff but starts with *"Assuredly I tell you . . ."* for added emphasis. He wants us to know in no uncertain terms that we can bind evil with our mouth and loose the ability of God through our lips.

God's Word in our mouths is the most powerful tool we have against the accuser. It is stronger than a two-edged sword for battle . . . even when our battle is within ourselves. Hebrews 4:12 (CEV) explains, *"God's word is alive and powerful! It is sharper than any double-edged sword. His word can cut through our spirits and souls and through our joints and marrow, until it discovers the desires and thoughts of our hearts."*

This vivid weapon analogy is backed up by Isaiah 49:2 (BSB), *"He made my mouth like a sharp sword; He hid me in the shadow of His hand. He made me like a polished arrow; He hid me in His quiver."*

> God's *Word* in our mouths is the most *powerful tool* we have against the accuser.

Swords can be used on the wrong side of the battle line too. Proverbs 12:18 (NIV) tells us: *"The words of the reckless pierce like swords, the tongue of the wise brings healing."* Reckless . . . hmmm . . . a pretty accurate description of what we become when we allow bunk to dribble out of our mouths, wouldn't you say?

This analogy of words cutting and piercing in a negative way is continued in Psalm 52:2 (NIV) *"You who practice deceit* (there's that word again), *your tongue plots destruction; it is like a sharpened razor."*

The enormous power your words have for either life or destruction . . . sinking in yet?

Let's stop slaying our health, our life and our family with our words and instead use them to destroy the accuser and his attacks *"without wavering"*!

CHAPTER SIX

Words (Part III)

Not Such a Fruitcake

Okay, so perhaps you have a better hold over your tongue than we did. Maybe you're not spouting off reckless words all the time and dribbling negative bunk wherever you go. Good job. But if you're not declaring His truths, then you're still not using your tongue for what it was designed for. A non-truth-declaring tongue has gone AWOL from its military post.

Have You Gone AWOL?

Perhaps the idea of being that girl who "declares" scriptures aloud over herself and over situations doesn't sit that comfortably with you. Honestly, when we first started our "I'm That Girl" journeys, both of us felt like literal weirdos speaking these things out loud, even without anybody else listening in. We were far more comfortable being quiet Christians . . . sweet little spiritual mutes we were.

Well, we had to get over that and so will you. We are here on this earth to destroy the works of the accuser. 1 John 3:8 (NLT) tells us why Jesus came to earth *". . . But the Son of God came to destroy the works of the devil."* If that was His mission, then shouldn't it be ours, as imitators of Christ and who He calls His body on the earth?

Look at this scripture from Matthew 16:18 (KJV), *". . . upon this rock I will build my church and the gates of hell shall not prevail against it."* We always thought that meant Satan's plans wouldn't be able to succeed against us if we trusted in the rock of Christ, but we were completely WRONGO! Look at it again . . . the gates of hell . . . gates don't go to war . . . gates defend. That verse actually infers we are to be the ones on the offense! We are the ones going to battle and doing damage to the accuser and his armies of darkness. We push against his gates, not the other way around! With God's Word on our lips, we get to push the accuser back, and his measly defense gates won't be able to stop us! How wonderful! Just look at you . . . you new creature you . . . Who knew you were destined to be such a fierce warrior queen?!

We are to be the ones on the offense!

Galatians 2:20 gives us more understanding, *"I have been crucified with Christ; and it is no longer I who live, but Christ lives in me; and the life which I now live in the flesh I live by faith in the Son of God, who loved me and gave Himself for me."* 2 Timothy 2:11 backs it up, *". . . for if we died with Him, we shall also live with Him."* We are here as His ambassadors in His stead. We don't go AWOL! We do like Jesus . . . He spoke the words of His Father. We say what He says! John 12:49 (KJV) shows us this obedience, *"For I have not spoken of myself; but the Father which sent me, he gave me a commandment, what I should say, and what I should speak."*

Why are we going on and on and laboring this point? Because again, we must repeat . . . it is the truth of God's Word that sets you free! But you have to profess it to let it set you free!! You can only unleash the sword by opening your mouth and declaring who He says you are . . . who He says your husband and children are! You need to hear it and they need to hear it. The accuser and his destructive armies need to hear it if you want to ram their gates over and push these forces of darkness back out of your life!

Power to Break!

Psalm 29:5 describes this power, *"The voice of the Lord breaks the cedars, yes, the Lord splinters the cedars of Lebanon."* The cedar trees were the pride and glory of the East, the mightiest and longest-lived trees of that area. Interestingly, modern science has revealed through brain imaging that our thoughts become literal physical matter (proteins, in fact) which resemble trees in form.

If the voice of the Lord can break the cedars of Lebanon, His word can certainly break heavily rooted trees of negative thought patterns in our minds. Long-lived thought circuits we assumed we could never break free from are nothing to the voice of the Lord. When His voice becomes our voice . . . when His Words are on our lips, we destroy and overcome previously undefeatable problems in our lives.

Perhaps you've said and believed you can never stick to healthy eating . . . you always fall off the wagon. God's words on your lips are the power to splinter that. Perhaps you've said and believed your relationship with your husband is broken beyond effort . . . beyond mending. God's words on your lips can break through years of relationship struggle . . . break the accuser's grand plans to pull you and your husband apart.

> His *word* can certainly break heavily rooted *trees* of negative thought patterns in our minds.

Revelation 12:11 gives us more of a glimpse into this insight *"And they overcame him by the blood of the Lamb, and by the word of their testimony, and they did not love their lives to the death."* We defeat the accuser by the precious blood of Jesus that gives us the authority to use His Name on our lips to conquer all oppression. We overcome by the Word, which we give testimony (the use of our voice) to. Jesus comforted the weak and the broken with words, so we do too. He sent demons to flight with the power of His words, so we use them too. He healed the sick with words, so we behave just like Him. Psalm 107:20 proclaims, *"He sent His word, and healed them."* Jesus is that Word and when we profess it, we deliver healing from our lips.

Jeremiah 23:29 (CEV) likens God's words to an unbeatable force . . . *"My words are a powerful fire; they are a hammer that shatters rocks."* This reminds us of Romans 8:31 (NLT) *"What shall we say about such wonderful things as these? If God is for us, who can ever be against us?"* The way God loves to *"be for us"* is by His words birthing in our hearts and nestling in our mouths. They are His power within us . . . but they're powerless when they're left unused in their sheath. A sword cannot protect, defend, or defeat if it is not used.

Got a feeling a bunch of rusty old swords are about to be cleaned up and put to use. Are you about ready? Do we hear somebody saying, "I'm that girl who is pumped"? Cue the choir! Can we get a witness in here!!!

Fruit Cake Follies

Okay, before we go smashing some accuser lies and "I'm That Girling" over everyone and everything, we gotta preface with a little wisdom. Some of your family and friends may love the changes happening in you as you learn to transform your speech and subsequently your identity. But it is possible others might start to consider you a little bit of a Quacker as we say down under . . . a Fruit Cake here in the US.

Here's the deal . . . you don't need to be obnoxious with your "I'm That Girl" declarations. Be wise as to when and where you say them around other people. For instance, there's no need for an "I'm that girl" retaliation to everything your husband says.

> Be *wise* as
> to when and
> where you say
> them around
> other people.

Husband: *"What are your plans for tomorrow?"*

You: *"I'M THAT GIRL WHO TAKES NO THOUGHT FOR TOMORROW!!! GOD TELLS ME IF HE CAN LOOK AFTER THE BIRDS OF THE AIR AND THE FLOWERS OF THE FIELD, THEN WHY SHOULD I WORRY ABOUT TOMORROW??? I'M OVER WORRYING ABOUT TOMORROW!!!"*

Husband: *"Ummm . . . You okay? You look sort of wild and feverish."*

Let's avoid that, shall we?

We know we just talked about the problem with being a spiritual mute, but one wise step at a time. The first, most important baby step as you start your transformation is to stop saying all the negatives. You'll soon start to catch yourself uttering them. Don't worry if, at first, you realize too late, and they slip out. If you're anything like us, they've been such a habit of your speech, so engraved into the core of it for years . . . likely even decades, you'll have to give yourself some grace. The more you start to become aware of these "idle" phrases, the more you'll be able to avoid blurting them. Don't get down on yourself for not being a perfect "I'm That Girler" when you're just beginning.

Once you start noticing the "idles" and getting them more under control, you can begin combatting them with truth declarations in your mind (unspoken) but also out loud, in the privacy of your own space with no ears around. Or perhaps just the ears of young children if they're always with you. This might be your bedroom, your car, your kitchen, or on a walk outside. You don't have to bellow them out in a thunderous voice. Just allow your own ears to hear them come from your own lips. Know that when you're speaking, spiritual forces are also listening and . . . according to the Word . . . obeying!

> The *more* you start to become aware of these "*idle*" phrases, the more you'll be able to avoid blurting them.

The goal is certainly for you to start uttering your declarations in front of others, but you don't have to start each one dramatically with . . . "I'M THAT GIRL!!!!" That phrase is actually more for your own private journey. It is a wonderful reminder of who you truly are in light of God's Word, but there's no need to start every sentence with it in front of your loved ones and friends.

Here's a non-fruit-cakey way to go about this in social situations:

Coworker: "This project is killing us. Don't they realize they've put way too much work on us? I've about had it!"

You: "It sure is a bigger project than we realized. But you know what? God has somehow given us the strength to face it so far. We're going to get through this. We're strong, you and I, and it won't kill us. We'll feel refreshed in the morning after a good night's sleep. We're going to rock this thing!"

In the above scenario, you gently put the curse your friend spoke (this project is killing us) in its place with the authority of your words, and you also spoke life into the situation! You avoided two extremes:

First Extreme—you avoided the danger of an untrained mouth, which would probably have previously agreed with your co-worker and cemented fatigue, a sense of being overwhelmed, worry, frustration, and sickness over both of your lives.

Second Extreme—you avoided coming off as a "cray-cray". You didn't reply with, "Don't be so negative! My God tells me I'm that girl who can do all things I put my hands to!"

Actually the . . . "I'm that girl who can do all things I put my hands to" is a fantastic declaration to say in your head. But saying it aloud would probably turn your friend off and diminish any further chances to speak positivity into her life. Telling her to stop being so negative would certainly have clinched the deal.

You'll learn to find that balance between wisdom and wacky. While you don't want to put people off by coming across as a total nutso with your declarations, this doesn't mean you should hide your light under a bushel. What does that old song say? "No! I'm going to let it shine!" Just the mere act of not allowing your speech to be full of negatives will pull you out of "normal speech" zone. People will begin to notice. That's okay. Let's always remember, our identity is in Christ, and we mirror Him and Him alone. Our identity as a truth declarer is not one who needs to "fit in". The Bible calls us a peculiar people. 1 Peter 2:9 (NIV) says, *"But you are a chosen people, a royal priesthood, a holy nation, God's special possession, that you may **declare the praises** of him who called you out of darkness into his wonderful light."*

> The mere act of *not* allowing your speech to be full of *negatives* will pull you out of "normal speech" zone.

Notice those words . . . *"declare the praises."* Most of us have declared our misery and our failings and extolled the power of the accuser over our lives. Declaring His praises pulls us out of normal speech and puts spiritual enemies to flight!

You carry around such a powerful force with your words of truth. God wants them put to use, but they will require discernment as you grow in this journey. Gauge how your friends and loved ones are responding. You don't want to turn them off to these powerful truths you are learning by overdoing the "I'm That

Girl" phrase and making them roll their eyes every time they hear or see you coming.

When It Fits . . .

There are certain times when making a declaration in public and starting it with "I'm That Girl" will be highly appropriate. If you want to gather together with like-minded women, all of you determined to change your speech and identity . . . then going around the room with each of you declaring "I'm That Girl" statements would be powerful encouragement.

Social media posts starting with "I'm That Girl," followed by a positive declaration, can encourage yourself and others too. Social posts are often dramatic declarations about ourselves, so hash tagging with "I'm That Girl" is fitting. And you can "I'm That Girl" to your heart's content on any of our Trim Healthy Mama social platforms without having to feel like you're a weirdo.

Regarding posts on your personal social platforms . . . online imprints are fantastic opportunities to bring previous wayward declarations back into line. Look at the difference between the following two social posts about dealing with a difficult toddler. (And whoa . . . did you see what we just did there? Here we are instructing you on how to avoid blurting idle words, but we're obviously still far from perfect ourselves as they just flew from our own lips. "Difficult toddler" is negative naming. It is giving that precious toddler a label God doesn't intend for them to wear. We're leaving this oops in, though, just to show you that we haven't yet arrived and that we're all still growing, learning, and changing along with you.)

The drag, doom, and gloom post— "Please be nap time already! My two-year-old is a monster!" #wineformommytonight

The life ain't a bed of roses, but I'm up to it post—"Mommy to a spirited two-year-old . . . what a ride but what a privilege!" #learningpatiencethroughastrongwilledkid

> Online imprints are *fantastic* opportunities to bring previous wayward *declarations* back into line.

> Your words *declare* to the world what sort of girl you are and what sort of *God* you have.

There are some key words to watch out for in your social posts. Catch yourself before making posts that start with "Ugh", or "Need to vent for a second", or "I'm sick of . . .". Nothing good usually comes after those except idle, reckless, deceitful (without God's truth) words. And remember . . . your words declare to the world what sort of girl you are and what sort of God you have. Socially media-ing a bunch of venting and whining or spewing viscous remarks . . . do not reflect the true you . . . not you the daughter of royalty . . . not the you who has been brought with the highest price and whose nature and patience level has been redeemed.

CHAPTER SEVEN
Words (Part IV)

Your Authentic Self?

But what if you're just not feeling these positive declarations we're encouraging? You're not feeling loved, at peace, not close to self-controlled, or even slightly filled with joy . . . isn't it a lie to speak what doesn't feel true? This will be answered in more depth in the upcoming *Promised You Some Science* chapters, but first we need to understand what God has to say about not feelin' it.

There's a current and very popular belief that we should always be our authentic selves. If we're in a not-so-great mood . . . go ahead and express it. Feeling angry . . . "I'm so angry right now," is well accepted . . . even encouraged. Feeling down . . . don't fight the gloom, no need to act otherwise. Feeling sick . . . focus in on your symptoms so you can describe them in detail to yourself and anyone else willing to listen. Feeling sorry for yourself . . . a pity party is okay sometimes. Feeling weak . . . go ahead and announce your weakness for a Dairy Queen binge whenever you're stressed.

Does God agree with this authentic self stuff? It is all too clear from the scriptures that we have already shared (and countless others we haven't) that He doesn't. In Joel 3:10, God says, *"Let the weak say I am strong."* If God agreed with this current trend of authentic self-expression, He would have said *"Let the weak say I am weak."*

The Psalmist's declaration in verse 2 of Psalm 91 is pretty interesting. He says, *I **will** say of the LORD, "He is my refuge and my fortress; My God, in Him I will* *trust."* Notice that word *"will"* used there? Our marriage vows use "will" too . . . "I will take you as my husband." So, for the days when we feel like loving our husband and for the days when we don't . . . we *will* anyway! Will is a verb. We do it . . . feelings don't have to come into play. In the same manner, we *"will say of the Lord"* . . . it is action . . . we declare His promises regardless of whether we feel like it or not. We do it because it is the correct choice . . . the life-giving choice.

> For the days when we feel like *loving* our husband and for the days when we don't . . . we *will* anyway!

If it feels untruthful declaring things such as, "I am pure and holy," or "I am strong and well," or "I honor my body with my food choices," when that is not how you actually feel or not even how you're measuring up, we get it. But as we keep drumming over and over . . . God's ways are higher than ours. His kingdom calls things into being from a state of nothing. The earth was dark, formless, and void when God said, *"Let there be light."* You know what happened next of course . . . light appeared! When our minds and bodies are lacking, when we're feeling dark and void of joy, we are to call far greater things into being.

> We declare His *promises* regardless of whether we *feel* like it or not.

While Psalm 42 is attributed to the "sons of Korah," David's musicians at the time he was King, the text is written in the first person, singular and it is thought David composed this Psalm. In it he was obviously feeling rather gloomy when he said in verse 11 (NIRV): *"My spirit, why are you so sad? Why are you so upset deep down inside me? Put your hope in God. Once again, I will have reason to praise him. He is my Savior and my God."* So, we're not saying you pretend you don't have any of these "authentic" feelings. Hey . . . they happen to all of us wearing earth suits. David admitted to them rather often, in fact. But he wasn't content to just go along with what he was feeling. He knew there was something better for him than his authentic self. He knew there was a path out, and he encouraged himself to take it. In modern language (with a little of our Down Underisms thrown in), he was all like . . . "Get it together, soul . . . God's got this . . . come on Davie mate, shove this misery and take hope in your awesome Savior . . . jolly well give Him some praise and glory, why don't ya'!"

We might not feel righteous but truth according to scripture is *"We have been made righteous through Christ."* We might not feel well, but truth, according to scripture, is, *"By his stripes we are healed."* We might not feel whole but truth, according to scripture, is *"Old things have passed away . . . all things have been made new."* We might not feel like choosing healthy food, but according to scripture, we have been given a *"sound mind."* And what does a sound mind do? It makes sound choices. We could go on and on and on, sharing scriptures that declare truth that we do not necessarily "feel", but our feelings do not negate His truth, and yet AGAIN, we say . . . God's truth is higher than our own!

Our *feelings* do not negate His *truth*

Should You Pretend?

In his legendary book, *Mere Christianity,* C.S. Lewis explains this concept of speaking and thinking other than what we are feeling a lot more eloquently than we can. Chapter 7 is titled, *Let's Pretend.* In it, he talks of how when Christ was asked by His disciples how to pray, he taught them to start with *"Our Father."* Lewis points out that praying this way is actually pretending. It is putting ourselves in the place of the son of God . . . He calls it *"dressing up as Christ."* To quote Lewis . . .

"If you like, you are pretending. Because of course the moment you realise what the words mean." He goes on to say . . . *"You are not a being like The Son of God whose will and interest are at one with those of the Father: you are a bundle of self-centred fears, hopes, greeds, jealousies, and self-conceit, all doomed to death. So that, in a way, this dressing up as Christ is a piece of outrageous cheek. But the odd thing is that He has ordered us to do it."*

We agree . . . it certainly is outrageous cheek! Let's just admit it . . . this whole "I'm That Girl" walk we're taking together . . . it's outrageously assuming! It's cheeky galore! All this acting and talking like we are something we are not . . . how dare we! Oh . . . but God urges us to take this dare . . . not only to dare . . . but to celebrate the daring! To joyfully and confidently dare! We are called to it . . . this unmerited favor to be something we are not . . . it is rightfully ours through the Cross! How crazy blessed are we girls! God tells us to pretend then makes it true!

Lewis goes on to talk about how there are two types of pretending. One is harmful, where someone pretends they are going to help you and they don't. But there is actually a good kind, where the act of pretending leads to the real thing. And this is what God has essentially called us to do. Lewis suggests that when you are not feeling particularly friendly, the best thing to do is to put on a friendly manner and behave as if you are a nicer person than you actually are. Soon, you find yourself feeling much friendlier than you were. He points to the importance of play-acting as grown-ups that children often do,

> This unmerited *favor* to be something we are not . . . it is *rightfully* ours through the Cross!

"*. . . all this time they are hardening their muscles and sharpening their wits so that the pretense of being grown-up helps them to grow up in earnest.*"

We can't really give the justice this 7th chapter of *Mere Christianity* deserves here, so we urge you to read it for yourselves. But in it, Lewis writes of how God actually does His own pretending. He chooses to look at us as if we are little Christs . . . not as the sinners we are. We so love what he says here on the last page of the chapter:

"*I daresay this idea of a divine make-believe sounds rather strange at first. But, is it so strange really? Is not that how the higher thing always raises the lower? A mother teaches her baby to talk by talking to it as if it is understood long before it really does.*"

Not a Stepford Wife Thing

In telling you all this, we don't mean you have to go around feigning that everything about your life is perfect. There's a label for that as there is for everything these days, "toxic positivity". If you barely slept last night because your newborn wouldn't allow it, of course it is okay to mention to a friend you only got two hours last night. You don't have to lie and tell her you feel perfectly rested when she asks how you're doing. But watch yourself for . . . "this sleep deprivation is killing me." sort of statements. They're not going to help you through this.

When exhaustion hits and you feel like you can barely go on, speak this over yourself . . . *"I'm that girl who can do all things through Christ who strengthens me"*. Then, girl . . . go take a nap with the baby! Snatch one whenever you can. This sleepless phase will pass but don't make it harder with your confessions. They can cause a focus on the negatives which can cause you to miss the beauty and joy of this wondrously special time.

Of course, even as that girl who speaks life over herself and her situations, we should all be able to reach out for help when we are struggling. In no way are we saying things like PPD (post-partum depression) are not real and there is absolutely no shame in seeking help for such things. Multiple places in the New Testament exhort us to bear one another's burdens and for a burden to be borne it must be passed along. But if it is just exhaustion or "baby blues" or another challenging situation you may be facing, keep in mind how powerful your words are even as you ask for help or share a struggle. Seek help from a friend or counselor who you know will encourage your spirit and help you live up to your cross-redeemed identity rather than commiserating with how weak you are. Ask them for encouragement rather than just blurting . . . "I just don't do this motherhood thing well. I wasn't cut out for it!" Remember what Proverbs told us ". . . *you are snared by your words.*"

> We don't *mean* you have to go around feigning that everything about your life is *perfect.*

> We should all be able to reach out for *help* when we are *struggling.*

Prayer Chain Woes

The goal is for you to not be that person continually on the prayer chain at church, the one whose life constantly seems to be involved in either drama, despair, or both.

You know "Woeful Joan"? **Sure,** you do . . . every church has one . . . (or many, many more than one).

DON'T BE LIKE JOAN!

Pastor: *Okay, before we wrap up our mid-week meeting, anyone have any prayer requests this week?*

Congregation: *All eyes turn to Joan, waiting for the regular update of all that went wrong in her life in the last seven days.*

(Look, before we make an example of Joan, we're not trying to be the mean sisters here; this is just a tad more of that tougher love you're going to hopefully thank us for later. We get that "Woeful Joan's" can be some of the sweetest people you'll ever meet. But sweetness does not mean an overcoming lifestyle. And yes, absolutely, we should pray for one another. What a fabulous privilege to be able to share our needs with those who are willing to petition God on our behalf. You're not a second-class Christian if you ask for prayer, but if you're always on the prayer chain, never getting victory in your life, then your confession and your identity are what need to change.

As your idle words *transform* into victorious, truth-centered ones over time, you'll find that you'll be the one *praying* for others

As your idle words transform into victorious, truth-centered ones over time, you'll find that you'll be the one praying for others rather than being that name on the list who is constantly struggling and defeated. For sure, you'll still have some prayer requests of your own, but even when you bring those, you'll phrase them differently from how you used to.

Maybe your prayer requests are not nearly as pitiful and as long as Joan's, but sometimes it is good to see things in others so we can then spot them in ourselves.

How to NOT Ask for Prayer at Wednesday Night Group

Joan: *I still need prayer for my family and my health. Regarding my marriage, I know you've all been praying for so long for us, but Craig and I have had another rough week. Honestly, right now . . . I can barely stand to be in the same room with him. Please pray that God will work on our hearts . . . both his and mine because we just can't seem to get along. He told me to go ahead and come alone tonight due to the argument we had this afternoon, but knowing us, we'll just pick it right back up when I get home. If God doesn't do a miracle in our marriage, I am afraid it might be over.*

Also, you all know our 17-year-old son Preston. There's a reason he hasn't been coming to church lately. He's in major rebellion. He's been mouthing off at me all week, and it's wearing me down. God just needs to grab his heart because he's out there running around making all sorts of bad decisions and ruining his life. He's so easily influenced, and just thinking about the crowd he's keeping heightens my anxiety.

Joan wipes a tear then continues: *Regarding my health requests to lift up this week, my allergies have been playing up. Stress always makes them worse, but that can't be helped because this issue with Preston has meant sky-high stress all week. I can feel it all through my body, and I'm not sleeping properly, which is not helping either.*

Can you also pray that I don't get that virus going around? With my compromised immune system, I'm just so fearful of it. Everyone is dropping like flies with it at work, and we've been so short-staffed, which again doesn't help with stress . . . I'm completely overloaded. I can't afford to come down with it, not only because I'm immune-compromised and it will take such a toll on me but because if I get it, that will mean at least two weeks off work. I had to miss a whole week last year when I got the flu, and that was bad enough. This year I've already used up my sick days, so now I'll be using my vacation time. I'd really covet your prayers for this as I don't know how I'm going to avoid it. I seem to pick up everything going around ever since I got that unexplained rash all over my chest, face, and arms a few months ago. It's all intertwined somehow.

One of my Docs thinks the rashes and a whole bunch of my other symptoms, including the fibromyalgia, might be an allergy to wheat. So, now I'm off all gluten, which is hard because it seems like it is in everything, and honestly . . . we just don't have the finances for a bunch of special ingredients. It looks like I can't do dairy now either, so I need prayer to be strong and not cave to dairy foods like I usually do. I've always eaten my emotions. It just feels too hard to change, you know? Also, please keep my fibro pain in your prayers. It's been flaring this week despite the steroids that I'm on, which are causing more weight gain and only making my moods more unstable.

Do you see how easily prayer requests can turn into a bunch of declarations of despair? Seeing this sort of prayer request in print seems a bit over the top and exaggerated. But, growing up as Pastor's kids, we've sat through plenty of meetings where we've heard it almost word for word! We've even said a few of those lines ourselves so don't think we're being too judgmental! Sad but true, prayer requests can be some of the worst opportunities for speaking *"idle* words," "deceit," and *"perverseness."* The accuser must love them!

> Sad but true, prayer *requests* can be some of the worst opportunities for *speaking* *"idle* words"

Jesus tells us in Matthew 6:8 that our Father already knows our needs before we ask Him. This doesn't mean we shouldn't come to Him when we have problems. We're His children. Of course, our Daddy loves for us to run to Him when we're having problems. He's the first we should turn to. But let's not pray a big dirge about the problem. In fact, we're crazy to pray the problem! Let's pray His answers . . . let our prayers be agreements with His Word, which contains all our answers of victory.

> Let's pray His *answers* . . . let our prayers be *agreements* with His Word

Yes, the old you and even the emerging new you may still have life and health challenges. But you can learn to speak about them appropriately both in life and in prayer. Claiming ownership of diagnoses such as "my thyroid problem" or "my chronic fatigue" works against you in both areas.

Though I Walk Through the Valley

To end this chapter, we need to recognize that sometimes there are very real . . . sometimes even unimaginable hardships in life. The loss of loved ones, miscarriages, accidents, and other tragic experiences . . . what should our speech reflect during these times? Must we pretend we're all golden and that unfathomable pain and loss do not exist?

Grief and mourning are natural, God-given emotions that are part of the healing process. Bitterness and despair are not. The Bible tells us that even *"Jesus wept"* (John 11:35), but in no place in the Gospel do we find Christ in despair or raising His fist at His Father God. He believed and trusted in God's goodness, even while sweating great drops of blood in the Garden of Gethsemane, before facing the cross. And even when He asked God to take the cup of wrath from Him three different times. But His Father remained silent.

There are some things we'll never understand in this life, but we can still proclaim His goodness. We have still been redeemed! His love never fails! His word is still true! These are the truths we can still stand on and declare through tear-stained eyes even in the most difficult times of our lives.

Psalm 23 teaches our mouths how to respond during the most excruciating of days. Many of us have this Psalm memorized, but look at it again with new eyes and ears in light of how to proclaim God's goodness in the face of immense hardship.

Verse 4 says, *"Though I walk through the valley of the shadow of death . . ."* Just imagine if that was the end of Psalm 23. What if it had said, "I'm walking through the valley of the shadow of death" then simply stopped and never continued with the declarations that come after it. That's sometimes how

> There are *some things* we'll never understand in this life, but we can still *proclaim* His goodness.

Ending without *promise* and *power* is never who He is or who He wants us to be!

we talk, right? But no, that is not our God! Ending without promise and power is never who He is or who He wants us to be!

What comes after this shadow of death statement are seven (God's number of perfection) of the most steadfast declarations in the Bible. Feast your eyes on these incredible proclamations of truth in times of trouble. May they ever be our words in our own valleys and shadows:

1. *"I will fear no evil; for You are with me;*
2. *"Your rod and Your staff, they comfort me."*
3. *"You prepare a table before me in the presence of my enemies;"*
4. *"You anoint my head with oil;"*
5. *"My cup runs over."*
6. *"Surely goodness and mercy shall follow me All the days of my life;"*
7. *"And I will dwell in the house of the Lord Forever."*

CHAPTER EIGHT

Thoughts (Part I)

Journey into Your Secret Life

Research suggests that we talk internally to ourselves at the rate of about 1,300 words per minute. That's more than ten times faster than the rate at which we talk out loud which is about 120 words per minute.

Some of us converse with ourselves in our minds in full sentences, others of us have more abstract mental conversations and rely heavily on images. Either way . . . state-of-the-art cinematography has nothing on the full-colored and special effect projections of our mental thoughts. They race through our minds with vivid imagery riding on their backs like skilled jockeys. Dr. David Stoop, a licensed clinical psychologist, explains that even one word in our thoughts can be so saturated with meaning that hundreds of verbal words would be required to explain it.

Thoughts are our inner speech, the first layer of our identity . . . you could think of them as cake. Our audible speech is the icing on that cake; it finishes it up. It lets us and others know if it is a carrot cake, chocolate, or lemon cake just by looking at it. But our inner thoughts . . . they're the foundation of who we are, the center of what we need to get right if we're to be a jolly awesome cake!

We hang out with thoughts and have long "yarn seshes" with them for as long as we are conscious. When we sleep, these messages we send ourselves all day fuse into our spirits, fuel our dreams and program our unconscious thermostat. Self-talk, whether you realize it or not, is a powerful, full force steam train that leaves the

> You are the *governor* of your mind. Or maybe we should change that to *sheriff*.

station at birth and takes you to destinations of either liberty or slavery, depending on how you govern the engine.

Please don't skim over that last phrase . . . "how you govern the engine". Truth be known, we just patted ourselves on the back for coming up with such a poignant metaphor . . . (if we say so ourselves), but we want you to dwell on it for a second. You are the "governor" of your mind. Or maybe we should change that to "sheriff". Better put a silver star on your shirt and don some spurs because there are bad guys that need clearing out of town.

You Just Got Deputized!

We know the feeling of out-of-control thoughts. Doesn't it sometimes seem like they take you on wild rides all day, and you are anything but in charge? But that was the old you (and the old us.) Wild West brain space where the bad guys have taken over can be set back into order. It just takes practice and persistence, and thankfully the Word tells us how to do it. (*Actual clinical depression is discussed in later chapters but not necessarily what we are talking about here.*)

> All your *thoughts* are not *you*.

Lots of thoughts will enter your head uninvited. These come from various places such as memory proteins, (yes, recent scientific research shows many of our thoughts and memories are made up of proteins), environmental stimulus, your own habitual thought pathways, and the spirit world. But here's what's important to understand . . . all your thoughts are not you . . . in fact, many are not.

Thoughts only become a part of you when you welcome them in and set up house with them. That's a great idea if they are productive house guests. But if they are pulling you down, wearing you out, messing you up, and making you sick, you need to send them packing. It is your choice as to who you are going to live with. You are not forced to live with any muck-making thoughts.

Sometimes we get so used to our most frequent thoughts, we think they come with the house and are not kick-out-able. They are. They are squatters, not owners. They don't want to go quietly sometimes, and they may try to keep barging back in, but you don't have to let them.

Thoughts only become a *part* of you when you *welcome* them in and set up house with them.

You Choose Your BFF's

2 Corinthians 6:14 (NIV) asks us. *". . . what fellowship can light have with darkness?"* This scripture is a segment of the famous *"unequally yoked"* verse that some people quote with a warning for Christians to avoid marrying nonbelievers. But what if there is another layer of meaning to this verse, we all need to apply to our lives?

The word *"fellowship"* in the original Greek language that the New Testament was written in is *koinōnia.* That means to communicate with, to be intimate with, or to participate with. Basically, when you're in fellowship with someone, you're hanging out, sharing meals, and getting all cozy with them. And this is what we do with our thoughts, right? We cozy up and become BFF's with them. Well, that is completely wonderful if they are God-acceptable thoughts, but if they're not, we have to stop being besties with them. They have to be booted.

We have to *stop* being besties with them. They have to be *booted.*

Psalm 19:14 says, *"Let the words of my mouth and the meditation of my heart be acceptable in Your sight, O Lord . . ."* Philippians 4:8 tells us what thoughts and meditations are acceptable. Take a look . . . *"Finally, brethren, whatever things are true, whatever things are noble, whatever things are just, whatever things are pure, whatever things are lovely, whatever things are of good report, if there is any virtue and if there is anything praiseworthy—* **meditate** *on these things."*

Okay . . . awesome, we have the list of acceptable. What then are the non-acceptable thoughts?

Any thoughts fed from the accuser fall into this non-acceptable category. Why? Because they are not true, they ain't noble, they sure aren't just, not a tad pure and definitely, not in the least . . . lovely. These include thoughts of worry, fear, doubt, bitterness, anger, resentment, despair, etc. Those are not thoughts from the Light . . . from Christ. We must identify them for what they are . . . not of us! We are of the Light; they are of the darkness, and we can't allow ourselves to get cozy with them in our minds.

1 Peter 1:13 tells us: *". . . gird up the loins of your mind."* Some modern translations change that to "get your mind ready for action." Both the King James version (KJV) and the New King James version (NKJV) have a more accurate translation in this case. They portray the important image of ancient Greek military attire that is totally lost in the modern "prepare for action" translations. This *"gird up your loins"* phrase refers to the act of lifting up and tucking in one's military tunic prior to battle. You couldn't have the bottom of your tunic, the hem, so to speak, dragging on the ground while you were running into battle or you'd trip! Basically, you had to gird it up to prevent it from "fellow-shipping" with the ground. You had to yank it up out of the dust!

> We have to stop our *minds* from dragging around in dusty, dirty, old and ugly *ground* thoughts.

Same goes for our thought life . . . we have to stop our minds from dragging around in dusty, dirty, old and ugly ground thoughts. Another way to look at them are as bottom-feeding thoughts. They're scavengers.

God transforms our lives by changing our junky thinking (nonacceptable) into brilliant thinking (acceptable). He can only do this by washing us with His Word.

His Word is living water. It washes those ground splattered, hem of our garment thoughts and helps us raise them up into brilliant fresh smelling, God-inspired ones. Ephesians 5:26 (KJV) tells us, *"That he might sanctify and cleanse it* (His body, the church) *with the washing of water by the word."*

CHAPTER NINE

Thoughts (Part II)

Be a Joy Grabber

In case you're thinking we're getting far too super spiritual and you need some down-to-earth application, let's bring it! Meet Ed. He is a literal voice in the minds of many people. He attacks, hurts, abuses, and betrays people all over this globe. He is a well-accepted persona . . . in other words . . . an actual dude, acknowledged by secular therapists and psychologists alike. Ed stands for "Eating disorder" and he has destroyed countless lives and killed millions of people.

Ed is a reminder that we should never allow ourselves to accept any accusatory voice in our heads and consider it harmless. The mortality rate associated with Anorexia Nervosa is 12 times higher than the death rate of ALL causes of death for females 15-24 years old. Sadly, without intervention and help, Ed still takes the life of close to ¼ of anorexics.

In the book, *Life Without Ed,* author Jenni Schaefer shares how she had to learn to disassociate herself from Ed and realize Ed wasn't her. She'd always thought the thoughts that told her she was fat, that she shouldn't eat more than 500 calories today, that she had to be the thinnest woman in the room or that she should go binge then throw up to ease her emotional pain were her own mind talking to her. Once her therapist helped her understand that Ed was a separate voice and that he was a liar and a betrayer, Jenni and many thousands of others who have learned to divorce themselves from Ed, found freedom and healing.

Here's a quote from *Life Without Ed:*

"The first step in breaking free from Ed was learning how to distinguish between the two of us. I had to determine which thoughts came from Ed and which ones belonged to

me. Next, I had to disagree with and disobey Ed. This was not easy. This took time, lots of patience, and a willingness to keep trying over and over again."

If you are a Bible believer, you've probably started to guess who Ed really is. Yep, he has many names in the Bible but don't be fooled; he's that very same accuser who 1 Peter 5:8 tells us, *". . . walks about like a roaring lion, seeking whom he may devour."* The accuser loves to find our weak spots, get into our minds and accuse, accuse, and accuse again. All his thoughts are bottom-feeding thoughts.

Perhaps in your case the accuser doesn't try to devour you with obsessive thoughts of diminishing your body size and controlling food. Maybe he's not actually Ed for you but are there other misleading voices in your mind that need to be ignored? Perhaps in your mind you have an entitled toddler you've been listening to. She says you get to have those potato chips and French onion dip whenever you want them. She lies and tells you that you need soda and sugar and binge eating sessions at midnight. That large fry and cheeseburger . . . the toddler demands them whenever you pass by the drive-through . . . waaaa . . . gimmee . . . gimmmeee! I neeed . . . I neeeeeed!!!

> A two-year old should *never* be in charge *...chaos* always ensues.

Hey . . . no condemnation here. We've all listened to the demanding toddler in our heads before. But a two-year old should never be in charge . . . chaos always ensues. Toddlers throw fits when they don't get their way, they make ridiculous choices and anyone who's ever raised one can testify that they don't possess the fruits of the Spirit including temperance and self-control . . . are we right, Mamas? Toddlers are never happy when they're in charge and when we give them authority, we're miserable too. A toddler needs a wise adult making decisions for them, gently shushing some of their ridiculous ideas.

There is a very inspiring talk on YouTube by a man named Andrew Taylor. He's also known as The Spudfit Guy (the YouTube is called Dr. McDougall Potato Diet Talk at the Advanced Study Weekend if you want to look it up). Andrew is an Aussie. We've never met him but we have a little in common accent wise, along with his passion to help people get well, trim and healthy (although we take a vastly different approach). Andrew was a compulsive eater, well over 100 pounds overweight, depressed and at the end of his rope. He'd tried everything but continued to return again and again to his food vices. He finally felt like he needed to do something extreme. He decided to try to beat his addiction by removing all food choices except for one food and see what happened. After much research, he found out potatoes would give him the best chance for well-rounded nutrition and discovered that during times of food scarcity, entire civilizations had flourished on potatoes for quite lengthy times.

Andrew ate nothing but potatoes for a year, dropped all his weight, his blood work became perfect, his depression lifted and it set him on a path to vital health and fitness (he eats more than potatoes now but he beat his addiction). His method sounds extreme and he acknowledges that. It is not something we'd advise but it worked for his very severe food addictions. We're saying all this to come to this point . . . although this man is most likely a secular guy, it is interesting what he said in this YouTube about the voice in his head that tried to constantly veer him off his course. He called it . . . "a devil." Later he called it "a junkie" then he even called it a "used car salesman". The take away is . . . a great part of Andrew's success was figuring out that voice is not him. Rather, it is a liar and a deceiver and it only wants to take him out. Just like Jenni who beat anorexia through identifying then ignoring Ed, Andrew beat overeating by refusing to listen to that same destructive voice. To quote Andrew:

"It was important for me to realize that devil on my shoulder telling me it is okay to have a slice of pizza or a piece of cake does not have my best interests at heart. This devil is not telling me something that is good for me. He never does."

"This is a junkie sitting on my shoulder who wants to get a fix . . . that's all he is. He's got nothing helpful to say. He doesn't care about my health or my happiness or my long-term goals."

"He's like a used car salesman. He doesn't care if he sells you a lemon and you have to spend all your money on trying to keep it fixed. He just wants you to buy the car and give him the money."

"When he pops up on my shoulder and starts talking in my ear about what I should be doing next I can go . . . 'Stop it.' I know what you're trying to do and it's not going to work."

So, if you identify with having a toddler in your head trying to tell you to constantly make unwise food choices . . . or perhaps yours acts more like Andrew's did . . . like a junkie or even a used car salesman out to sell you a lemon . . . permission to ignore!

What about the voice of "Fear"? It tells us to be worried about tomorrow or to be anxious about that upcoming meeting or doctor's appointment. The Bible actually calls fear a spirit.

Permission to ignore!

Again . . . permission to ignore.

Or maybe the voice is "Hurt". Hurt tells us to be offended about what our friend or co-worker said, to be broken about our past, or to be angry because of our husband's insensitive words.

Permission to ignore.

Let's not forget "Gloom". Gloom tells us we are going through a hard period and things are only looking like they are going to get worse.

Ignore . . . Ignore.

Perhaps we've been listening to "Shame". Shame tells us we're disgusting for eating 3 cupcakes on our 9-year old's birthday. We'll never meet our goals because we have absolutely no self-control. Shame also tells us we are dirty and defiled from past sexual relationships or from childhood abuse.

Absolute permission to give shame the boot.

Most of us have been living our whole lives under the impression that these voices are the true us. But just like the author of *Life Without Ed,* once this realization hits that they're not, it is like breathing a sigh of relief. We thought we had to listen and obey them . . . we actually don't????!!! Totally empowering. The more we ignore them, the more they lose authority over our lives.

The more we *ignore* them, the more they lose *authority* over our lives.

Have you ever read the first verse of Psalm 1? It starts off like this, *"Blessed is the man Who walks not in the counsel of the ungodly . . .".* This is usually taken to mean that we should not listen to people who oppose God's ways. But it was a huge realization when it hit . . .

our own mind can house ungodly counsel. We need to be as careful to allow only true, wise counsel in our minds as we are from outside sources. As we toss the junky, ungodly stuff out of our heads . . . a blessed life is what is waiting for us!

So, let's nutshell this:

We're no longer that girl who buddies up with destructive thoughts.

How do we break the relationship?

We disagree with them . . . we refuse them.

Then we speak the truth of the Word to them and declare: "I no longer give my thought space to lying voices. I put on my helmet of salvation and my breastplate of righteousness and repel all lying darts from the accuser with the truth of God's Word. The accuser wants to bring gloom, shame, and terror, but I'm that girl who doesn't negotiate with terrorists. I'm that girl who refuses to open the accuser's clickbait . . . even a crack."

> We need to be as *careful* to allow only true, wise *counsel* in our minds as we are from outside sources.

Can We Talk Depression?

We just mentioned gloom, so it feels about the right time to talk about the D-word associated with it. As we'll do when we revisit this subject again (but in a different way) in the upcoming science chapters, we need to first acknowledge that medications may play an important role in mental illness. We're not necessarily discussing clinical depression here, nor are we pretending to give any advice for mental health conditions such as schizophrenia, bipolar and other issues. And can we please acknowledge that just as physical illness is a real thing, so too is mental illness? But just because it is real, this does not mean it needs to become our "precious" nor our banner. Both physical and mental illnesses were taken by Christ through the stripes on His back that He received. Claiming them as "my depression" or "my anxiety" only cements them deeper and deeper into our DNA.

What we do need to discuss here are negative thought patterns that many times are swept into a big bucket labelled "depression." It represents unhappy or "feeling down" thoughts. The Word calls them a *"spirit of heaviness."*

There are many good doctors hard at work trying to tackle depressive thoughts from a medical perspective. Sometimes brain chemicals and hormones are out of balance and need addressing. Diet can also play a role. Important brain nurturing nutrients are often missing from our culture's standard, sugar-filled and nutrient lacking diet. But while our physicality certainly needs tending to, the Word tells us the spirit world is where the real battle rages. We can do many positive things to fight negative thoughts physically, and yes, sometimes that fight includes important medications. But it is only in the Spirit where this war can be fully won. Ephesians 6:12 (CSB) speaks this plainly, *"For our struggle is not against flesh and blood, but against the rulers, against the authorities, against the cosmic powers of this darkness, against evil, spiritual forces in the heavens . . ."*

Can we *please* acknowledge that just as *physical* illness is a real thing, so too is *mental* illness?

Let's be reminded of what the book of John tells us about the accuser, *"The thief comes only to steal and kill and destroy. I came that they may have life and have it abundantly."* Satan's very nature is thievery. He'll use any chance we give him to steal our brain space and fill it with lies of gloom, fear, and dismay. It is not super-spiritual nonsense to acknowledge there are spirits intent on eradicating our joy and filling our minds with depressive thoughts. The scriptures often mention spirits associated with both mental and physical conditions. Let's not pretend these things don't exist. Hopefully we're not coming across as Cray Cray's here and saying you are demon possessed if you have gloomy thoughts and you need an exorcism! But there's no doubt that spirits will bother us if given the chance. The Bible says King Saul's

While our physicality certainly needs *tending* to, the Word tells us the spirit world is where the real *battle* rages.

mind was afflicted by a spirit. David, a young man at the time who was full of faith and praise, was the only one who could bring relief to Saul's malaise through dispelling the evil spirit with praise filled songs on his harp.

Zechariah 4:6 (NLT) tells us where we get our ultimate deliverance. "*It is not by force nor by strength, but by my Spirit, says the LORD of Heaven's Armies.*" Demons *"believe and tremble"*. James 2:19 tells us. It is only God's Spirit that can break the chains that hold our minds in this bondage of despair. Isaiah 61:3 (KJV) reveals this truth *"To appoint unto them that mourn in Zion, to give unto them beauty for ashes, the oil of joy for mourning, the garment of praise for the SPIRIT OF HEAVINESS; that they might be called trees of righteousness, the planting of the Lord, that he might be glorified."*

Even Jesus himself experienced the whisper of Satan's lies, and He too had to fight them off. How did He do it? He spoke the Word! So, we do the same. Or we can sing the Word with worship songs, or even shout the Word if we feel the need to . . . or go ahead and whisper it if that's more your style. Doesn't matter which way you do it. The Word is the power to defeat the spirits of darkness who seek to destroy your peace of mind.

> The Word is the *power* to defeat the spirits of darkness who seek to destroy your *peace* of mind.

No More Fainting Minds

No one needs to walk away weak and hungry from our Savior. When Jesus broke bread to feed the multitudes, He multiplied it. He said about that large crowd that had followed him in Matthew 15:32 (AMP) *". . . I do not want to send them away hungry, because they might faint [from exhaustion] on the way [home]."* Many of us today have *"fainting"* minds. Our minds grow weary and exhausted on the journey because we forget to partake of His provision . . . His Bread which is His Word. His Word is full of the spiritual nutrients our minds need to stay well . . . to stand strong against spiritual attacks from the accuser and his spirits. God's Word is full of His JOY, which according to Nehemiah 8:10, is our STRENGTH.

So, let's take that next step. Let's not only be that girl who refuses to allow our minds to be a nest for the accuser's lies which is Step 1, but let's take Step 2, which is to then be that girl who grabs joy. Isaiah 51:11 (NASB) puts us right, *"So the ransomed of the LORD will return and come with JOYFUL SHOUTING to Zion, And EVERLASTING JOY will be ON THEIR HEADS. They WILL OBTAIN GLADNESS and JOY, And SORROW AND SIGHING WILL FLEE AWAY."*

Did you catch that in that last scripture? *". . . they will obtain gladness and joy . . ."* You don't obtain something without stretching for it . . . reaching for it and scooping it up. Joy doesn't suddenly fall out of the sky, and all of a sudden . . . wow . . . we feel joyous. No, it is the "swap" we keep talking about. We purposefully put off lies of despondency and then purpose-fully put on the truth of joy . . . no matter the circumstances.

> We purposefully put off *lies* of despondency and then purposefully put on the *truth* of joy

We no longer have to sit under the old thought banners of gloom and oppression. We might be proficient at sighing and moping from much practice, but now we can practice something different . . . joy! When we fret and frown and trudge along despairingly, we can catch ourselves in these old habits and consciously rebound our minds back into redeemed thinking . . . into joy!

Sighing is not for us . . . not if we're wearing our new redeemed identities. Sitting under the old sighing tree actually undermines the magnificent magnitude of power and grace bestowed upon us. Let's not be known as that girl who sighs. When we *obtain gladness* . . . when we jolly well grab for it . . . the awesome-ness happens . . . the book of Isaiah tells us sighing flees away!

> Let's not be *known* as that girl who *sighs*.

A Reverent Frown?

Perhaps it feels like we can't or shouldn't immerse our minds with this joy because of all the sadness in the world . . . all of the suffering, all the chaos, pandemics, political craziness, and all the persecution we hear about. To be joyful might feel like we are giving an indifferent slap in the face to the sad state of our culture or to those who are suffering more than we are. Maybe we should keep the frown so we can give honor to so much pain in life?

The truth is that those in far less than perfect situations who are filled with Christ and are suffering for His Name are some of the MOST JOYFUL people you could ever meet. Richard Wurmbrand was a severely persecuted Believer and author who fondly remembered his time of trial. In his writings, he recalls with nostalgia the Heavenly Father's beautiful, comforting presence so richly fragrant inside his prison cell. He actually missed those times!

His is just one tiny testimony of millions of "Joy Grabbing" believers who are happier under persecution than we sometimes are filling our grocery carts at the store or pressing "buy" on our Amazon carts. Come on . . . you know we're right! Not finger pointing at you alone. We're jolly well speaking to ourselves here too. Instead of falling into sadness when considering the tumultuous times we live in or all the horror and abuse that the accuser has run around inflicting on the innocent, we can instead dwell on John 16:33 (ESV) *"I have said these things to you, that in me you may have PEACE, In the world you will have tribulation. But TAKE HEART; I have overcome the world."*

Our God has crushed the accuser underfoot so we, empowered by His LIFE in us, continue in His footsteps. He is the creator of joy, and we look to Him as our example. This means we grab joy no matter if our political party is in power or not, no matter if cities are burning or mobs are destroying and looting.

This means we *grab joy* no matter if our political party is in power or not, no matter if cities are burning or mobs are destroying and looting.

None of this makes us feel joyous but Hebrews 12:2 (NIV) shows us how to emulate Christ who came to the world in a very non-joyous time: "*. . . fixing our eyes on Jesus, the pioneer and perfecter of faith. FOR THE JOY SET BEFORE HIM, he endured the cross, scorning its shame, and sat down at the right hand of the throne of God.*"

(We want to end this chapter with an important note—the accuser and his spiritual army are so intent on our mental despair . . . they'll go for the ultimate . . . the loss of our very lives if given the chance. If thoughts of suicide are attacking, we urge you to reach out and let someone know. A therapist or a friend or family member . . . someone you can count on to take you seriously, to pray with you, and to speak life to you. You need someone who will check in on you frequently and help you seek medical attention if necessary. This book is not a detailed handbook on how to overcome suicidal thoughts . . . there is much more thorough help for that elsewhere, and we encourage you to seek it if you're in this situation.)

CHAPTER TEN

Thoughts (Part III)

A Tale of
Three Lynda's

Meet Lynda. She is musing. She's doing that 1300 words a minute thing in her mind we all do. You're about to get a glimpse into her internal dialogue. Choose (honestly) which Lynda best represents your current thought life: 1, 2, or 3.

All three Lynda's in this chapter are facing the same challenges, which are, of course, completely made-up scenarios. They may not be exactly what is going on in your life but again . . . getting a glimpse into the inner workings of others allows us to see ourselves with new eyes.

Lynda 1:

I can feel the anxiety again . . . like a pit in my stomach. Seems like I'm just anxious all the time these days. What if this is the first month that we can't actually pay all of our bills? That's not only frightening . . . it's embarrassing. We'll have to ask Tom's parents to help, I guess . . . again. Well, Tom will have to do that by himself as he got us into this mess. I'm not going to go groveling to them.

This whole financial stress is tearing down my health. Swallowing feels more painful than yesterday . . . awful scratchy throat . . . definitely worse today . . . how long has it been? Two days with this dry, scratchy feeling . . . probably means I'll come down with that cold going around. Hard to avoid it when you have a 2-year-old and a 4-year-old with runny noses. Just my luck, and it will be Strep throat.

No wonder my health is suffering. I really don't have help with the kids, and that wears me down. There's never any "me" time. Yes, Tom's working longer and longer hours to try to get us out of this financial hole, but that means I'm left to carry almost all of the load of our family life. You'd think his parents would offer to help out more . . . take the kids now and then or something. They know what my mother has been going through, what with her chemo treatments last year and now looking after Aunt Margaret while she goes through the same thing. She can't help with the kids like she used to.

It's hard to go to that Moms of Toddlers group every Wednesday and hear how other moms have such great help from their parents or in-laws or how their husbands pitch in and give the kids baths or read them stories at bedtime. I hate hearing about how they actually go on dates! Can't remember the last time Tom and I went on a date. He's basically a zombie when he gets home. You'd think he'd at least try for the kids. Jack is ten now. He needs more from his dad. About the only thing they do together is watch football and eat junk food. Pretty sure it is this lack of quality "dad time" that's contributing to all his new behavior issues.

I guess Tom does hug the kids and listens to their chatter about their day for a few minutes when he gets home, but I can tell he just wants to zone out and head for the basement. That look on his face tonight when I asked him to take out the trash . . . I mean, he did it . . . but I could tell just me asking him made him mad. Doesn't he realize I work hard all day too? Feels like he totally takes me for granted. My day doesn't stop until the children are in bed and finally asleep. That's getting later and later with Jack wanting to stay up later now that he's older. Nice for Tom that he gets to come home and zone in front of the TV . . . I don't have that luxury.

He's not the same guy I married. He used to want to be with me every evening. We'd actually talk! I rarely get adult talk anymore. I talk to preschoolers all day and a moody 10-year-old boy in the afternoon. Then Tom pretty much ignores me every evening.

Why is it that lately, almost every night by dinner, I seem to have this headache? No doubt it is stress related. The constant tension between Tom and me is not helping. I know it's mostly due to all the stress of the bills, but the fact that he hates this new job is part of it. But why did he have to try that home business anyway? I told him it wouldn't work. He had a good job, I know it wasn't his dream job, but now after the failure of his business, this new one he's had to take is worse. He should listen to me more. I'm not an idiot, although these days he looks at me like I am one. We wouldn't be in this predicament if he'd listened to my gut feeling on this.

Not even sure we'll be able to keep the house now. Where will we go? I told him I refuse to move in with his parents, and he just got that look and stormed off. Surely, he can't expect us to do that! What's worse is his dad's been filling his head with talk of helping him restart the business again next year . . . that's crazy! It failed sensationally once; we can't go through that again. His mom secretly dislikes me; I'm sure of it. She tries to act like there's nothing wrong between us, but I know I don't measure up to anyone in his family.

There's no way I could live with those people. We'll have to rent an apartment, I suppose. I don't know how we'll do it. The kids will hate it. I always thought this house was too small, but now when I think of all of us squished into a two-bedroom apartment, I can't bear the thought of it.

I suppose life is just tough, and all this is my cross to bear. I'm a realist, and that means I better prepare myself for even tougher times ahead. If last year seemed difficult with mom's cancer treatment, the failure of the business, and the beginnings of Jack's behavior issues . . . this one feels even harder. Why is it that every year things feel like they are getting more stressful? Everyone has their wilderness time, but it doesn't seem fair that our wilderness time seems to have no end. My faith has been so tested. Hard to trust in a loving God when things are this rough. I'm full of doubts because it feels like He doesn't hear my prayers anymore.

I can't shake this foreboding sense about our future. Mom's breast cancer was a huge scare, and I have this nagging worry that it will be me going through it in twenty years. What do they say about it running in families? Those percentages are pretty high . . . I need to Google that again to find out exactly. How can I even hope to avoid it if both mom and Aunt Margaret got it? Runs in the family for sure. I better start checking for lumps far more intensively now that I'm in my mid-thirties. But what if I get it even earlier than mom? Maybe that's the real reason I'm so tired all the time and why I keep getting these chronic headaches. What do they say . . . a stressed and inflamed body is more susceptible to cancer? Yes, that's it. What if I actually have the beginnings of breast cancer now . . . like the tiny seeds of it are inside me, and they're growing. Tom hates that I've been spending so much time after the kids are in bed on symptomchecker.com, but I'm scared for the kids! They need me here! I can't leave them without a mother.

I guess it means I should exercise more and eat better. But I hate how the women in Zumba class are acting more and more snooty to me. Since they found out we might lose our home (I should have never told them), I get the feeling they look down on me for it. Poor Lynda . . . fat, dumb Lynda with the doofus of a husband who couldn't keep a business alive. Probably what they're thinking. I saw how Judy gave Clara that quick, awkward look when I came in the door last week. Obviously, they can tell I've put on weight. That look was like . . . "Here comes the fat cow, wonder how much weight she's put on this week." I don't think I'll go anymore. They have no idea of the stress I've been under. They can't know what it is like as a person who eats her emotions. They're probably perfectly happy eating egg white and spinach omelets with their perfect little lives and their perfect husbands.

I have that quart of Häagen-Dazs in the fridge for tonight. Maybe I am a fat cow . . . no, I know I am. I deserve the name . . . but honestly, I'm past the point where I care or have the energy to do much about it. Life feels far too stressful to worry about eating all granola-mom-ishy right now, and our love life is in the trash, so it's not like I'm about to wear something sexy for Tom. My nighttime binges while I'm at the computer once the kids are finally asleep are about my only comfort.

Lynda 2:

No use wasting time worrying about this. It doesn't help . . . just gets me down. I know there are outstanding bills and other things pressing upon our spread thin budget, but Tom and I are doing all we can do, so that's that. We can't change anything, so why stress it? I'm just going to watch a funny movie with the kids tonight and zone out. We'll all dig into that gallon of chocolate ice cream Tom brought home last night, and we'll all feel better.

I guess we've all put on weight since the loss of the business . . . not just Tom and I but Jack too. Maybe he's learning some not-so-great food habits from us that aren't the best for a ten-year-old, but I'm not going to get on a guilt trip over that. Jack's anger outbursts have gotten worse in the last year. Sitting with his Dad drinking soda and eating chips while they watch football actually seems to calm him down. I'd be crazy to put a stop to that as he needs "dad time" any way he can get it. I'm sure there will be a time in the future for tightening up our diet when things are easier around here. I'll try to set everyone straight then, but we need our comforts now.

Besides, it's Tom's love language to bring home junk food for all of us, and goodness knows he needs some sort of happiness and affirmation right now. Poor guy. He'll probably make a beeline for the basement again tonight once he finally gets home, but he works such long hours these days! He deserves some man cave, chill time. I'm trying to get the kids to understand that daddy is going through a rough time right now, that's why he seems a bit grumpy, but things will get better down the road, as I always say.

Then again . . . darn . . . maybe I shouldn't have that ice cream tonight. They say sugar's no good for the immune system, and I've got that annoying scratchy throat thing. Been bothering me for 2 days now. Hopefully, it won't turn into that cold going around. Well, I've always had a strong immune system, so maybe I'll fight it off. Anyway . . . the ice cream will feel good on my throat, so perhaps it might help after all. The positives will probably cancel out the negatives. I'll just take some ibuprofen for this headache, and that might take care of the throat thing, too. Oh, well . . . at least I know this puny feeling is coming from the extra pressures we're under these days. Things will lighten up when the sun comes out, so to speak. (Starts humming theme song from *Annie . . .* "*The sun will come out tomorrow . . . bet your bottom dollar that tomorrow . . . there'll be sun.*")

I know Tom's taking this the hardest. He's shouldering all the blame for the failed business, but it's not like it's all his fault. It wasn't solely his decision. When he asked me about starting the business, I told him he might as well give it a try. Guess neither of us was smart enough to see the future, but that's all spilled milk. What's done is done. I just wish he would stop feeling so much guilt for it. Probably why our love life is pretty nonexistent right now. Since the bankruptcy, he just doesn't feel good about himself. I keep telling him not to blame himself for it . . . "you win some, you lose some." I keep saying. But he still seems pretty down in the mouth. Oh well. I gotta let him have his funk. He'll get over it. He usually does.

Looks like we'll have to move in with his parents for a while if we lose the house. I know it was hard for Tom to tell his dad about the bankruptcy. He was always so proud of how he was able to provide for our family . . . his parents raised him that way. And honestly, we always had that dream of our future in common . . . I'd stay home with the little ones; he'd bring home the bacon. Well . . . it was a good run. Maybe I'll just have to put the toddlers in daycare and get a job to help out. Tom hates the idea, but we've got to do what we've got to do.

Yes, his parents are being so great about all of this, but there's only so long we can keep borrowing money from them. Good thing they have that big house and that his mom and I get along pretty well. It would be hard to move in with awful in-laws like some other women have. I lucked out with Tom's family. And at least by staying there, we won't have to find an apartment while we get back on our feet. His Dad's talking about helping Tom start the business back up again next year . . . being a silent financial partner. Tom's just too gun shy to even consider that right now. He might hate his current job, but he hated watching the business go under even worse. Maybe he'll come around to the idea when he's out of this funk.

It stinks that Mom had to go through the whole cancer thing last year. She hasn't been the same energetic person she always was, but it's a good thing she caught it early. She's still here, and I'm grateful for that. She made it through like a champ. She always told us, "Keep your chin up." and she showed us how to do that big-time last year. Now Mom will be there for Aunt Margaret, who has to face that same grueling chemo. Nice that they have each other through this. I don't have Mom helping out as much with the kids because Aunt Margaret needs her, but I understand. I'll just keep my chin up, too. If Mom can, I can.

Oh . . . tomorrow's Tuesday. I have that Zumba class! But this scratchy throat . . . hmmm . . . not sure I'll go this week. Also, Judy and Clara have been acting a little weird toward me whenever I turn up. Probably because I keep skipping weeks now when I used to be so committed. They can probably tell my eating habits have not been that great either. But if they're going to be that shallow and only be friends with me if I turn up to classes and eat only lean chicken and salad all week, they're just not worth it. I'll give them a hall pass for now. But if they turn out to be true jerks, then I'll just move on and find new friends like I always do. Making friends has never been hard for me.

It will all work out . . . no sense getting my knickers all tied up in a knot about everything going crazy in my life right now. Just got to get through this day . . . I can't wait until all of this struggle is behind us. Hopefully, there'll be better times ahead, and life will calm down. Looking forward to putting on my favorite PJ's, snuggling up on the couch tonight with the kids, and laughing at Mrs. Doubtfire.

Lynda 3:

I don't understand all that is happening in our lives right now, but I refuse to partner with any thoughts of fear and anxiety. Those thoughts are from the accuser, but he has no right to my brain space. Putting a big stop sign up in front of them right now. Father, thank You that You have not given me a spirit of fear but of love and of power and of a sound mind. I'm going to follow Your Word which tells me to lift up the hem of my mind and take all thoughts captive that do not line up with You, my Prince of Peace.

Thank you, Father, for pouring Your peace over my life; peace that Your Word says is beyond my own understanding. You have told me that Your perfect love is what casts out fear. You do love me perfectly, and I am that girl who rests in Your love and Your peace while all is storming around me. I don't even know how we will pay the house mortgage this month, but Tom is working as hard as he can. You will take care of the rest Father. I'm not going to worry about the bills as Your Word declares You are Jehovah Jireh, our Provider. You tell us You will never leave us or forsake us. I stand on that promise right now and rest in Your loving arms.

We are so blessed to have Tom's parents offering their home to us. It will be an adjustment moving in with them if that is what it comes to, but hey . . . I know I can do all things with God's strength. Actually, the more I look at it in a new light, I'm realizing it will be great for the kids to be living with their grandparents for a few months. I'll have more help with them, so it could even turn out to be a bit of a win-win. Tom's mom loves being with the little ones in her own home. With live-in babysitters, we might even get a date night now and then!

The Word tells me, "It is a good thing to give thanks unto the Lord" and that "we enter His gates with thanksgiving in our hearts", so I'm going to do that right now. Thank You, Father, for family that are being so supportive during this time. Thank You for Tom's dad and his wisdom as he speaks into Tom's life and encourages him to keep up his faith in You during this challenging time. He even talked about helping him start the business back up again next year after we figure out all the financials more thoroughly and get together a far more detailed business plan projection this next time around.

I love that I'm beginning to see glimpses of Tom finally starting to look at this as a learning experience toward doing even greater things in the future rather than as a failure that will forever keep him from his dreams. It has taken a while for Tom to realize God does not see him as a failure as a provider, but as a man still trying his best for his family. I'm going to keep reminding him of this.

I know Tom doesn't love the new job he's had to take. Father, please comfort him and sustain him as he does something all day long, he doesn't enjoy just to support our family. I speak peace over my precious husband, who works so hard for us. You know me, Father, and You know my past. Thank You that You helped me last night when I could have taken the way Tom acted about taking out the trash as an offense. He was tired and so was I, but God, somehow You let me see his heart rather than being blinded by hurt like I always used to do. Thank You that You later nudged my heart toward him and gave me the opportunity to initiate making love. That was always a struggle for me in the past, but I am a new creature in Christ, and little by little, I am becoming more and more the blessing I was created to be for my family.

It's amazing that as I bless others, You are pouring the blessings back into my life, Father. I could tell this morning from Tom's demeanor that our intimate time together was just what we both needed. He winked at me as he left for work. I actually got that little flutter in my heart again that I had when we were dating! That's crazy considering our current circumstances. But you are the God of the impossible! The stress of all this would have worn me down in the past. But, Father, You are sustaining me and growing me and doing incredible things in my marriage through all this. I declare health, vigor, and renewed strength over my husband. God, I ask that you increase his vision for our future and restore his losses into greater things than he ever could have hoped for. I thank You that you are teaching me to not get constantly hurt and shut down, but rather to love unconditionally as You do.

Once again, I want to give thanks for that word "remission" that Mom got a few months back. It was hard to watch her go through the treatment. I hated seeing my mother's beautiful hair disappear, but somehow God, you gave us moments of pure joy in the journey. I have that special memory of us both trying on wigs. We laughed till we cried . . . people thought we were nuts. Oh, that felt good! My mom is alive! You are a good God. How I would have mourned and missed her if she left us, but I still would have declared You good for that is who You are. But she is here! You guided the surgeon's hand through her surgery, and You sustained her through her treatment. Thank you for upholding Your Word that I spoke over Mom every day that "no poison shall harm her" based on Mark 16:18. I know chemo can be toxic to the body, Father, but I thank You that You used it to heal rather than harm.

*Thinking about healing . . . I accept the beautiful promises of healing given to me through the stripes that Jesus bore on the cross. This scratchy throat . . . I'm not going to go down with it. It has no right in my body, for Galatians 3:13 tells me, "Christ has redeemed us from the **curse** of the law, having **become** a **curse** for us (for **it** is written, "**Cursed** is everyone **who** hangs on a tree"). He took all of the curse on the cross . . . both sins and sicknesses. If He took it, that means I don't have to wear it! Yay! I am made whole and healthy through Jesus' stripes that He bore for me. I'm not going to concentrate on the pain of this throat and do like I used to and examine how bad it is or how far it is progressing into a cold. I'll just shoot for an earlier night, take some immune helping herbs, and some extra vitamin C. Thank you, God, for Your provision* *of healing herbs and for doctors and medicine You have provided for us on this earth. If medicine is needed, I won't feel shame in using that, too . . . anything that contributes toward my healing is from You, Father, for You sent Your son to heal and to save. I thank You for Your healing power, and I accept it in my body right now.*

Don't think I'll go to Zumba class tomorrow. Resting my body when it needs it is as important as moving my body. I'm sure the girls will understand, but I better text Judy and Clara to let them know. They've been so encouraging to me on my health and weight loss journey. I thought there was an awkward moment in one of our conversations a couple weeks ago. In the past, I would have really worried about what they were thinking. Thank You, Father, that You have freed me from presumptive thinking and from nursing hurt. I'm so done with judging expressions and presuming negative intentions about people. Getting together with friends, sweating, and dancing to music with the girls always makes me feel so great afterwards. I also love that they have childcare there at Zumba. It's amazing that the church offers it as a free service and an outreach. I want to reach out more to some of the young moms who've been turning up there. What was that one girl's name . . . Susan? Yes, I think so. She has a sweet two-year-old girl, too. She was rather shy when I said hello last time, but I'll try again. I should ask her over so our little ones can play, and we can chat. Got a feeling she could use a friend.

Maybe I can't exercise right now as I walk out of this sore throat, but I can make healthy food. Yeah, I kinda caved yesterday and had that shake at the drive-through since the toddlers were so hungry and wanted chicken nuggets after errands, but that was yesterday, and this is today. His mercies are new every morning. If God can give me that never-ending mercy, I can offer it to myself.

I refuse to listen to guilt and shame and the accuser's garbage that says I'll never be able to conquer binge eating or reach my health goals. Well, guess what? I didn't have the fries . . . I didn't have the burger. I had one small shake. I came home and had a healthy meal last night. I am rocking it!!! You know what . . . doesn't even matter if I had caved to the fries yesterday. Even that could not deter me from a brilliant future. The scale, with its ups and downs, does not define me, and my identity is not in my failures. My identity is in who He has called me to be, and He says, "I have been made more than a conqueror!" I am that girl who honors this body He has given me. I'm reminded that in the book of Joshua, God gave the choice of life or death, but He told us to choose life. You bet I am choosing life. I choose life in my thinking. I choose life in my marriage.

I choose life on my plate. I choose life in my cup. In every area of my life, I will choose and nourish life.

I think tonight I'll try that healthy meatloaf recipe Judy texted me last week. I'm not going to make a big deal about how it replaces the white breadcrumbs with ground flax seed and almond flour to Tom. That just wigs him out. Judy swears her whole family inhaled it, so I'm just going to serve it, and if it doesn't go over, I'll try something else next time. I'll make a salad and some broccoli with it. Maybe some brown rice tossed with butter and shredded cheese for the kids. Tom is eating broccoli . . . I can't believe it! The key was roasting it with coconut oil and lots of seasonings. Who knew! Sure, he's still eating some junk food, but it is less . . . we're making strides.

This is me now . . . I'm That Girl who feeds her family healthy meals . . . whaaaaat???!!! I buy ingredients like flax meal, and my grocery cart is full of leafy greens, healthy proteins, frozen berries, lentils, beans, and other stuff I never saw myself buying. The old me doesn't even recognize this new me! My cart used to be boxes of cereal, packs of chips, sodas, and single-serve mac-n-cheese for the microwave. I didn't think it was possible to eat healthy on a tight budget, but it is . . . I just had to say I could do it, then do it! Even Jack is trimming down. Thankfully we'd never made a big deal about his weight, but it is naturally melting with the changes I'm making to our family meals. He's slowly starting to come around to some of the new foods I've been serving up, though it hasn't been easy removing the sodas and so many of the sugary foods he was used to. Since his sugar consumption has gone down, his behavior has improved too. I think encouraging him to join the baseball team has also been great for him. And whenever Tom can get to a game . . . Jack's grin at knowing his dad is watching him . . . I love seeing it.

Sometimes the accuser's voice tempts me to partner with thoughts of despair. I'm tempted to look at all that we've been through as a long and rough two years, but I refuse those thoughts. I see how much Tom and I have learned through this trial. There's been huge growth in our lives we wouldn't have experienced without going through what we have. I am determined to look at the future with hope and delight. I remind myself of that scripture . . . Jeremiah 29:11 (NIV), "For I know the plans I have for you," declares the Lord, "plans to prosper you and not to harm you, plans to give you hope and a future." That's me . . . I'm that girl full of hope.

CHAPTER ELEVEN

Thoughts (Part IV)

Let's Reflect

So . . . Lynda 1 from the last chapter . . . anything in common? Okay, perhaps her thought life is a bit more extreme in the stinkin' thinkin' department than your own. Her thoughts are *really* stinking up the room with a noxious, negative odor. Maybe your internal dialogue isn't quite that toxic, but if we were betting women, we'd wager it's come close a time or twenty. Of course, we only know that because we used to have quite a bit in common with Lynda 1 ourselves.

People like our first Lynda are sometimes labeled "naturally negative". But really, there's no such thing. Naturally negative just means someone has done a lot of agreeing with negative thoughts over the years, and those thought patterns have become entrenched. If you see yourself in Lynda, no need to despise yourself. You were made for so much more and God wants to lead you out. Those hopeless, dismal thoughts aren't you. They're from the accuser. As you start seeing those mud-caked thoughts for what they are . . . not your own, you can start detaching yourself from them and filling your mind with wiser, truth-filled, Word-washed, life-building ones.

"Glass half full" Lynda was next. Thank God for the "life is rosy" Lynda's of the world, right? Chin up and all that. Lynda 2 has some great natural instincts. She is determined to laugh through her struggles (laughter is scientifically healing). She gives grace to her husband and children (studies show grace given in relationships results in longer-lasting and deeper ones). She keeps hoping that things will get better. (Hope is a powerful force that can lead to faith and real change.)

The *truth* of the Word is the ultimate *weapon* that can slay the yuck and mess of life.

But while second Lynda's life is better overall because of her attitudes, she's still missing the full picture. The truth of the Word is the ultimate weapon that can slay the yuck and mess of life. John 8:32 tells us that it's this truth that "shall make you free". Lynda 2 is having to pull her big girl socks up and drag herself through her current life struggle like a Navy Seal, whereas she could rest in the revelation that God's got it. She doesn't have to wish it all over. Wishing it over causes her to miss out on seeing the promises emerge that God has for every problem. It causes her to miss out on growing and learning and changing through the storm of a struggle. It causes her to miss out on the deep soul rest no matter the circumstances; the basking in God's peace as He takes her hand as whispers to her, *". . . all is well . . . I have overcome the world"* (John 16:33).

Don't get us wrong. Everyone is blessed by positive people. They don't drain the energy out of their family and friends (or themselves). But there is a bit of a flaw with positivity when it isn't grounded by the Word. It is not surety. It is not confidence. It is limited to hoping for the best; but hope without FAITH is not the currency of expectancy and harvest. Proverbs 3:26 (ESV) states the truth, *". . . for the LORD will be your confidence and will keep your foot from being caught."*

The Far Better Offer

What if the glimpses into Lynda 1 and Lynda 2's internal dialogues were the only two we had to show? What if there was no example of Lynda 3 . . . no offer of something far better? We would have had to say something like . . . "See how much better Lynda 2's marriage seems to be? While Lynda 1 is possibly heading for divorce, Lynda 2 is likely to go on and have a long, amiable marriage. Notice how she's not shutting out her kids or filling her mind with toxic thoughts about friends and family? She still has hope for the future, and that will go a long way to help her and her family through this trial. We all need to be more like Lynda 2 during times of trouble."

Hmmm . . . maybe somewhat true and slightly helpful words. But there have been plenty of positive thinking, self-help type books written over the years saying much the same thing. We're offering (well, God is offering, not us, but you get it) something far greater. Not all of us can turn ourselves into Positive Polly types. To truly turn our lives around, we need something stronger than "keep yer chin up" bumper stickers that Lynda 2 probably has on her minivan. What we need is the powerful, electrical charge of TRUTH to "shock start" dead hope and happiness and give life back its pulse.

Enter Lynda 3 and her transformed mind musings. Doesn't matter what her thought life used to be like in the past. Doesn't matter whether she considered herself a naturally negative or positive person. Doesn't matter what label she ended up with after taking all the trendy personality tests. Whether INGF, introvert, number 5, Autumn, or Type 3 . . . none of that matters a whiff! In fact, in her past, she may have even given our first Lynda a run for her money, stinking up the room with her thinking. She's simply not that girl anymore.

> To truly turn our *lives* around, we need something *stronger* than "keep yer chin up" bumper stickers

Lynda 3's new thoughts are directed by the Word, not by any part of her nature. She is truly a "new creature" when it comes to how she thinks. Her mind has been renewed through training it to agree with the truth of the Word. She is that girl who has found the secret place written about in Psalm 91 (NIV) . . . *"Whoever dwells in the secret place of the most high, will rest under the shadow of the almighty."*

This secret place is in her mind . . . her thought life aligned with God's Word. And did you see what it says happens to those who find this secret place? They get to rest! Where is that rest? Right under the beautiful shadow of Almighty God! Verse 4 goes on to say that He will cover them with His feathers, and under His wings will they find refuge. Honestly, that whole Psalm is so encouraging and beautiful. Go read all of Psalm 91 when you have a chance.

But it is not just knowledge of the Word alone that renews Lynda 3's mind. Memorizing scripture for memorizing sake or doing Bible reading by the clock to mark off on a to-do list is not how she is renewed. It's by hunger and appetite . . . it's by feeding on the Word. Matthew 4:4 (ESV) tells us, *". . . It is written, 'Man shall not live by bread alone, but by every word that comes from the mouth of God'."* Lynda 3 has fed on the WORD, and after feeding, she has PRACTICED the Word . . . like a weight trainer would train his or her muscles. At first it feels foreign and quite challenging, but then a rhythm happens, muscles slowly build and are able to lift more and more weights. In the same way, new pathways of truth start building in the mind. They get stronger and stronger the more they are used. Practicing the Word like this, as Lynda 3 has done, and continues to do, is being a doer of the Word like James 1:22 encourages us to do. *"But be doers of the word, and not hearers only . . ."*.

At first it feels foreign and quite challenging, but then a rhythm happens, muscles slowly build.

Lynda 3 smiles at the future and does just like 1 Peter 5:7 (NIV) encourages, *"Cast all your anxiety on him because he cares for you."* This casting cares is not a little dusting off of the burdens on our minds and hearts. It's a lot more dramatic than that. The word *"cast"* used in this verse is the Greek word *epiripto*, which is a compound word made up of *epi* and *ripto*. The first word means "upon", and *ripto* means "to hurl or violently throw" or "to fling something with great force." It is a picture of a burdened and exhausted traveler, literally chucking off their heavy bundles onto a beast of burden like a donkey. They are determined to be rid of them as they can't carry them any longer.

Solid Ground, Not Utopia

Please know that by showcasing Lynda 3's thoughts, we are not trying to pass off a made-up formula for a perfect life. This is no *"think these certain things and you'll get these certain results"* SHAZAM recipe! Well, ahem . . . there's actual scientific truth to that, as you'll discover in the upcoming *Promised You Some Science* chapters, but the goal here is not to magically get a smooth and easy life. The Word promises solid ground for the wise; it doesn't promise Utopia. It reminds us that we will face trials and temptations. Through them, we can exercise weaker spiritual muscles until they strengthen, and we grow in grace and truth.

Lynda 3 has real and lasting positive changes happening in her life, but just because she has chosen to *"gird up the loins"* of her thought life does not mean her life is suddenly perfect. Her husband is not sweet to her all the time. Her Zumba friends mean well, but maybe they are a tad two-faced sometimes. Her children can still be challenging, and the financial crisis is still very real. But through all of this, she now chooses the truth, which tells her that peace, joy, and contentment can be hers in the midst of the storm.

The *goal* here is not to magically get a *smooth* and easy life.

Does this mean she never cries? Oh, she does. This is not robot Lynda who stuffs emotions. God is with those who mourn, the scriptures tell us. Tears are a pure expression of human feeling. Jesus Himself shed them, and they can be cleansing and even healing. But Lynda is comforted. She knows the difference between a good, needed cry and despair. Despair is from the accuser, not her Heavenly Father. In His *Sermon on the Mount*, Jesus tells us in Matthew 5:4, *"Blessed are those who mourn for they shall be comforted."* Do you see the two parts to that verse? What begins with mourning ends with comfort. "I'm that girl who is comforted" can be the declaration we wear over our lives.

She *knows* the difference between a good, needed *cry* and despair.

Does Lynda 3 never get weary? She does . . . she *really* does. This is not Superwoman Lynda, who takes on too much and refuses to take time to meet the needs of her mind and body. But she is strengthened. She knows giving up is what the accuser wants her to do, not her Heavenly Father.

Does she never slip up and revert to old thinking habits? She sure does . . . too many times to count. This is not perfect Lynda who affords herself no room for error. This is Lynda who has learned to give herself grace and forgiveness and just get back to it. She knows it is the voice of the accuser that says . . . "you'll never get this," not her loving Heavenly Father.

Head to Baggage Claim

We love that famous quote by William Wordsworth that says, "Your mind is the garden, your thoughts are the seeds. The harvest can either be flowers or weeds." This quote actually stems from the Word. Look at Galatians 6:7, *". . . God is not mocked; for whatsoever a man sows, that he will he also reap."* Lynda 3 is not by her own strength saying, "I'm that girl who doesn't live under the cloud of worry." It's a gift; it is grace upon her life. The Greek word for grace means "love gifts". Lynda 3 is now that girl who has freedom from oppression because of LOVE gifted. But the gift has to be opened, and it all starts by opening the seed of the Word. Lynda 3 is simply that girl who decided to unwrap these beautiful gifts God had already given her.

There are over 8,000 promises in the Word that are ours to claim. But they are not handed to us like a gift already unwrapped on our laps. Like Lynda 3, we have to do the unwrapping. It's our turn to move! We have to say, *"YES, I want them!"* Lynda 1 is not receiving these precious gifts that could transform her life, only because her gifts are still sitting there . . . in their gift bags!

> There are over 8,000 *promises* in the Word that are ours to *claim.*

2 Corinthians 1:20 (HCSB) explains, *"For every one of God's promises is "Yes" in Him. Therefore, the "Amen" is also spoken through Him by us for God's glory."* Our Father has already said His "Yes". He is just waiting for ours.

We have to first identify that the promises are ours. We have to, through faith, see our name tag written on the bag of goods. When we discover that we are "that girl" who owns these promises (which will be a "no brainer" when we get familiar with the Word), then we can confidently march up to baggage claim, grab the hefty bundles of *"great and precious promises"* off the carousel and take them home to be gratefully opened and used in our lives. If anyone gives us any trouble or a side glance of skepticism as we are stride up to take the spoil, we can show them our identity badge of crimson love . . . "that girl" who is a blood-bought daughter of the King. Jesus tells us in John 16:15 (BSB), *"Everything that belongs to the Father is Mine. That is why I said that the Spirit will take from what is Mine and disclose it to you."*

Our Father has *already* said His "Yes". He is just *waiting* for ours.

CHAPTER TWELVE

Broken -vs- Victorious (Part I)

The Intro

An intro is needed here because . . . oh, boy . . . where we're about to go with you right now is such a touchy subject. We know you want to dig right into the science chapters, then take the fun dive into the *Sides* and *Desserts* part of this book . . . the actual declarations, but we can't move on until we all settle something.

It's time to tackle it.

If you're a Christian . . . should you be broken or victorious?

We broached this subject in the *Appetizer* chapters, but now it is time to dig much more deeply into it. Because you see, you can't go any further in this book . . . you can't start making all sorts of specific "I'm That Girl" declarations if you're not certain of what you believe. No use in declaring things that are not cemented in your heart. That would be what James 1:8 calls *"double-minded."* If one minute you're declaring, "I'm that girl who is walking out of this autoimmune disease" . . . and the next wondering if God is the one who gave it to you to teach you some well-needed lessons . . . you've got some sorting to do.

You need to be fully persuaded in your declarations and convictions if they are to be rooted in faith and therefore transformative in your life. So, let's talk this out and see if we can all come to some friendly agreement together.

We don't love debates, but this is a raging one between believers . . . are we broken, poor and needy, or are we whole, restored overcomers?

We *really* wanted to write this chapter as a "reach across the aisle" . . . "we see both sides" . . . "let's all get along" chapter. Because the thing is, both sides do have truths. But, in the end, we just couldn't be neutral. Although we gel with many

> We simply had to pick *Victorious*. There is *no* other place for us to land.

aspects of the "broken" argument, after much scripture diving, soul searching, and life experience, we simply had to pick VICTORIOUS. There is no other place for us to land.

Repercussions for Victorious?

Before we start talking about all the glorious treasures found in the land of victorious, we need to walk you through how we got here and why we're inviting you here with us. But yikes . . . even writing the word VICTORIOUS . . . it feels sort of politically incorrect (or more like churchically incorrect) to dare utter these days. It also comes with the threat of being lumped into the hyper faith doctrinal bandwagon . . . you know the stigma . . . where all the kooks manifest with crazy dances and cackles. Well, perhaps we shouldn't be too quick to judge there either. King David comes straight to mind. He's the one who God called a man after His own heart, yet David was documented as being a right crazy dancer. In fact, he danced in the streets before God *"with all his might."* Second Samuel tells us he was wearing nothing but *"a linen ephod"* (his loin cloth or what we would call his tighty whities).

Biblical scholars argue back and forth whether he really was dancing in just his underwear or whether it was something slightly more covering like a onesie tunic-type thing that soldiers wore under their armor. But either way, he looked completely undignified, and we know this because his wife told him so.

And Christian cackles? Hmmm . . . well, nope. We can't exactly bring any scriptures to mind supporting that one. But maybe only because we haven't looked hard enough. But kooky or not, whatever your beliefs, maybe we need to all stop judging one another for the way we worship and express our own, unique communication with the Father.

Some of us want to stand still in a holy hush and be reverent, quiet, and thoughtful. Others of us want to dance and holler and get all sorts of out there! Some of us want only the hymns . . . others of us only want the hip, modern worship tunes. As pastor's kids, growing up in nondenominational, charismatic-style church services, we'd seen it all, or so we thought. And, as is often typical for pastor's kids, we became more than a little jaded. We developed a judgy, "only we know best" attitude as to how people should express themselves in worship services. The "all their crazy might" worshippers were way over the top in our minds . . . and the ones who couldn't even raise their hands? Well, they were far too rigid.

Why couldn't all the wackified types be as "Christian cool" and balanced as us? Why couldn't the stiff and starchies loosen up and learn to clap a little and sway appropriately to the music (using mostly shoulder action . . . not too much hip . . . there are suitable Christian dance moves, of course—wink).

Good riddance to all that pride and judgement we carried . . . all ways of worship are fantastic. If someone is singing a bit too loudly or laughing in a suspiciously kook alert cackling way . . . perhaps dancing their best "Jerusalem Arise" movements, waving a homemade Feast of Tabernacles banner, and jigging with a tasseled tambourine . . . more power to 'em!

For real on the "more power to 'em" thing. The coming *Promised You Some Science* chapters will reveal that laughing, singing, and dancing are all incredibly physically healing behaviors for our bodies. And dare we even mention shouting? Oh, how we used to cringe in church services when someone would get all worked up and start SHOUTING FOR GOD! But, guess what? We, the cynical *shoutees,* were in the wrong. The *shouter* was only being Biblical. Zechariah 9:9 says . . . *"Rejoice greatly O daughter of Zion, shout O daughter of Jerusalem."* King David said in Psalm 71:23 (NASB), *"My lips will **shout** for joy when I sing praises to You."* In fact, there are multiple places in the Bible where we are specifically told to *"shout for joy."* It is actually a command. *Hmmm.* Makes you kinda feel a little less judgy about the so-called "kooks" in church, right? They got it right. Us? Not so much.

So, we're still going ahead with this victorious thing. If we come across as kooks, well . . . we're in good company with the psalmist who was viewed as the same.

> Good riddance to *all* that pride and judgement we carried . . . all ways of worship are *fantastic.*

> Laughing, *singing*, and dancing are all incredibly physically *healing* behaviors for our bodies.

Or, what about this . . . gasp . . . what if we end up getting lumped in with the prosperity doctrine folks . . . or gulp . . . if we get boxed in with "new thought" theology peeps?

No worries . . . we'll survive.

Speaking of "new thought" theology . . . if you're not familiar with it, it is the phrase given to Christians who embrace New Age theories. We want to go on record as saying we don't embrace New Age theories. We'd much prefer to call some of these "age-old truths," which we actually do embrace and which we'll talk more about in the science chapters.

But let's clear this up now, so you don't think we've gone off the deep end . . . No, we are not little gods (as New Age theology teaches). We are children of God. We don't worship ourselves; we worship the One who created us and gave His life for us. But God is the One who created all physics, energy, matter, electricity, meridians, crystals, sound therapy, magnetics and other so-called woo-woo stuff, eons before the New Agers claimed ownership of them. The cross paid the price to redeem us from all of our diseases. Ultimate healing comes only through the finished work of the cross. But this doesn't mean there are not wise eating principles, herbs, electric frequencies, and things like grounding your feet in the soil or sand to slurp up those amazingly charged ions that are simply a wonderful part of Divinely created nature to benefit our bodies. There's a sad case of "throwing the baby out with the bath water" in Christian culture around this issue.

> You sure won't find us throwing stones at the *gift* of financial *prosperity*.

While we're at it . . . might as well go on record to say while we're not actually part of any prosperity doctrines either. But we can't deny that we've been able to be a blessing to far more people since we have been financially blessed. Both of our families were once extremely broke, as in "Yikes, looks like we might need food stamps for a while" broke. For many, long years we had to pinch pennies and scrimp and scrape to get by. There were valuable lessons to be learned during those tight years, such as contentment and true joy found without "stuff." But God blessed our business (Trim Healthy Mama) beyond our wildest dreams, and that enabled us to bless many other lives through hiring hundreds of people and giving liberally when there are needs. So, no . . . even if we don't ascribe to "prosperity doctrines", you sure won't find us throwing stones at the gift of financial prosperity.

Word of Caution

But as we go forward in the next few chapters and discover the importance of opening ourselves up to receiving God's gift of victorious power in our lives, we want to make sure we're not steering you down a wrong path.

We never want to get wrapped up in gifts and forget that it is the Giver that we seek. Matthew 6:33 (NLT) tells us, *"Seek the Kingdom of God above all else, and live righteously, and He will give you everything you need."* God's victory and the other gifts He has for us are not really "things" at all; they are a Person, the Personhood of Christ.

A longing to know God is understood in the Hebrew word for "know", which is *yada*. It describes an intimate relationship and deep understanding through friendship as shown in Jeremiah 29:13, *"You will seek Me and find Me when you seek Me with all your heart."* This seeking to know Him with *"all your heart"*, described in the above scripture, ushers in the abundance of good gifts into our lives. Daniel 11:32 reminds us, *". . . but the people who* **know** *their God shall be strong, and carry out great exploits."*

The natural and divine way of things goes like this . . . If we seek an intimate relationship with the Author of love, we can't help but be drowned in His deluge of Perfect Love. *"Perfect"*, used as a description for this Divine Love that casts out fear, is the Greek word *teleia*, which means absolutely complete.

If we seek to be bestest of BFF's with the Prince of Peace, then there is no holding back a double portion of His Perfect Peace. The Hebrew word for *"peace"* in the scripture that says He will give *"perfect peace"* (Isaiah 26:3) is the word *shâlôm shalom* or peace peace. It is double peace that God pours out. He always works in abundance!

If we seek to fully know the Source of all happiness, rather than just ease of life and happiness through circumstance, we don't just find happiness . . . we find it multiplied to us. The Hebrew word for *"happy"*, used in Proverbs 16:20, and many other scriptures, is *esher* which is never singular but plural. It is better translated as "how happy" or more than just happy. You might say it also equals double happy.

If we seek the Father of Joy, He will swell joy up so powerfully within us that it affects the very physical matter and earth around us. The word *"joy"* used in multiple places in the scriptures and here in Psalm 126:3 (NLT), *"Yes, the Lord has done amazing things for us! What JOY."*, stems from the word *sameach* which means rejoice and be glad. It is the same word in 1 Kings 1:40 where they rejoiced *(sameach)* and the ground was rent and split by the sound. Such a POWERFUL word for JOY!

Our Daddy Is a Giver

While we always want to seek God's heart, not just His hand, His hand cannot be stopped from blessing us when we desire to know (aka *yada*) Him. Denying our Father the joy of giving to us by turning away His hand would be destroying this intimacy since giving is God's very nature. He holds nothing back . . . even His only Son. John 3:16 reveals the depth of His generosity, *"For God so loved the world that he GAVE His only begotten Son . . ."*. LOVE GIVES. It cannot be stopped. We are reminded of 2 Peter 1:3-4 (NLT) *"By His divine power, God has GIVEN us EVERYTHING we need for living a godly life. We have RECEIVED ALL of this by coming to know Him . . ."*

Giving is God's very *nature.*

A victorious mindset and its reality of blessing is the natural consequence of this "yada-ing" (our made-up Hebrew/English word) God. It follows us dying to ourselves and taking His mind into our own.

Matthew 16:25 (ESV) explains, *"For whoever would save his life will lose it, but whoever loses his life for my sake will find it."* Galatians 2:20 (ESV), *"I have been crucified with Christ. It is no longer I who live, but Christ who lives in me. And the life I now live in the flesh I live by faith in the Son of God, who loved me and GAVE himself for me."* This correct and God-ordained order of Who and What we live for is the difference between this victorious GOOD NEWS the Bible expresses and yucky "prosperity doctrines" that stink of self-gain and a red Ferrari to ride our puffed-up selves on a pride parade through downtown "Self" Street.

Being favored through a close friendship with God, instead of just grabbing His stuff with no intent on a relationship with Him, changes the smell of things entirely. There is no "something is rotten here" stench from being a natural, beloved, and rewarded daughter of the King of Kings! It's His way, His personality, to reward the ones who seek Him (Hebrews 11:6). This inherited shoe of blessing fits perfectly onto our heiress's feet . . . no forcing or squeezing necessary. To give you another analogy (you know we love 'em), let's not confuse a bridegroom's lavish love gifts on His bride with the desperate and selfish "give me, give me" grabbing of a girl who will take expensive jewelry but refuses to give her heart away to the one who loves her.

> There is no "something is rotten here" stench from being a natural, *beloved,* and rewarded *daughter* of the King of Kings!

Our real treasure is in "yada-ing" our God. Seeking stuff and victories for the comfort and promotion of "self" is grotesque and only leads to poverty of our spirits. Matthew 6:19-20 (NLT) encourages us, *"Don't store up treasures here on earth, where moths eat them and rust destroys them, and where thieves break in and steal. Store your treasures in Heaven, where moths and rust cannot destroy, and thieves do not break in and steal."*

Receive So We Can Give

The next few chapters will hopefully show that we cannot Biblically describe a true believer's life without abundance and blessing, but let's also keep in mind that this is sooooo much more than uber prosperity that may or may not even manifest in monetary riches. God has financially blessed us, and we believe He can and certainly wants to help pull you out of debt and financial struggle, if that's where you are.

> This whole *beauty* of receiving is the ability to have so we can *give away.*

But, His most awesome riches are far beyond mere finances. 1 Corinthians 2:9 (WEB), *"But as it is written, 'Things which an eye didn't see, and an ear didn't hear, which didn't enter into the heart of man, these God has prepared for those who love Him'."* Our Father's gifts extend into realms beyond our physical sensibilities and these remarkable blessings can only be understood and opened by our spirit. Our spirit is awakened by "yada-ing" with the Spirit of God. When we know Him, we receive Him.

This whole beauty of receiving is the ability to have so we can give away. It is reproducing . . . multiplying love . . . a beautiful circle of giving and receiving so we can give and receive again. LOVE knows no end. We receive our daily bread so we can break it and give it away . . . no matter how small, He can multiply it to bless five thousand. Whatever we receive, we sow into others.

Opting for a "broken" identity prevents this identity of a "giver". We want to be that girl who receives from Daddy so she can pass it to others. This is our redeemed nature as true daughters, emulating our Heavenly Father.

Taking Our Stand Without Standing on Others

So, VICTORIOUS is still our only choice. The accuser would love to prevent us from standing to our full height in God and sharing this good and victorious news with you, but too bad for him . . . it's about to go down.

In taking this stand though, we sure don't want to be part of Christian camp culture. Know what we mean, right? No, not like summer camp . . . we're talking about all these divided camps in modern church society that set up doctrines on opposing sides and basically shout Christian insults to each other 24/7. There are far too many YouTubes, social media rants, and podcasts calling out and then pulling apart teachers, churches, and entire ministries over this "Broken -vs- Victorious" issue (and lots of other issues . . . gentle parenting -vs- traditional parenting, homeschooling -vs- regular schooling, predestination -vs- free will, old earth -vs-new earth, etc.). Ouch . . . dare we even mention these topics without making half of us irate at the other half?

These are all prickly issues, but come on . . . there are valid truths on both sides. We can all disagree on things, but we can keep our love! Families, friends, and churches are dividing over these arguments. But being harsh, right up in your space . . . "you unbiblical person, you" type of disagree-ers only gives Christ a bad name. John 13:35 ". . . *by this all men know that you are My disciples, if you have love one for another."*

> We can all *disagree* on things, but we can *keep* our love!

You can certainly disagree with some of the things we say in this book; hope we can still be friends if we meet. Take the parts here that you are ready for and that will bless you and put the rest on the shelf. Heck (Can we say "heck"? You okay with that?), even the two of us sisters aren't twinsies with our theology. We have some pretty vast theological disagreements. Don't even get us going on old earth -vs- new earth or whether we are part of the lost tribes of Israel or not . . . or what about this one . . . ha ha . . . whether those *"men of valor"* Jude talked about in the Bible were Satan's fallen angels or not . . . you bet we don't see perfectly eye to eye. We used to argue with each other 'til we were red in the face then get all prickly and hurt after our "Christian debate" sessions. Now, thank God, we have learned to be open enough to actually listen to the other side (well, for a few minutes before we butt in). But even after listening, we still frequently just end up agreeing to disagree and love each other through our differences. We have the cross in common and that's what counts.

So, please . . . let us do the same thing here. Allow us to lay out our case for victorious. We hope to do it with grace and without name calling or name naming (not gonna mention certain pastors or teachers that may disagree with us as their hearts are usually good and we are all on a journey of learning and growing).

Common Ground

To those of you who have adopted a Christian mindset of brokenness . . . so much love and respect for you! You're so right that our Christian walk should focus on the cross rather than on drummed up, baseless, hyper faith, or obsession with signs and wonders. You're right, we need to be broken vessels before we can be restored. 100% agreement that we must first humble ourselves before Christ can be lifted up in our lives. Yes, we must also be crucified with Him and take up our cross daily. We're on the same page that God is sovereign and that sometimes, for reasons that we'll only find out in heaven . . . physical healings do not always happen despite much prayer. We're with you that these unanswered prayers don't automatically mean sin in someone's life or that someone didn't summon enough faith. (Although, let's not pretend the Bible doesn't continually encourage the prayer of faith . . . not the prayer of the worried.)

> We're with you that these unanswered *prayers* don't automatically mean sin in someone's life or that someone didn't *summon* enough faith.

We agree that just because we're Christians, we shouldn't expect or pray for perfect little lives where we never go through challenges and battles and times of testing. You're spot on that we should rejoice in times of trials. Hey . . . God wants us to have a merry heart in both the hard and easy seasons of our lives! So, yeah . . . let's absolutely rejoice! Who could argue with Paul in Philippians 4:12 (ESV) when he said, *"I know how to be brought low and I know how to abound in any and every circumstance, I have learned the secret of facing plenty and hunger, abundance and need."*

See how much we have in common already? And you've probably got many other huge God-inspired downloads that we haven't fully grasped yet ourselves. So, we hope what we're about to share in these next few chapters do not come across as looking down our noses at you or anyone else. We're still learning and growing and are far from final "authorities" on God's Word.

But . . . we've been on a journey. We've walked both sides of this faith and belief path and in doing so, some truths eventually settled peacefully down in our hearts. We've come to realize that the cross is not a half-finished work that leaves us broken and limping along. The notion that it elevates God when we concentrate on and lament about our utter broken and pitifulness cannot be one that we personally identify with.

Hold on . . . let's stay friends here. Don't ditch us yet. Can we reiterate . . . we agree that there are many beautiful attributes that develop in the hearts of Christians who seek a walk of brokenness. They are encouraged to be grateful and perseverant in times of trials . . . this is absolutely scriptural. They are encouraged to have a contrite heart, one that is quick to repent. Spot on! So long as it doesn't give us a sin-minded nature. But again, we have to differ on one thing. When there is little to no encouragement to believe for a breakthrough . . . to believe for healing or to believe that we can overcome . . . this is when we say, "Hey, what's going on here?"

> The *cross* is not a half-finished work that *leaves* us broken and limping along.

And here comes the ouch . . . **when it is considered saintlier . . . nobler . . . dare we say . . . Godlier to suffer through illness or other trials than to believe that God can heal, rescue, and restore . . . the magnitude of the cross is diminished.**

We've been right there in the broken mentality, so we pray this isn't coming across as high and mighty finger pointing. But we are there no longer. We came to a place where we had to ask ourselves the following question . . .

"Are we Believers or not?"

CHAPTER THIRTEEN

Broken -vs- Victorious (Part II)

Believers Believe!

The word "Believer" is basically interchangeable with "Christian". Christians are known as "Believers". But notice that root word, **believe**? To be a Believer means we naturally do just that . . . believe! If we believe Christ took our sins through the shedding of His blood, we can't leave out the stripes He took on His back for our healing part. That is only partial belief, and we can't pick and choose. He cleanses sins and He heals diseases; they go hand-in-hand in the scriptures.

God's Word shows over and over that it is just as much God's will to heal our bodies as it is to heal our souls. I Peter 2:24 says, *"Who Himself bore our sins in His own body . . ."* Not so much trouble believing that for most of us. He took our sins . . . they are gone! Insert happy dance or at the least a jolly good fist pump! But it doesn't make sense to get all fist-pumpy about that and remain blasé about Matthew 8:17, which tells us, *"He Himself took our infirmities And bore our sicknesses."* This is equally deserving of belief and exuberance on our part.

David starts Psalm 103 by saying, *"Bless the LORD O my soul, and forget not all His benefits."* "ALL" is a key word here. A broken Christian mentality is at risk of forgetting *ALL* His benefits . . . His miraculous healing power being a major one of them. We do the cross an injustice by remembering only half of what it accomplished. The fullness is what we need to remember. Not only remember, but celebrate and anticipate because He is still at work.

Many of us as Christians . . . we do our devotionals and we go to our services and our support meetings, but we don't live plugged into the ultimate power source of the Spirit of God . . . the electrical outlet. Our spirit gets all plugged up with doubt, human reasoning, and past experiences. Those cause us to no longer **believe** the WORD at face value. 2 Timothy 3:5 (NIV) spells out how this *"having a form of godliness but denying its power . . ."* ain't great. That same scripture puts denying His power in the same group as those who are *"without love, unforgiving, slanderous, without self-control, brutal and not lovers of good . . ."* the list goes on describing all sorts of not-so-stellar behaviors.

> We do the *cross* an injustice by remembering only *half* of what it accomplished.

The Word of God has the POWER to change our lives, but only when we believe it! Ephesians 1:19-20 (NASB) reveals the apostle Paul's heart on this matter, *"I also pray that you will understand the incredible greatness of God's power for us who believe him."*

Sadly, too often, the story goes like this . . . we know someone (or maybe ourselves) who got prayed for and never received their physical healing. Doubt crept in and snuffed out our belief in God's miraculous and transformative power. We started to think . . . *Well, perhaps we are here just to endure and grow in grace. Healing is one of those things we can't really count on God for. Perhaps the sickness was part of God's divine plan.*

But it is not true *"godliness"* to doubt healing, redemption, and deliverance because the WORD plainly does believe in them, as we'll soon show. Paul encouraged us to be like him in our spiritual walks. If we're to do so, we'd all better get on the power page because Paul was definitely a power sorta guy. Look at what he said in Colossians 1:29 (NASB), *"For this purpose also I labor, striving according to His POWER which MIGHTILY works within me."*

Due to this *"form of godliness"* that denies the POWER of God, there are beautiful children of God who think that being "saved" means only saved for heaven, not saved from a depressed and oppressed life here on earth. They have forgotten *"ALL"* of His benefits. (Insert the two of us in that group in former times.)

The saving starts now!

Legally Victorious

LOVE hung there on the cross until death and spiritual darkness were defeated and won for us an incredible victory. We get to share the spoil! The legal side of our redemption is completed and perfectly fulfilled in Christ. Romans 4:25 (ASV) gives us a peek at what Jesus accomplished for us, *". . . who was delivered up for our trespasses, and was raised for our justification."* But the story doesn't end with the legal side of us now being able to get a ticket to heaven.

John 1:16 says, *"And of His fullness have all we received."* We don't have to wait for heaven to receive this fullness. It's been done! Past tense, baby! In the eyes of justice, we are no longer LOST, but FOUND. No longer broken but RESTORED. No longer struggling but OVERCOMING. And, yes . . . despite what you might have seen or what doubts whisper to you, no longer sick but HEALED! Doesn't even matter if our bodies have not received that healing yet. Isaiah 53:5 clearly says, *". . . And by His stripes we are healed."* 1 Peter 2:24 even puts the healing in the past tense, *". . . by whose stripes you were healed."*

It got good and done on the cross, mates! (Sorry, our "Down Under" speak comes out stronger when we are excited.) Our job as Believers is to simply believe it. Let God take care of the rest. He is the Healer; we are the Believers.

We love Colossians 2:10, *"And you are complete (whole) in Him, who is the head of all principality and power."* There are so many scriptures in the New Testament which talk about the touch of Jesus making people WHOLE. Matthew 14:36 says, *". . . as many as touched it were made perfectly well."* Luke 8:48 says, *". . . your faith has made you well."* As Christians, we are those whose lives have been touched by Christ. It is not fitting for us to be "broken". You can't find the depiction of true Believers as "broken" in the Bible. We must have found it somewhere else . . . like maybe theology rewrites to fit the logic of our finite mind.

We don't have to wait for *heaven* to receive this *fullness.* It's been done!

The **full** and glorious story is that we were redeemed from being lost children to being born again daughters of Father God with His very nature STAMPED on the inside of us. The redemption story is about a love relationship to be ENJOYED NOW . . . to bring heaven to earth (as described in the Lord's prayer) NOW and to live and love like our Savior NOW . . . so that we can draw other lost children to our Redeemer.

Let the Dead Stay Dead!

The "old us" or our old me-centered, doubting selves were crucified with Christ on that cross, the book of Galatians tells us. This means they are dead. No, we need to say it again because growing up in the church, we'd heard that a thousand times, but still didn't get it until just a few years back and perhaps you're in the same boat. THEY ARE DEAD!!!!!! Why do we resurrect our dead self and allow her to constantly say things like, "I'm that girl who is just struggling right now . . . I'm not doing well at all."

Dead *people* really need to *stay* dead!

These days it is rather PC, quite trendy in fact, to say "I'm struggling", but the truth of the matter is we are allowing a dead woman to talk. We need to shut her up and let only our new girl speak!

Okay, we're starting to sound a little heated but finally understanding this was a huge light bulb moment for us. Dead people really need to stay dead! Let's look at that full scripture in Galatians in a new light. If you've been a believer a while, you've heard this scripture preached many times but take another gander at it and let it fully sink in. Galatians 2:20 (ESV), *"I have been crucified with Christ. It is no longer I who live, but Christ who lives in me. And the life I now live in the flesh I live by faith in the Son of God, who loved me and gave himself for me."* Ephesians 4:22 backs this up . . . that mind-blowing "put" verse we mentioned back in Chapter 1. It tells us to make the simple swap . . . to **put** off our old self and **put** on our new one.

So, what would the new one say, the new girl who has Christ living in her and is His very mouthpiece? It would make no sense for her to say she's struggling because Jesus never said it. In fact, He said the opposite. He said, *"I have overcome the world."* So pretty sure in the face of trials, the new, resurrected girl would be more like Lynda 3, who would say something more along the lines of "God will help me overcome this struggle." Or "I can do all things through His strength." Or "He promises to be my very present help in times of trials."

It would make absolutely no sense for our resurrected selves to say, "I'm just so scared." Why? Because Christ lives in us and there is no record of Him ever saying that. In fact, He said . . . *"Do not fear"* in many different ways at many different times.

So, while it might be all current and hip theology to "feel all our feelings", it is just not Biblical truth. Sure, our old selves want to fear. And, our old selves would love to voice that fear, but despite current hipness, we can't just go along with them. Instead, we have to practice hushing them. They're actually getting rather smelly and tiresome. Dead people do tend to stink, ya' know? They certainly do not make for good dinner companions.

> While it might be all *current* and hip theology to "feel all our feelings", it is just not *Biblical* truth.

Crucifixion was the highest price God could pay for us. Through it, He purchased us a new nature . . . a new set of lips. Why . . . why . . . why . . . do we allow our old lips to speak and keep the new natured lips zipped? Is it because it feels like we are more humble to say we are struggling than to say, "God is my ever-present help in times of trouble?" Is it because it feels like we are being more honest to say we feel alone than to say, "He will never leave me or forsake me?"

Honesty and humility are important virtues, but our old nature can't be trusted with them. Our new nature will bear those attributes simply because Christ is honest and humble, and He now lives in us and speaks through us! We no longer have to try for honest and humble because He's done the work for us. He does a much more bang-up job of honest and humble than we ever could anyway. If we believe and speak His words, those attributes will naturally be expressed.

Yes, we died with Him, and yes, we do identify with His shame and agony and the suffering of the cross. But what do we identify with those for? For just a ticket to heaven?????? For that we are grateful, but there's far more . . . TO BE

> We have been given the most amazing *gift* . . . the very spiritual *DNA* of the Father.

RAISED WITH HIM. To have Ephesians 3:16-20 at work in us, *". . . that you may be STRENGTHENED WITH MIGHT through His Spirit in the inner man."*

Our inward selves no longer have to wear a fallen identity. We can now be new creations, strengthened with power! Can we get a WOW? We have been given the most amazing gift . . . the very spiritual DNA of the Father. We have His life and nature of love at work within us by the Spirit and through the Word. He is growing us up more and more to walk and talk like Him as we live NOW upon the earth.

Don't Stay in the Grave

Let's grasp this AMAZING REALITY . . . we are no longer lost and lonely sinners. We are actually and accurately redeemed daughters of the Almighty God. If we died with Him and then were raised with Him, staying down there in the grave with our old rotting selves makes no sense. Colossians 3:1-3 inspires us . . . *"If then you were raised with Christ, seek those things which are above, where Christ is, sitting at the right hand of God. Set your mind on things above, not on things on the earth. For you died, and your life is hidden with Christ in God."*

The purpose of the cross is to get HIS VERY LIFE INSIDE OF US and get our old doubting, struggling nature out. The cross gives us our true identity . . . an identity of power over the enemy, through HIM and HIS triumph of LOVE. Let's say, "Yippee!" Let's go pray for someone and smile with Life and Light, as overcomers in this world instead of being the downtrodden, needy, always on the prayer chain, and always on the counselor's appointment book.

Hey, please don't write us a Christian doctrinal error ticket for that last statement. Prayer is great; you know our hearts on this by now and counseling is often helpful. But God wants to grow us up . . . to get us eating the meat of His Word, rather than constantly sucking milk down while others feed us a bottle. Walking in His nature . . . speaking His words in our minds and through our lips rather than the words of our old dead selves . . . this is what is truly going to bring us into victory!

This is not too good to be true. What is the New Testament actually called? The Good News! Luke 2:10 (ESV) says, *". . . Fear not, for behold, I bring you GOOD NEWS of GREAT JOY that will be for all the people."* The price has already been paid for this good news. Now we just have to own it, LIVE it, and spread it. Romans 10:15 (ESV) tells us our mission: *"How beautiful are the feet of those who preach the GOOD NEWS!"* The words of Isaiah 61:1 (NASB) jump off the page, *"The Spirit of the Lord GOD is upon me, Because the LORD has anointed me To bring GOOD NEWS to the humble; He has sent me to bind up the brokenhearted, To proclaim release to captives And freedom to prisoners."*

> We just have to *own* it, *live* it and *spread* it.

Broken Chains Not Broken Children

Did you catch all those words from Isaiah? LIBERTY and FREEDOM!! They sure don't sound like the "broken and needy" phrases and words that come out of our mouths sometimes. We can become that GOOD NEWS kinda girl who speaks of overflowing cups instead of glass half empty talk and pits instead of cherries. Come on, girls . . . we have something far better than even the sweetness of red cherries; we have the CRIMSON RIVER OF CHRIST'S BLOOD flowing through us and redeeming us fully from the curse. Check it out in Galatians 3:13 (ESV), *"Christ redeemed us from the curse of the law by becoming a curse for us . . ."* This is our gospel. Let's wear the shirt!

Matthew 6:10 (NIV) states our Father's desire, *". . . your kingdom come, your WILL be done, ON EARTH as it is in HEAVEN."* His will is to have the will of Heaven manifested here on earth. The will of Heaven is for every chain to be broken . . . not for His precious children to be broken! Isaiah 58:6 makes this clear, *"Is this not the fast that I have chosen: To loose the bonds of wickedness, to undo the heavy burdens, to let the oppressed go free, and that you break every yoke?"* It is not fasting from your smile and wearing a "holy sigh" that is pleasing to our Father. His fast is to be so victorious in your life through His POWER in you that you can be a chain breaker.

Let's become that girl who refuses to use the pen or the keyboard to journal the "broken" journey. This sort of journaling only cements defeat and negative emotions that totally rob, steal and destroy our joy.

Remember who it is that robs and steals? The accuser. God is the giver of joy and every other good thing. You want to journal? Journal His Light and Love and Power in your life. Let the new you speak. The old you has no legal right to express doubt, fear, and failure. She is in the grave, and that is where she needs to remain.

The new you just might start a journal entry like this . . .

"Dear Diary," (Couldn't resist . . . do people still say that?)

"What a fantastic day it was watching God at work. Let me begin to count the ways I saw His hand move in my life . . ."

> Let the *new* you speak. The old you has no *legal* right to express doubt, fear and failure.

CHAPTER FOURTEEN

Broken -vs- Victorious (Part III)

Extra Crispy

In this chapter, we'd like to clear some things up that seem to encourage the broken robe many of us have worn, thinking it "humble Christianity." But just before we do, let's do a wee recap.

Our old selves are scripturally viewed and legally seen as DEAD. We are not meant to be dredging up all that the cross paid to bury. We sure aren't meant to give the lime-light to what we thought was "humility talk", but in reality, is only a bunch of yackity yack about all the flaws of the old us. We are meant to be skighting (that's our Down Under word for boasting) about our God in us, His FULL-NESS and GLORY!!! It's a fact for sure that we are no-hopers without Him, but if we are born again, we are reborn with GOD inside us. We are awesome new creatures "in" CHRIST! His nature is certainly something to "skight" about!

> We are not meant to be dredging up all that the cross *paid to bury.*

Some refer to Paul's boast about his weaknesses in his letter to the Corinthians as an example of a "broken Christian thing to do". 2 Corinthians 12:9 is the verse most often used to perpetuate this broken mindset, but it can be misunderstood when we don't read all the way through to the final point being made. The entirety of this verse is truth, not one stanza pulled out and left hanging alone. The NLT translation reads: *". . . My grace is all you need. My power works best in weakness.*

So now I am glad to boast about my weaknesses, so that the power of Christ can work through me."

Too many of us have been caught up with the weakness part of this verse and missed the awesome ending to it . . . the power! Look deeper at what Paul is doing here. He's literally boasting about the power of Christ working through him despite the condition he was in. Paul was beaten up at the time he wrote Corinthians. In the previous chapter (which is the setup for this 12th chapter and focuses on the same topic), Paul talked about all the physically taxing experiences he'd endured as an apostle for Christ . . . he'd been beaten, whipped, and shipwrecked all several times. Then earlier in this 12th chapter, he'd talked about how a thorn in his flesh had been making problems for him. All he tells us about this thorn was that it was a spiritual messenger, one of Satan's guys who'd set up some trouble for him (no, contrary to church legend and what most of us were taught in Sunday School . . . Paul's thorn wasn't that he needed reading glasses . . . wink). Many Bible scholars agree; Paul had probably been beaten to the point where his eyes were black and bruised and almost closed shut.

We don't know his exact physical state at the time of writing this verse, but it is obvious Paul's body was extremely weak. Imagine if he had written, "I need to vent, I'm just really struggling right now. I've asked God three times already to remove this thorn in my flesh, yet it's still tormenting me. Well, I'll just endure all these trials, I guess. I'm feeling so weak, but nobody said life was going to be easy. Y'all pray for me."

Hmmm . . . that would have been Paul's old nature talking, and that would have encouraged neither Paul nor any of us. But lookie at what Paul's new nature boasts about to end verse 10. He totally "I'm That Guy's It", and makes Joel 3:10 his identity by saying . . . *"But when I am weak, I am strong."* Gotta love us some new natured Paul!

We have nothing to boast about regarding our old dead selves with all their weaknesses and mistakes. Paul didn't either . . . heck, he went around killing Christians for goodness sakes before God knocked him to his senses! Talk about getting it wrong. But the power of Christ in Paul as a resurrected man . . . Yeah, Paul knew that was worth talking up! God doesn't start with perfectly self-controlled, superhero individuals to shape into His children. He just needs regular, old, earthly hunks of dirt like you and I or a guy like Paul who was fighting for the total wrong side . . . or some stinky fishermen apostles who were always quarreling amongst themselves.

In these Corinthians chapters, Paul shows us how to be victorious while still being relatable rather than stuck up. Confessing our weaknesses is sometimes fitting but when we do it, let's never forget to point to God's transformative power in our lives. We sure don't have to pretend we got it altogether . . . but we sure should do like Paul and tell how we've been turned from losers into winners!

Oh . . . one last little interesting point to ponder about Paul's confession during these tough times. He actually called them "light

> God doesn't start with perfectly self-controlled, *superhero* individuals to shape into His *children.*

afflictions." Paul wouldn't even give his troubles the dramatic adjectives they probably deserved in reality. And what were these light afflictions he was talking of? 2 Corinthians 11:24-25, *"From the Jews five times I received forty stripes minus one. Three times I was beaten with rods; once I was stoned; three times I was shipwrecked; a night and a day I have been in the deep."*

Kind of makes you go, "Hmmmm . . ." We've called our days "rotten" just because the air conditioning wasn't working well enough.

Beauty for Ashes Amps Up Our Praise

Can we labor the point for a minute . . . just so we all clearly get it? (We did warn you this is no quick read. Growing up as pastor's kids, our dad loved to belabor the point in his sermons until the point was extra crispy, verging on a tad burned . . . so we're chipping off the ol' block.)

His STRENGTH is made perfect in our weakness. Paul was entirely spot on with this. God's grace is absolutely astounding! You see, we, like Paul, should be eager to say that by ourselves (in our own strength), we are truly losers. But . . . and it's the big BUT . . . we only talk of our weaknesses to point to the big WHAMMY . . . the main climactic pinnacle of this scripture . . . that THE POWER OF CHRIST WILL WORK THROUGH ME. POWER THROUGH ME!!!!!

We should never stop at weaknesses . . . we should never stop at broken . . . we should never stop at sick! We only use those words as fuel to amp up our praise and gratefulness towards God. Then we, like Paul, keep going to proclaim God's strength, His wholeness, and His deliverance. "I'm That Girl who might be enduring some light afflictions, but I'm also that girl who has God's power working through me!!" Any conversation about our weaknesses needs to end with a Paul-inspired type of big finale . . . "When I am weak . . . you betcha' He makes me strong!"

The freeing lines of 2 Corinthians 5:17 dance around our minds, ". . . *Old things have passed away; behold, all things have BECOME NEW.*" We can say . . . "I was a mess, but thankfully I'm that girl He has given *beauty for ashes.*" (Isaiah 61:3).

King David got it right when he said, *"My soul shall make its boast in my God. The humble shall hear and be glad."* The Hebrew word for humble there more accurately means oppressed or afflicted. Many translations actually use the word "oppressed" in place of humble. Unless we start boasting about the powerful lives, we live with Christ in us, the oppressed will stay oppressed. They won't hear the good news and be able to get glad. And sometimes, it is our very own selves who are oppressed. We need to also tell ourselves this glorious good news. Our ears need to hear it from our own lips. How about boasting these beautiful and whammy-filled words from Psalm 40:2 when oppression threatens? "I'm that girl who *has been lifted from the pit of despair, out of the mud and the mire. He set my feet on solid ground and steadied me as I walked along.*" That's Psalm 40:2 (NIV).

> We only *talk* of our weaknesses to point to the big WHAMMY . . . the main climactic pinnacle of this scripture . . . that THE *POWER* OF CHRIST WILL WORK THROUGH ME.

"I'm struggling" is simply not a boast in our God. We have to get our eyes off our old broken selves and onto our victorious Savior who is birthing new LIFE inside of us.

We can't, not for even one second, look at our new, redeemed selves as shameful sinners! If we are struggling with sin, repentance is essential. Let's do that, then get on with the journey. We don't stay down in the muck of shame when God's blood is faithful to cleanse us of all sins. If we are struggling with addictions, depression, illness, or other afflictions, we'll want to reach out to others for prayer and wise support. But we don't leave it there . . . we then make sure to do what the Word suggests. We start boasting about God in us. We boast in Christ's righteousness that is laid upon us by His incredible GRACE.

> We don't just boast when we *feel* like we got it all together. No, we *boast* when we're weak.

We are "That Girl" who gets to the point that is worth making . . . the point of His POWER at work through us despite our weaknesses! We don't just boast when we feel like we got it all together. No, we boast when we're weak. For then we are made strong! YAY AND YAY!! Can we get some sort of "Amen" out there, sisters? Sure hope we're not high-fiving alone on our Hilltop in these Tennessee woods. Hoping there's some high-fiving in Texas, California, Canada, Down Under, and well . . . all over the globe! What a life-changing gift we've all been given!

No Time for Fruitless Boo Hoo!

So, as new women, we no longer give voice to useless, non-edifying dribble like "I just can't seem to do anything right!" No, we get to the point that boasts of Christ's strength, and we declare awesome stuff like Psalm 60:12, *"Through God we do valiantly, and it is HE, who will tread down my enemies."* In modern speak it goes something like this . . . "Through

> We no longer give *voice* to useless, non-edifying dribble.

God, I'm that girl who is on top of the world. I AM TOTALLY EMPOWERED! He works in me to destroy and have victory over addictions and heavy spirits, and all chains that bind me. I'm more than alright, mate . . . l am jolly awesome!" (Well, maybe you talk like this if you come from Down Under. You can put in your own favorite words.)

We can also say, "I'm that girl who was a dried-up plant but now harvests victory and plucks ripe promises." That's all deliciously backed up by John 15:5 (ESV), *"I am the vine; you are the branches. Whoever abides in me and I in him, he it is that bears much fruit, for apart from me you can do nothing."*

Brokenness in God's Tool Belt?

Another pitfall that falsely gives us license to celebrate the title of "broken" is the idea that God is the One who gives us this "brokenness." It saddens us that He gets such blame . . . or at times, such credit (depending upon a person's way of viewing things), for things He had no part in. Sometimes God is even given raised hands and praise and glory for things that have only come from the accuser himself or from choices we have made in our own lives.

This very prevalent belief that our Heavenly Father gives us sickness to perfect our character, heartache to teach us empathy, and temptation to humble us is gaining more and more traction. Sickness can indeed deepen our character; heartache can give us compassion for those who've experienced the same, and temptation can indeed humble a soul confident in her own strength. But these are not methods that are in God's tool belt. Romans 2:4 tells us the opposite, *"Or do you despise the riches of His goodness, forbearance, and longsuffering, not knowing that the goodness of God leads you to repentance?"* James 1:13 reminds us that temptation never comes from God, *"Let no one say when he is tempted, 'I am tempted by God'; for God cannot be tempted by evil, nor does He Himself tempt anyone."*

Yes, God will always bring beauty from out of the ashes because He is in the business of restoration. He makes us whole by the power of His SPIRIT birthing LIFE inside of us. But we have to remember the ashes are ours, not His. He gives us beauty in exchange if we are willing to swap with Him. And that is the key . . . our willingness. Sickness and troubles have just as much opportunity within them to weave more bitterness, resentments, brokenness, and even impatience into our character than before they turned up on the scene. That is their purpose of ill intent from the accuser. Let's put it on repeat . . . he has come to kill and steal and destroy. Our Savior has come to bring LIFE and life more abundantly.

If we allow God to swap with us, He can use the storms we go through both physically and spiritually to harvest much beauty because He always turns around what the devil meant for harm and creates GOOD. Genesis 50:20 (GNT), *"You plotted evil against me, but GOD TURNED IT INTO GOOD . . ."* He makes GOOD from our obedience to His words of LIFE and TRUTH and our identity in HIS WHOLENESS. "I'm That Girl who is made WHOLE through Christ!" Now that's something to journal about or share with a friend over coffee.

And let's never forget what Christ did when he awoke to a storm when he was in a boat with his disciples. He told it to hush. We can do the same to stormy sicknesses and troubles in our lives.

> If we *allow* God to swap with us, He can use the storms we go through both physically and spiritually to harvest much *beauty.*

Divinely Giftwrapped Sickness?

Time to tackle some tough questions. Does God plan cancer for our benefit? Does He receive glory from our suffering? Is it part of His mysterious higher purpose to give us disease so we'll rely on Him more than our own strength? Does He give leukemia to a precious one-year-old child so you as parent can learn some well-needed lessons and become well and truly broken before Him?

Let's really get to the bottom of this now because this "God is breaking me" theory is rampant. So many are thanking God for putting certain diseases upon them or their family members when He was not the giver of them in the first place.

We can be thankful for the way He helps us through and even right out of times of illness, but thanking God for them . . . perhaps it's time to rethink that. We understand this is a very tender topic. We don't pretend to understand why some of our babies die before they are born or why other extremely hard things happen to us and our loved ones while we are clothed in these earth suits. But just accepting disease as God's plan for our lives results in an identity of submission to sickness. Christ overcame our diseases by the stripes He took on His back, so why should we submit to them as His will for our lives? Sicknesses, like our sins, were nailed to the cross. We don't submit to sins, so why should we look at sicknesses differently?

If we fall into anger or jealousy, does that mean He doesn't forgive us our sins? If the answer to that is no, a big NO, then just because we get sick does not mean that He does not heal. He needs us to continually believe by faith and be confident in His full work of salvation so we can receive both forgiveness and healing.

> Accepting *disease* as God's plan for our lives results in an identity of *submission* to sickness.

Sickness is not God's tool to grow His children up into Him so we can be equipped with strength and power to be His witnesses on the earth. In fact, many times it does the opposite. This is why we must do our best to honor our bodies by eating wise foods and include movement so we can stay strong and healthy. As strong and healthy people, He is able to use us to be blessings to our families and others He places in our lives. And while we can still boast about our God during times of physical weakness as Paul did, sickness often robs us of opportunities to be a light and life to a needy world. Yes, you can share God's goodness wherever you are . . . even in a hospital bed, but tell us . . . is God glorified more by your healing or your sickness?

Ouch . . . are we being too harsh? We're not saying you or your loved ones will never get sick, but we are saying you don't have to live a life of submission to sickness. And we're not trying to come against what your pastor or teacher speaks from the pulpit here. He or she probably has a beautiful heart to help during times of crisis and illness. As pastor's kids, we know just how hard it can be for church shepherds to hold and comfort those who have just lost loved ones. Pastors are often the ones called to be there when the worst happens to people . . . usually when they face extremely tough diagnoses or tragic accidents. It is difficult for them to know what to say in such times. So please, if some of these truths start resonating in your heart and they differ slightly from what your pastor teaches, don't leave your church over this.

But the fact still remains . . . Jesus healed everyone who came to Him needing it during His time here on earth. He didn't pick and choose depending upon their maturity of character. Imagine Christ in the crowds of thronging people pushing in around Him. So many needed healing. Jesus points someone out and says, "You, I can heal as you seem to be mature enough already." Then to another . . . "Sorry, you've still got some learning to do . . . best to keep your leprosy, as it can teach you some needful lessons."

Just nope. Not the way it happened.

Likewise, if Paul really wanted us to dwell on our weaknesses and stay content in our diseases in order to be stronger Christians, as many believe, why did he (through Christ's power) heal **all** those who were afflicted with a plague on the Island of Malta as described in Acts 28? Wouldn't it have been more prudent to let some of them keep their sicknesses so they could mature and develop better temperaments?

It is not sickness or temptation themselves that strengthen us. God's Word does it. Sometimes sickness can push us into His Word . . . send us searching for and then finding our God-given authority. The Word clearly gives it to us through the power of the cross. But that authority, that salvation, was already there in the Word waiting for us. Sickness has just as much potential to leave us despondent and even more lacking in faith than it does to build us in faith.

> Jesus *healed* everyone who came to Him needing it *during* His time here on earth.

We must be very clear that salvation is not in sickness itself.

Now, can we allow God to pour into us His fruits of the Spirit and clad us with His armor so that we can fight trials and illness valiantly? Absolutely! Can we allow Him to work through us to overcome the works of the evil one through His blood and His name and His power as we declare His word on our lips? A thousand times YES!!!! We can be stronger in every way after a battle with sickness, if we press into the Word. But, it is only our willingness to cling to God and have faith in His ability to be our refuge and rescue that makes us valiant.

God hasn't promised us a life of ease. But He has *promised* us a life of *victory*.

Just because we may learn some wonderful spiritual insights and get our priorities straightened out through these "broken" times does not mean the attack and onslaught of hardship was ordained by God. God hasn't promised us a life of ease. But He has promised us a life of victory . . . grabbing that victory is up to us. He will use our mess and our ashes, or the devil's plans for harm and recycle them all into wonderful beauty, strength, and salvation.

We can't give up, give in, roll over, and shape our doctrine into one that considers sickness to be from God. If we do that, why have faith to be healed? If God were actually the one who gives sickness to us, wouldn't Jesus have been undoing His Father's will when He went around healing all that came to Him? Nuh-uh. He told His disciples that He came to do the will of the Father, and then He went and healed the masses. Look, it's right there in Matthew 9:35 (ESV), *"And Jesus went throughout all the cities and villages, teaching in their synagogues and proclaiming the gospel of the kingdom and healing every disease and every affliction."*

Let's be careful not to *willingly* open any sickness package, thinking it is *gift wrapped* from God.

Let's be very careful not to willingly open any sickness package, thinking it is gift wrapped from God to break us for His glory. One of God's seven Hebrew redemptive names is "Jehovah Rapha", which means, "I am the Lord that heals." Let's check . . . nope, not one of His other six Hebrew names means "I give My children sicknesses to break them."

No Need to Help the Cross Out

So, are we saying this whole following and speaking God's Word thing means you'll never be touched by sickness? No. We live in a fallen world, one with germs, toxins, viruses, and imperfect bodies. Scripture tells us there will be trials. We have not been strangers to life-threatening illnesses in our own families. We have prayed and stood in faith, battled the accuser and his spirit world and have seen incredible healings. But we have lost loved ones, too. We came to that same choice so many of us arrive at . . . our prayers were not answered in the way we longed for. Do we leave our faith on the floor, or do we pick it back up and believe?

Do we leave our faith on the floor, or do we pick it back up and believe?

We pick it back up, baby! That's our commission . . . believe! And our loved ones . . . healed and whole in heaven . . . you bet they are cheering us on. If sickness knocks on the door, we know what the WORD says and are obedient to believe it! We're not that girl who surrenders to disease and calls it her cross to bear. Why? Let's repeat the answer once more . . . because Jesus took all disease upon Himself at that very cross!

The cross wasn't endured to give disease, but rather to take it away. We gotta stop grabbing things down from the cross and calling them "ours."

Christ's work at the cross was completely finished. So, these afflictions so many of us call "ours" . . . our arthritis, our depression, our anxiety, our fibro pain, our cancer, our thyroid disease, our migraines, and so on . . . we got that all wrong . . . they're no longer ours . . . the cross took them! "My Hashimoto's disease" is a completely untrue statement according to God's Word. Hashimoto's may be battling for authority in your body, but Christ defeated it at the cross. Don't sign your name on the

We gotta stop grabbing things down from the cross and calling them "ours."

dotted line for it, like it's a FedEx delivery you've been waiting for. That's handing over all authority to it.

Christ doesn't need our help attempting to bear anything for His glory that the cross already took care of. Our Savior doesn't need us to "break'" by staying under the weight of bondage to suffer as a "cross" bearer for Him. He went through the "breaking" of His own flesh (our Bread of Life) already. It's already been accomplished! He broke His body, to put ours back together. How incredible!

Most of us (if we're Christians) have had the following scripture about taking up our cross drilled into us over and over again. Can we look at it in full for a minute? Luke 9:23 (NIV), *"Then he said to them all: "Whoever wants to be my disciple must deny themselves and take up their cross daily and follow me."* But what if denying ourselves is not exactly all that we've been led to think it is? What if it looks more like denying the habitual and comfy trip down unbelieving, negative lane and dying to those natural tendencies sewn within the fabric of regular humans ruled by their senses?

> Our *Savior* doesn't need us to "break'" by staying under the weight of bondage to *suffer* as a "cross" bearer for Him.

What if denying ourselves and picking up our cross looks more like taking off our own dirty backpacks filled with doubt, worry, sickness, negative moods, and bitter resentments and making room to place His cross on our backs . . . which is our new nature of VICTORY, BELIEF, HOPE, LOVE, AND HEALING. In Matthew 11, Christ tells us to take His yoke upon us, and He describes it as being *"light."* Sickness and depression are not light . . . they are not Christ's beautiful yoke that He wants us to wear. Look at the verse in full . . . Matthew 11:28-30 (NIV), *"Come to me, all you who are weary and burdened, and I will give you rest. Take my yoke upon you and learn from me, for I am gentle and humble in heart, and you will find rest for your souls. For my yoke is easy and my burden is light."*

Let's crisp our point up one final time and phrase it a little differently since our dear ol' dad might think it isn't quite sinking in just right yet. The cross is not a

burden of heaviness. It is not a physical affliction or a particular challenging circumstance
that is ours to bear. It is the most triumphant
accomplishment in history!

Finally, it is clear . . . struggle is not the
cross we take up every day; REST is! Not a
day at the spa but DEEP SOUL REST! This is
the green pasture we walk in that the Psalmist
talked about in Psalm 23.

Struggle is not the cross we take up every day; *REST* is!

Don't Be an Eeyore

As cute as he is, we are not supposed to emulate Eeyore. Excuse the sudden rabbit trail into the Hundred Acre Wood, but picture this: Eeyore gets up in the morning, straps a big burden to his back and says (in his very dreary Eeyore voice), "Oh, well . . . guess it's just my lot in life. Gotta carry this big ol' burden around for the Lord. Just doing my part and wearing this disease to bring Him glory and honor. If He heals me, I'd probably just get it back anyways."

John 1:1 tells us that Christ is the Word; they are one and the same. Psalm 107:20 also tells us, *"He sent his Word to heal them and delivered them from their destructions."* That healing is still for us today. Believing that is taking up our cross! Day in, day out . . . we are to cast off doubt, sickness, and fear and strap on the yoke of His complete, not partial, resurrected work which includes belief, healing, and a sound mind.

This belief doesn't depend on whether we've seen every person healed that we've prayed for or if not one has been healed yet. We're still growing up in faith, girls . . . we have much to learn, and we ain't perfected yet! Remember the story in the Gospel of Matthew where the

Day in, day out . . . we are to *cast* off doubt, sickness, and fear and strap on the yoke of His *complete*, not partial, resurrected work.

disciples prayed but couldn't heal the boy who suffered from seizures, but Jesus came on the scene and healed the boy instantly? The disciples asked Jesus later about why they couldn't heal him. He basically told them they could have; that mountains can be moved by a mustard seed of true faith.

So, let's be "grower uppers" in faith, not faith decliners! Let's shed the Eeyore talk and just keep on practicing His promises. Even if our own bodies are still living with daily pain from a condition, we don't quit believing. We take up our cross and hold fast to the truth that He is the Healer. We cast off the burden of doubt that wants to snatch this promise from us. The Word never promised our answers to prayer would be in short order. Our job . . . just keep believing! Just keep standing!

If It Be Thy Will

Many of us have asked God for physical healing using "if it be Thy will" to begin or end our prayers. In years past, we prayed this in earnest, hoping to sway God's heart to heal, but willing to be content with our affliction if not. Inevitably, these prayers lead to thoughts wondering if the highest form of faith may not actually be to believe for healing but to trust that times of illness are part of our spiritual journey. What if greater faith simply means we shouldn't expect anything else from our Father than what we already have? Perhaps it is more Christian to just journey on as wounded soldiers under the burden of our lot in life?

We can't be the only ones who've wondered these things, right? But how scripturally accurate are they?

It is not our job to sway God into compassion to heal.

While it might be common practice, we stopped saying the "if it be Thy will" phrase in any petition prayers for healing once we realized it leads to uncertain prayers, stripped of the knowledge of who God really is. After thoroughly searching the scriptures, we came to understand that "if it be Thy will" has often been taken out of Biblical context. It is not our job to sway God into compassion to heal. We don't have to plead with him and we certainly don't have to change His mind to heal as His mind is already made up! We only have to get on the same page with

Him as He already desires to do it. He doesn't need us to sway Him . . . He needs us to start agreeing with Him!

So, how has this saying come to be so frequently used then? From what we can tell, it is pulled from a few different places in the Bible. In the Lord's prayer, Jesus says, *". . . Your will be done on earth as it is in heaven."* Let's quickly deal with that: God's kingdom is not one of sickness and disease; Satan rules that kingdom. During the Lord's prayer, Jesus was definitely not calling sicknesses down to earth from Heaven because Heaven contains no disease. In Matthew 10:7-8, Jesus was talking to His disciples about the power He was about to give them. He said, *". . . And as you go, preach, saying, 'The Kingdom of heaven is at hand.' Heal the sick, cleanse the lepers, raise the dead, cast out devils. Freely you have received, freely give."* See that? Heaven is at hand. Heal the sick. Clearly, Heaven's will is never to give disease, but to take it away.

> Heaven's will is *never* to give disease, but to *take* it away.

Next, Jesus prayed in the garden before surrendering Himself to the cross . . . *". . . nevertheless . . . not my will but yours be done."* But here, Christ was not unsure of God's will to send Him to the cross. He wasn't wondering about it, hoping to change His Father's mind if God wasn't entirely set on it. Revelation 13:8 tells us that Jesus was the Lamb *"slain before the foundation of the world."* It was always the plan that Christ would endure the cross. Jesus knew this and had already shared this piece of information on several occasions to His disciples. Christ's words here in the garden were only affirming God's perfect will for Him to go to the cross despite the knowledge of the agony He'd have to endure.

Another verse that trips people up over the "God's will" dilemma is 1 John 5:14, *"Now this is the confidence that we have in Him, that if we ask anything according to His will, He hears us."* God's Word is His will. It's time to establish once and for all whether the Word clearly shows if it really is God's will to heal or not because . . . it really matters. Your prayers for healing will have no substance of real faith to them if you have to wonder what is going on inside God's mind when you ask Him to heal. And honestly . . . that just doesn't work. God doesn't gel with it. James 1:6-7 tells us how to ask things of God, *"But let him ask in faith, with no doubting, for he who doubts is like a wave of the sea driven and tossed by the wind. For let not that man suppose that he will receive anything from the Lord."*

Your prayers for *healing* will have no substance of real faith to them if you have to wonder what is going on inside God's mind when you *ask* Him to heal.

The will of God for healing can be found all over the scriptures, but let's just look at a few . . . 1 John 3:8 says, *". . . For this purpose the Son of God was manifested, that He might destroy the works of the devil."* Every time Jesus healed someone, He destroyed the work of Satan, not the work of His Father. Remember the leper in Matthew 8:2 who was unsure of Christ's will to heal him? He said, *"Lord, if You are willing, You can make me clean."* Jesus straight away dealt with the "if" word. He replied, *"I am willing; be cleansed."* Jeremiah 30:17 (NIV) also reveals God's will for both spiritual and physical wholeness, *"But I will restore you to health and heal your wounds,' declares the Lord."* The 3rd book of John 1:2 (NIV) says, *"I pray that you may enjoy good health and that all may go well with you, even as your soul is getting along well."*

Crispy enough?

Battered Belief

Some of what we've been saying here may be inviting some more hard questions. Perhaps you're thinking, *What about God in the Old Testament? Wasn't He frequently putting all sorts of plagues and pestilences on people?* King Nebuchadnezzar is another example. Most of us have heard that Bible story of him turning crazy and eating grass like a cow. Didn't God give him mental illness to teach him humility?

We'd have to take a whole book to delve deep enough into Old Testament scriptures to support the belief that God is Healer rather than sickness giver there, too. There is not enough room for all that here, but we'll try to summarize what we've learned in just a few paragraphs. (The following is that nitty-gritty stuff we talked to you about in the intro chapters that you might find yourself wanting to skip but you're not allowed to . . . hang in there . . . we'll be out of the woods soon.)

First, we need to preface that there are differences of opinion even between those who believe that God is not responsible for sickness. Some believe Satan is completely to blame for all disease and sickness as he is the prince of this world with all its problems. Others believe that while Satan can (and scripturally has been shown to bring about sickness as in the case of Job and others), this world is fallen, meaning it is not perfect. And while Satan and his kingdom of darkness may often be responsible, there are many things that contribute to disease. Without being too dogmatic that we're right and everyone else is wrong (he he), this is about where we land on the subject. Unwise eating habits, genetics, toxins, sedentary lifestyle, negative emotions, and destructive thinking . . . all of these things can also contribute to ill health.

Now let's attempt to summarize how our God is the same in the Old Testament as the New. He is the same yesterday, today, and forever. Jesus said, *"If you have seen me, you have seen the Father."* So, if Jesus healed everyone who asked and if He rebuked sickness and disease, how does this gel with God in the Old Testament "putting" disease on people?

The ancient Hebrew language that the Old Testament was written in uses hundreds of idioms, otherwise known as figures of speech. These are phrases that had meaning to the Hebrew people who understood the colorful aspect of their language but are lost to us through translation into English. When we read some of these scriptures, we read the work of translators who have had to substitute English words for the original Hebrew. Though the words might be there, the initial meaning is lost. We read in the Old Testament of God hardening people's hearts and sending pestilence, but the intent of the original Hebrew was not God causing these things but permitting them.

Many Bible scholars understood this causative -vs- permissive idiom a couple of hundred years ago, but somehow these truths have become lost in modern church theology. You can do a Google search on scholars who understood this subject, if you are so inclined. Your search engine will bring up a lot of fascinating quotes from great Bible scholars of the 1800's who well understood these matters. Book-wise, if you ever want to do a deep dive study into idioms, E.W. Bullinger's *Figures of Speech Used in the Bible* is an enlightening, even if long, read. This book was written over

The *intent* of the original Hebrew was not God causing these things but *permitting* them.

200 years ago, but wow . . . Bullinger knew his Hebrew stuff! Look at how he describes the difference between permission and cause, *"Active verbs were used by the Hebrews to express, not the doing of the thing, but the permission of the thing which the agent is said to do."*

Look at how this verse in Deuteronomy 28:61 has been translated in the King James Bible, *"Also every sickness, and every plague, which is not written in the book of this law, them will the Lord **bring** upon thee, until thou be destroyed."* Dr. Young, author of *Young's Literal Translation of the Bible,* explains that it has been translated with a causative verb, "I will bring", but it actually should have been translated with a permissive verb, "I will permit." It should, in fact, read, *"Every sickness and every plague, which is not written in the book of this law, them will the Lord **allow** to descend upon thee . . ."*

This permissive -vs- causative translation is prominent throughout the Old Testament including cases such as Nebuchadnezzar's mental illness. Understanding the idiom allows us to see that God was merely allowing, not causing. Sickness

Not once in the entire *Bible* could we find an instance where sickness is shown as God's *blessing* or one of His gifts.

has always been part of the "fallen world" or "dominion of darkness" (whichever you would like to call it) that Adam and Eve entered into through their entanglement with the accuser. Whenever God took His hand of protection off to "allow" disease, the curses of sickness and pestilence had instant access to invade.

But let's be clear, the Old Testament never portrays sickness as a blessing as some have chosen to view it these days. We've looked . . . hard . . . but never . . . not once in the entire Bible could we find an instance where sickness is shown as God's blessing or one of His gifts.

In the Old Testament, though, it was clearly sometimes a consequence for choices. Look at God's heart in Deuteronomy 30:19, *"I have set before you life and death, blessing and cursing: therefore choose life . . ."* When God's people pulled away from Him, disease was an inevitable result, but it was never God's heart to inflict it.

Disease was also the consequence to nations or people who rose up against God's chosen. In all these cases, illness was permitted, but it was far from God's initial will. Dare we think God enjoyed allowing the plagues to come upon Egypt? God loved Egypt and its people too! He could have wiped them out in one plague, but no, it was chance after chance. Pharaoh just kept hardening his heart, and more plagues were the result.

Many years before the time of Moses and the slavery of the Israelites, God had blessed and favored Egypt. In Genesis 41, we read how He had given Pharaoh a dream of which Joseph was able to interpret and save the nation from starving through a time of famine. Pharaoh even became a worshipper of God! The problem came later on when Egypt forgot all about Joseph and God's goodness to them. But even after all that, God still loved Egypt. Look what He said about them through His prophet Isaiah some years later . . . *"And the Lord shall smite Egypt, he shall smite and heal it. They shall return even to the Lord and he shall be entreated of them, and shall heal them."* Here we see God's heart again . . . always longing to heal. And again here, let's not miss the idiom used . . . "shall smite" is more accurately interpreted as "allowed to be smitten".

> God *loved* Egypt and its people too! He could have wiped them out in one *plague,* but no, it was chance after chance.

Dare to Bring Belief Back

So now we've seen God's heart on the matter. We know that His will is to heal. I think even our dad would agree this chapter is sufficiently charred and can come off the grill. But before we turn off the gas, can we ask one last question . . . what did you stop believing God for?

Perhaps you're still wrestling . . . not quite ready to pick belief back up again? Perhaps you're sitting there . . . memories are swarming . . . excruciatingly hard questions are forming before you can make the leap back to belief.

Serene and Pearl, this all sounds well and good, but I have been infertile for 12 years. I have longed and longed for a baby, and God has not heard my prayer. It hurts too much to hope and believe anymore.

Or

Serene and Pearl, nice for you to talk about healing so flippantly. We prayed and believed for my father, yet he died a painful death from pancreatic cancer. How can you ask me to believe God will magically heal those I love when I've been through that?

Or

Hey, sisters . . . perhaps you've never watched your baby take its last breath. Until you do, you may want to show a bit more understanding for those struggling in their faith.

While our hearts grieve to think of some of the hardships that have led to these sorts of questions, we have only one reply to them. It is simply a repeat of what we said in the last chapter . . . Believers believe. Perhaps, on an intellectual basis, this doesn't give you all the answers you're desperate for. But we are not God. He is the One Who has called us all to this sort of belief even when nothing about it makes sense to our human minds. But as Believers, we can't change doctrines to suit what our eyes have seen or because we now think too much time has passed to believe for victories anymore.

We are called to stand on His promises without doubting and let our loving Father do the rest. Hebrews 10:23 reminds us to "*. . . hold fast the confession of our hope without wavering, for He who promised is faithful.*" Our natural minds want to waiver, but we must do the swap . . . **put off** those doubts,

> He is the One Who has *called* us all to this sort of belief even when nothing about it makes *sense* to our human minds.

put on the mind of Christ, and hold fast. God will be our keeper until the fullness of His promises are received. To the end, we believe . . . no matter the outcome, right up until *"Well done, thou good and faithful servant . . ."* That's when we'll no longer see through a glass darkly, and all will be revealed.

Until such time . . . we only believe.

CHAPTER FIFTEEN

Broken -vs- Victorious (Part IV)

Royalty Baby!

The trouble with even a little embracing or identifying with a "broken" spirit or the tinsiest bit of nursing the "lonely tribulation road" is that negativity grows. It's a thorny weed. Brokenness bears brokenness . . . like produces like. It creeps so quickly through your emotions and infects your spirit, soul, and body before you even realize the damage done.

Galatians 5:9 (ESV) says, *"A little leaven leavens the whole lump."* Leaven was the old-fashioned word for yeast or starter for bread. In the Bible, it is used as an analogy for sin. While it is not our place to go as far as labeling negative talking and thinking as actual sin, it sure is not being obedient to the Word, so come to your own conclusions on that. The Word tells us to dwell *". . . only on things above and that which is of good report and not on the cares and ugliness of this world."* (Philippians 4:8) (Colossians 3:2) (Matthew 13:22). We need to become aware of and then weed out any "leaven thoughts and words".

Crumbs or Crowns

Let's look at just a few of the names we can replace "broken" thoughts and words with. Our wonderful Savior has coined some of them for us Himself. We are *"daughter"* (1 John 3:1), *"chosen"* (John 15:16), *"blessed"* (Ephesians 1:3), *"saint"* (Romans 8:27), *"His possession"* (Ephesians 1:13-14), *"loved"* (Romans 8:38-39), *"righteous"* (Isaiah 61:10), *"forgiven"* (1 John 1-9), *"upheld"* (Psalm 37:24), *"strengthened"* (Philippians 4:13), and *"protected"* (Deuteronomy 31:6).

To top all that off, 1 Peter 2:9 (ESV) declares, *"But you are a chosen race, a royal priesthood, a holy nation, a people for his own possession, that you may proclaim the excellencies of him who called you out of darkness into his marvelous light."* Royalty baby! We are princesses. We gotta proclaim it! Let's wear this victorious crown! It's a crown of life because He wore the thorns for us. It's a crown because we are seated at the right hand of the Father in Christ Jesus and are reigning with Him victoriously. Let's get out our spiritual diamonds and shine them up! Let's use our King of Kings Father's two-edged sword against deception, fear, anxiety, and negativity. Let's look in the correct mirror, not the one that shows us our old dead selves, but the one who shows us who we now are!

The book of Matthew talks about a Canaanite woman who begged and cried aloud . . . *"Have mercy on me, O Lord, Son of David!"*

The Lord answered, *"I have been sent only to the lost sheep of the house of Israel."* Basically, he was saying, "This is not your provision . . . not your bread at this time."

The Canaanite woman (in our own personal paraphrase) cries back, "But I'll scrape up all the crumbs!"

> Let's look in the *correct* mirror, not the one that shows us our old dead selves, but the one who *shows* us who we now are!

Jesus answers her, *"O woman, GREAT IS YOUR FAITH! Be it done for you as you wish."* And her daughter, who had been cruelly plagued by a demon, was cured from that moment.

We share this story to express the determined attitude of this woman to receive all she could from God. She was not even of the house of Israel, but she was tenacious and bold. She was eager to take hold of all that Jesus would give her. Jesus responded to her need, her bold expectancy for a return, and honored her faith and desire. He filled her appetite for Him . . . giving her far more than just the crumbs.

We are the redeemed. We are that girl who is part of God's precious family, yet too often, we don't want to presume upon Him for even the crumbs of a blessed and overcoming life. We, like poor little Simba from Lion King (before he got straightened out), consider it too presumptuous to walk in all of our Father's blessings . . . that's not carrying our cross and suffering enough to honor Him. We wouldn't want to be greedy and take too many good things that the scriptures say are ours . . . perhaps some sin cleansing and throwing up a petition prayer or two will do us . . . can't impose on God's goodness too much. Gotta stay humble.

Phooey to all that! We honor Him by wearing **ALL** that His cross accomplished. Let's just put it on repeat . . . He broke so that we no longer have to be broken! He gave us salvation, healing, redemption, and a victorious life through the cross, and He wants us to joyfully put these new clothes on, not leave them hanging in the closet like Woeful Joan, who keeps asking for prayer because she keeps wearing the wrong clothes!

> He *broke* so that we *no longer* have to be broken!

We need to start putting on **ALL** the special redeemed robes of righteousness and all the victory sashes that our Savior hung there on that rugged cross to provide. We adorn ourselves with Him and crucify our old "complaining, lost, and lonely sinner" selves to the cross where He died. And now we live the resurrection "new creation" life THROUGH HIM, and WE AIN'T NO INSIPID, DESPERATE GIRLS NO MORE!

Yelling is indeed happening. Okay, we'll calm down.

It's just that this, "I don't need or want anything from you, Jesus," talk is such a trend in Christian culture these days. Many of the latest popular church songs are all about requiring nothing from Him. "Just wanna sit in Your presence, Lord, don't expect a thing from You," type songs are all the rage. Hanging with Jesus, but not seeking a thing from Him, might be "Christian cool", but Jesus wants us to receive from Him. It's His very nature to give and keep on giving, and He longs for us to receive all He has to offer. Look, its right there in John 16:24, *"Until now you have asked nothing in My name. Ask, and you will receive,*

> It's His very *nature* to give and keep on giving, and He longs for us to *receive* all He has to offer.

that your joy may be full." If we go back a couple chapters to John 14:14 (NLT), we see Jesus insisting yet again, *"Yes, ask me for anything in my name, and I will do it!"*

Actually, this receiving . . . this taking from Jesus rather than just sitting there thinking sweet thoughts about Him is the better, humbler action. We're not talking seeking wealth and privilege here of course but we are talking seeking victory, knowledge, and wisdom. Look at what the psalmist said in Psalm 27:4, *"One thing I have desired of the LORD, That will I seek: That I may dwell in the house of the LORD All the days of my life, To behold the beauty of the LORD, And to inquire in His temple."*

In the above verse, David desired something from God. He sought something from God, and he inquired something from God. What did God think of all this presumptive asking from David? Did He tire of it? No, He called David a man after His own heart. He loved that David desired things from Him. He blessed him for it. In fact, Hebrews 11:6 tell us that God is a rewarder of those who *"diligently seek him."*

If you grew up in Sunday School, you know the story in the Old Testament of how Jacob was a bit tenacious. Actually, more than a bit. He refused to accept anything less than the ultimate birthright inheritance. He ended up receiving that because he valued it far more than his brother Esau did. Jacob did get it through some shady dealings, but that's beside the point. God honored his determination to receive everything he could from his Maker . . . to not settle for anything less than all of it! Look at Jacob's behavior here in Genesis 32:26-28. He had just wrestled with an angel (most scholars believe the angel was actually Jehovah God Himself) all night and still wouldn't let him go. He said to the angel, *". . . I will not let You go unless You bless me!" So He said to him, "What is your name?" He said, "Jacob." And He said, "Your name shall no longer be called Jacob, but Israel; for you have struggled with God and with men, and have prevailed."*

God loved Jacob's determination to receive. The scriptures actually make a point of saying this specifically in Malachi 1:2, *". . . Jacob I have loved."* God rewarded Jacob greatly for his persistence to **take** all he could from Him. Through Jacob would come the line of Jesus, and through Him all the nations would be blessed. Listen to the words of Luke 12:32 (NIV), *"Do not be afraid, little flock, for your Father has been pleased to give you the kingdom."* Pleased . . . He's tickled pink to give us all these marvelous, overcoming gifts!

Why should we ever settle for crumbs when He has set a place for us at the King's table? Even in the presence of our enemies, He prepares us a table. Psalm 23:5 rings in our ears, *"You prepare a table before me in the presence of my enemies; you anoint my head with oil; my cup overflows."* Overflows . . . that is the exact opposite of half empty! He is our portion. Isaiah 58:11 (ESV) thrills our hearts: *"And the Lord will guide you continually and satisfy your **desire** in scorched places and make your bones strong; and you shall be like a watered garden, like a spring of water, whose waters do not fail."* He tops up our cup! Jeremiah 31:25 (ESV) boldly cries out, *"For I will satisfy the weary soul, and every languishing soul I will replenish."* The kingdom of heaven is for the tasting now! We can partake of its LOVE, POWER, and VICTORY while we journey on this earth walk.

> Why should we ever *settle* for crumbs when He has set a *place* for us at the King's table?

Just Peachy?

Yes, we will all go through trials, but it doesn't have to be gloom and doldrums for us! He has provided a table to strengthen us when we are surrounded by the enemies of depression, of fear, of anxiety, and every other evil force. We are that girl who is sustained . . . that girl who has bountifully received all the goods to overcome even in the midst of chaos. There may be a storm about us, but it is NOT INSIDE US! Our hatches are all battened down with Jesus, and the skirts of our minds are hemmed. We stay unfazed within His warm embrace.

Life will not be all peaches and roses. Quite the opposite. But in the face of all challenges, we can have joy and victory because of His power at work within us. This way, we speak to the storm as Jesus did instead of sigh and cry and curl up in a fetal position defeated.

> There may be a *storm* about us, but it is NOT INSIDE US!

Who are we kidding? We are not capable of "broken" with God alive inside of us! The accuser is having a heyday if we allow ourselves to accept a broken identity . . . to believe we are that girl who's trudging along all desperate for a drop of water or a crumb of bread. John 6:35 (NLT) dispels this deception with the truth, *"Jesus replied, "I am the bread of life. Whoever comes to me will never be hungry again. Whoever believes in me will never be thirsty."*

Fully sustained . . . that's us. We don't roll around in the darkness lacking sight. We see through faith . . . we rejoice because our God has overcome the world and because Romans 8:37 tells us we are more than conquerors. A conqueror is jolly amazing, we think, but merely being a conqueror is not good enough for God's desire for us. He wants us to enjoy the victorious life of being that girl who is actually MORE than a conqueror.

This place of MORE than conquering is the position set aside for us in Christ. It is not some weird, new age, positive thinking, hyper-faith doctrine. It is plain and simple, God's WORD for us. Living anywhere beneath *"more than a conqueror"* is belittling our abundant life as a Christ-follower.

> Merely being a *conqueror* is not good enough for God's desire for us. He wants us to enjoy the *victorious* life of being that girl who is actually MORE than a conqueror.

Adopted to Receive

We are no longer orphans. Let's feel the heartbeat of Romans 8:15 (WEB), *"For you didn't receive the spirit of bondage again to fear, but you received the Spirit of adoption, by whom we cry, "Abba! Father!"* We are not adopted into our Father's family only to be left at the awful orphanage to scrounge for a corner of the blanket in the cold dormitory or still have to fight for our morsel of dry and moldy crust. Adoption means we get all that is our Father's as it says in John 16:15, *"All things that the Father has are Mine; Therefore, I said that He will take of Mine and declare it to you."*

Our families, here on our Hilltop in Tennessee, have first-hand experience with adoption. (I, Serene, adopted 5 children from a Liberian orphanage.) These children were pulled from tragic and broken circumstances. Imagine if they did not want to accept all that is now theirs by wearing the family name? Becoming Allisons meant love, shelter, good food, laughter, financial provision, inheritance, hugs, guidance, clothing, prayer, and cups of tea and chicken broth when mending from a cold.

Adoption means we get *all* that is our Father's.

If our adopted family members did not want to identify with their new life of blessing . . . did not want to receive the acceptance and wear the honor of their new family name . . . if they identified with their old lack and heartache instead of their new life of love and provision, that would be odd, wouldn't it? So why do we do the same when it comes to all that God has given us? He wants us to step into His fullness, bask in His refreshing river of delights, and dance among His abundant blooms of joy buds.

No more crying about the old, empty, spiritual tummy that was ours back in the orphanage. Let's start enjoying the satisfaction of the gift of plenty that we get in the family of the King.

Let's take just a glimpse at His provision for His children:

Philippians 4:19 (AMPC), *"And my God will liberally supply* (fill to the full) *your every need according to His riches in glory in Christ Jesus."*

James 1:17 (KJV), *"Every good gift and every perfect gift is from above, and cometh down from the Father of lights, with whom is no variableness, neither shadow of turning."*

Psalm 34:8-10 (KJV), *"O taste and see that the Lord is good: blessed is the man that trusteth in him. O fear the Lord, ye his saints: for there is no want to them that fear him. The young lions do lack, and suffer hunger: but they that seek the Lord shall not want any good thing."*

Psalm 65:11, *"You crown the year with Your goodness, and Your paths drip with abundance."*

Psalm 107:8-9, *"Oh, that men would give thanks to the Lord for His goodness, and for His wonderful works to the children of men! For He satisfies the longing soul, and fills the hungry soul with goodness."*

2 Peter 1:3 (NIV), *"His divine power has given us everything we need for life and godliness through our knowledge of him who called us by his own glory and goodness."*

Psalm 23:1 (AMPC), *"The Lord is my Shepherd* [to feed, guide, and shield me] *I shall not lack."*

Deuteronomy 28:2, *"And all these blessings shall come upon you and overtake you, because you obey the voice of the Lord your God."*

Psalm 68:19 (KJV), *"Blessed be the Lord, who daily loadeth us with benefits . . ."*

Psalm 84:11 (KJV), *". . . No good thing will he withhold from them that walk uprightly."*

Psalm 37:25-26 (NIV), *"I was young and now I am old, yet I have never seen the righteous forsaken or their children begging bread. They are always generous and lend freely; their children will be blessed."*

His Divine Nature Birthed Within

You are staring into the mirror of the WORD. Your reflection is beautiful. You're that girl who has laid to rest all characteristics of her old self with her weaknesses, fears, failings, and constant cowering to earthly circumstances. You are NOW FREE, through Christ's life within you. You see clearly. You can now say:

"I'm that girl who is no longer a slave to her old self."

"I'm that girl who is redeemed out of the hand of the enemy."

"I'm that girl who receives the richness of His Grace, His Love, and His Ability."

"I'm that girl who has passed out of the accuser's authority into Christ's love." Colossians 1:13 (DARBY), assures us of this, *"Who has delivered us from the authority of darkness, and translated [us] into the kingdom of the Son of his love."*

Let's keep going . . . you can now say:

"I'm that girl who has Christ's Divine nature birthed within me." 2 Peter 1:4 (ESV) reveals this splendid truth, *". . . by which he has granted to us his precious and very great promises, so that through them you may become partakers of the divine nature . . ."*

You can take a deep breath and finally say:

"I'm that girl who is no longer mentally whipped but who now has taken on the mind of Christ." Philippians 2:5 backs this up, *"Let this mind be in you, which was also in Christ Jesus."*

Are you getting a clearer picture of who you are as an adopted daughter of the King of Kings? Remember Proverbs 23:7 which reveals that what someone thinks within himself becomes his truth. Let's start thinking correctly. We can no longer let our own concepts and opinions get in the way of TRUTH. 2 Corinthians 10:5 (NIVUK) says, *"We demolish arguments and every pretension that sets itself up against the knowledge of God, and we take captive every thought to make it obedient to Christ."*

You're *that girl* who has laid to rest all characteristics of her old self with her weaknesses, fears, failings, and constant cowering to earthly circumstances.

IN HIS NAME

Saving the best for last here. As adopted children, we have been given a legal right through the redemption of Jesus to use His name. His name is above all names, and at His name, every knee will bow! In the name of Jesus, the knee of depression will bow . . . the knee of anger . . . the knee of stress eating . . . the knee of anxiety . . . the knee of addictions . . . they must all bow. And you bet the knee of cancer must bow, too! Compared to the name of Jesus, it is not the Big C, so let's stop calling it that. It is puny compared to the name of the Lamb Who was slain before the foundation of the world to cleanse our sins and heal all our diseases. Call it the little C if you want. Or if it is coming against you, call it something you are walking out of through the powerful name of Jesus. Just don't call it yours! Your mind, spirit, and body have been redeemed through the cross. Stand on His Word and declare the name above all names over your body.

The Hebrew (Old Testament) word for "name" is *shem,* and in the Greek (New Testament) it is *onoma.* Many modern translators see these Greek and Hebrew words as synonymous with the word "people". In ancient Biblical days, a person's name wasn't just a bunch of letters strung together. Names were more than something to distinguish one from another; they depicted their very essence of personhood, their character, value, will, reputation, authority, and so much more.

Proverbs 18:10 says, *"The name of the Lord is a strong tower: the righteous run to it and are safe."* This means that the Lord Himself is a strong tower. God's Name is equal to God's Person. Psalm 9:2 (ESV) exclaims, *"I will be glad and exult in you; I will sing praise to your name, O Most High."* We praise His very personhood and all that His name describes, not the mere letters set in a certain order. We look again in the book of Psalm 91:14 (ESV), *"Because he holds fast to me in love, I will deliver him; I will protect him, BECAUSE HE KNOWS MY NAME."* We are protected by the knowing of the ONE who the name describes. Psalm 106:8 tells us, *"Nevertheless, He saved them for His names sake, that he might make HIS mighty power known."*

> Call it something you are *walking* out of through the powerful *name* of Jesus. Just don't call it yours!

In Hebrew times, writing and speaking "in the name of" meant you carried the authority of the name. You represented someone when you came or acted "in the name". "Blotting out" someone's name was the same as destroying them. Even today, a name is way more than our culture leads us to believe.

What is the point we are getting to here? We can't get away with mindless labels. We can't carelessly label ourselves and others with names and titles that describe defeat, failure, sickness, and oppression. We have the name of our God instead.

Brace yourself because here comes the ouch . . . all those negative, even half-kidding 'one liners' we name ourselves are in essence forgetting Him. "I'm an idiot," even said in self-deprecating jest is not a fitting name for you. Maybe you behaved in a foolish manner, but neither you, nor your child, nor your husband should ever have to wear the name . . . "idiot", "dumb", "stupid", or for that matter . . . "doofus" . . . even it that one sounds a bit cuter and funnier.

Maybe we sound over the top here, but God says He has given us the mind of Christ. We have His name and His mind, so calling ourselves "stupid" is undermining this gift to us. There's no neutrality on this. No fence to sit on. You will fall off one side or the other and land in the pasture that belongs "to the name of" _____ fill in the blank. God says there are only two pastures . . . two choices . . . LIFE and DEATH. When we choose His name and His Word, we choose life.

The Girl with the Choice

Are we going to be that girl who believes the voice of the all-powerful God and what He reveals about His name within His Word or that girl who believes more in the words of man, peers, doctors, or even devils? When many words of negative persuasion prowl around our ears and in our minds, let's stand on this truth from Romans 3:4 (CSB), *"Let God be true, even though everyone is a liar . . ."*

Look at Philippians 2:9-11 (ESV), *"Therefore God has highly exalted him and bestowed on him THE NAME THAT IS ABOVE EVERY NAME, so that at the name of Jesus every knee should bow, in heaven and on earth and under the earth, and every tongue confess that Jesus Christ is Lord, to the glory of God the Father."*

Will we dare believe John 14:12-14 (NIV)? It says, *"Very truly I tell you, whoever believes in me will do the works I have been doing, and they will do even greater things than these, because I am going to the Father. And I will do whatever you ask in my name, so that the Father may be glorified in the Son. You may ask me for anything in my name, and I will do it."*

> We can't get away with *mindless* labels. We can't carelessly label ourselves and others with names and titles that *describe* defeat, failure, sickness, and oppression.

Jesus, with His own lips, said that He has authorized us to use His name in Matthew 10:8 (NASB 1995) to *"Heal the sick, raise the dead, cleanse the lepers, cast out demons. Freely you received, freely give."*

The world is desperately needy and waiting for us to rise up to all we are in HIS NAME. His life-changing words, His caring touch, His healing power, His creative wisdom . . . they are all ours to partake of and to share.

CHAPTER SIXTEEN

Broken -vs- Victorious (Part V)

But Wait . . .

Now to encourage you (and ourselves) to do one of the things most difficult for all of us . . . to WAIT!!! We've established that believing, speaking and standing for victory in our lives is what we're called to do as daughters of the King. But this doesn't automatically mean we'll see our victories physically manifest in short order. While instant miracles can certainly happen if God is willing, more often, victories are fought for and believed for over time.

But in the wait, there is a choice. We can choose to wait with hope and joy. Or we can do the other . . . and the other usually causes one or both of two things.

1. Our theology changes to . . . "This wait has been too long . . . I guess God doesn't deliver. I can no longer believe Him for this."

2. We wait in a state of broken misery, focusing on the struggle and how hard we have it rather than anticipating our victory.

This whole "broken road" camp we just talked about in the last three chapters? Many of us ended up choosing it because we lost hope during the wait. **But having to wait does not mean God doesn't deliver!** Let's not be that girl who throws in the towel because our answer is not immediate.

We've established that not so easy and not so fun stuff happens in life sometimes. No use sticking our heads in the sand and saying, "Bad things don't happen to Believers." The Word makes it clear that things won't always be perfect. John 16:33 (ESV), "*. . . In the world you **will** have tribulation. But take heart; I have overcome the world.*"

The question we need to *ask* ourselves during times of trials is not "Why me?" but rather . . . "What does God want to give and *equip* me with through this?"

Patience is the *bridge* that links us to our *promises* in God.

Hopefully, we've been careful not to give the impression that these trials are never permitted or used by God. But the question we need to ask during times of trials is not "Why me?" but rather . . . "What does God want to give and equip me with through this? What is the promise He wants me to actually unwrap and experience through this trying time? What am I going to grow into as I wait expectantly for the victory?"

The Word is clear that we are not delivered from struggles instantaneously. Patience is the bridge that links us to our promises in God. Patience is a good gift. It is one of the gifts of the Spirit. The accuser doesn't have any of it and he *really* doesn't want you to have any of it. He slyly whispers for you to give up, but Romans 12:12 (NIV) tells you to, *"Be joyful in hope, patient in affliction, faithful in prayer."* And again, in Romans 8:25 (NIV), *"But If we hope for what we do not yet have, we wait for it patiently."* Hope birthed in trial and fed by patience breeds victory. Galatians 6:9 (NIV) encourages, *"Let us not become weary in doing good, for at the proper time we will reap a harvest if we do not give up."*

Not Yet Is Not the End

God wants us to get our hopes up then keep our hopes up for what we do not have . . . YET. Not Yet is not the end.

The biblical reality of a struggle and a wait for God's eventual plan of complete deliverance does not mean God's miraculous power is "broke". There is nothing "broke" about a perfect plan of redemption through the wait. Ecclesiastes 3:11 says,

"He has made everything beautiful in its time". If a follower of Christ has a story that is not yet beautiful . . . the story ain't over yet, baby cakes!

Our God is the God of the epic turnaround. We eagerly await . . . even if it be over 25 years as it was for Abraham to see God's faithfulness take physical form when Isaac was born. Abraham focused on the promise even more as the years stacked up and screamed the loud silence of unfulfilled desires. Faith is tried and tested in the wait. 1 Peter 1:7 (ESV) tells us, *". . . so that the tested genuineness of your faith—more precious than gold that perishes though it is tested by fire—may be found to result in praise and glory and honor at the revelation of Jesus Christ."*

A wait for God's *eventual* plan of complete deliverance does not mean God's miraculous *power* is "broke".

His will for us during the wait is not that we cave to a pit of despair and accept unbelief, depression, and gloom as our parking lot . . . but rather to HOPE and then HOPE some more as Psalm 71:14 encourages, *"But I will hope continually."* We can even do some REJOICING in HOPE with full assurance that *". . . he rewards those who diligently seek Him."* (Hebrews 11:6

Hebrews 11:1 tells us, *"Faith is the substance of things HOPED for . . ."* Faith sees! It actually forms substance. Faith moves mountains, but it is powered by the emotion . . . the electric energy of HOPE. Depression and despondency do not have to be our partners in our times of WAITING; joyful HOPE can be our co-pilot!

Depression and despondency *do not* have to be our *partners* in our times of WAITING

Hope shouts at the storm clouds that there is something far better, brighter, and totally brilliant on the horizon. The psalmist writes in chapter 25:5 (NLT), *"Lead me by your truth and teach me, for you are the God who saves me, all day long I put my HOPE in you."* Notice that *"all day long I put . . ."* part? Once again, the scriptures urge us to do the swap . . . to *"put"* off our doubts and *"put"* our hope in

God. Doubts will come . . . that's a given, but let's just do like David and practice this "put swap" all day long. We'll eventually be "put swap" masters.

Waiting Is Action

The word WAIT and its other variations, WAITED and WAITING, are mentioned close to 150 times in the scriptures. The most frequent use of the word "wait" in the Bible defines the attitude of earnest expectation. We think of waiting as doing nothing but that's not right. It is a soul leaning into the deliverance and promises of God. This powerful, non-passive action of waiting is weaved through the entirety of the scriptures. This type of WAITING is never a state of limbo but a pressing into and persevering in HOPE.

His *desire* is not that we wait passively but instead with joyous, *hopeful* gusto!

Once again, we can see that God's ways are so much higher than ours. Our authentic selves find the wait tedious. "Why can't this just be over," we wonder? But if we nurse those thoughts, we lose our joy, and we lose our power. God has a different desire for us during these seasons of wait. His desire is not that we wait passively but instead with joyous, hopeful gusto! We are to be waiting doers . . . not waiting crybabies! (Massively preaching to ourselves here, too.)

This joyous wait can be applied to all aspects of our lives. We can take joy as we wait for our physical transformations to unfold. No need to get down and despondent during stalls or slow weight loss. Press in . . . grow in wisdom and maturity as you learn what works for your unique body. Don't throw up your hands in despair when your journey takes longer than you thought it would. You'll miss so much treasure if you give up now.

We can take joy as we wait for broken relationships to heal. Love never gives up, Ephesians tells us.

We can even take joy as we wait for healing from sickness. His stripes on the cross healed us, but our healing may take time to manifest.

It Ain't Just You

Noah WAITED for the rain and then for the dry land. Abraham WAITED for a Son. Jacob WAITED for Rachel. Joseph WAITED in slavery and prison before his dreams were fulfilled. David WAITED to become King of Israel after being anointed. The prophet Simeon and Anna WAITED many decades for the fulfillment of the Messianic promise . . . the birth of Jesus. It is quoted in scripture that Simeon was WAITING for the consolation of Israel. Mary, the mother of Jesus, WAITED for the time when her Son would fulfill the words declared to her by the angel.

Most of these examples were not short waits. We already mentioned the quarter-century time between God's promise to Abraham and the time Isaac was finally born. Joseph's promise of blessing and position of power was not a quick turnaround either. It was fulfilled after 10 long years of slavery. God did not cause Joseph's brothers' jealousy that sold him into slavery, but He definitely recycled it to initiate the beautiful yet lengthy process of strengthening and molding Joseph's character. He grew him up to be the man of the hour to help save the starving nation of Israel.

> Most of these *examples* were not *short* waits.

This process of God delivering us from ourselves through the things the enemy throws at us is genius. We can humbly submit to these God lessons but not to the plans of the accuser himself. Likewise, God can use a fight against cancer to grow us into deeper and mightier places in Him, but this doesn't mean we have to accept the cancer as His will.

Jesus himself had to WAIT for His Father's time . . . He said, *". . . My time is not yet come . . ."* (John 7:6 KJV). And even creation WAITS! Romans 8:19 (NLT) says, *"For all creation is waiting eagerly for that future day when God will reveal who his children really are."* Notice that? *"Waits eagerly."* That's how we wait . . . not losing hope, but full of belief and anticipation, resting and trusting in our God for His perfect timing.

To top it off, our Father waits. Isaiah 30:18 (NASB) tells us, *"Therefore the LORD longs to be gracious to you, And therefore He WAITS on high to have*

> That's how we wait . . . not *losing* hope, but full of *belief* and anticipation.

compassion on you. For the LORD is a God of justice; How blessed are all those who long for Him." The word *"long"* is birthed in a lengthy WAIT. You can't long for something if it is instant. We learn the power and preciousness of longing for God only in a wait. And by waiting on God, we learn to seek and we who seek find (Matthew 7:8). And what do we find? A God who "longs" back . . . who looooooooongs to bless us. Yay! Waiting is good then, aye? We are not gonna be that girl all broken up and abandoned, losing the plot because our promise hasn't arrived yet . . . it is just getting fattened up and ready for our patient, hopeful, overcoming selves.

Are You a Promised Land Citizen?

The whole magnificent storyline of the Bible . . . first in the physical (as told through the Israelites) but also in the spiritual, is all about the "Land of Promise". When we read the story of the children of Israel, we see a bunch of battles and loads of WAITING on the way. These battles and waits . . . they can so easily knock a bunch of us off our hope track. In fact, most of the Israelites lost their faith and simply stopped believing. Joshua didn't, though. Remember him in the Bible story? He refused to quit . . . he saw himself as a rightful citizen of the Promised Land. God honored him for his belief and took him right into the land of promise . . . but it sure didn't happen overnight.

Promise Land citizens may still be waiting for their promises, but they see who they really are through the eye of faith, and they carry on with hope. They may get dirt flung on them from the "land of problems" (which we refuse to capitalize). They may even get knocked down a few times, but these courageous "People of Promise" have learned the art of bouncing back.

Actually, they have learned a little secret. The inertia of bouncing back from problems, catapults them to an ever-higher place of abiding in the Promised Land. The very thing that is purposed from the enemy to take them lower, they let God use as the "lift" so they can soar in Him.

Isaiah 40:31 (ESV) says, *"But they who WAIT for the LORD shall renew their strength; they shall mount up with wings like eagles; they shall run and not be weary; they shall walk and not faint."* Did you notice there that the words "WAIT" and "STRENGTH" are nestled together in this verse? A "wait" does not mean a "NO" from God. A "wait" is just the road to His "YES!"

We love this quote from Graham Cooke (a wonderful Bible teacher, speaker, and author). He writes, "A crisis attracts the power and strength of God." This is the power and strength that fuels the WAITING and the HOPING and the leaning and the learning that builds a person into a VICTOR . . . a true resident of the Land of Promise. Let's be that girl who is a Promised Land citizen, by faith at first and finally by its harvest.

1 Corinthians 15:57 (NIV) shouts, *"But thanks be to God! He gives us the VICTORY through our Lord Jesus Christ."* This Victory is ours. It may not be immediate. But it always comes to those who hang on to God. It is inevitable for those who refuse to let go of Him . . . like a wolverine who's clamped on and cannot be shaken off. This grit and tenacity reminds us again of Jacob, who wrestled with God and said, *"I will not let You go unless You bless me!"* (Genesis 32:26) The awesome news is . . . God loooooooooongs to bless us. But He also loooooooongs to instill in us faith, spiritual grit, and overcoming, promise drilling, blessing-cracking perseverance.

A *"wait"* does not mean a "NO" from God. A "wait" is just the road to His *"YES!"*

Wait . . . Wait . . . Wait

Here is a small sample of scriptures to encourage us in our waits.

Psalm 33:20, *"Our soul WAITS for the Lord; He is our help and our shield."*

Psalm 130:5, *"I WAIT for the Lord, my soul does wait, and in His word do I HOPE."*

Psalm 62:5-6 (KJV) cheerleads, *"My soul, WAIT thou only upon God; for my expectation is from him. He only is my rock and my salvation: he is my defence; I shall not be moved."*

Proverbs 20:22 counsels, *". . . WAIT for the Lord, and He will SAVE you."*

Micah 7:7 (NASB 1995) declares, *"But as for me, I will watch expectantly for the LORD; I will WAIT for the God of my salvation. My God will hear me."*

Lamentations 3:24-26 (NASB 1995) builds hope's case, *"The LORD is my portion,"* says my soul, *"Therefore I have HOPE in Him." The LORD is good to those who WAIT for Him, To the person who seeks Him. It is good that he WAITS silently For the salvation of the LORD."*

Psalm 39:7 (BSB) encourages, "And now Lord, for what do I WAIT? My HOPE is in You."

Waiting is weaved everywhere throughout the inspired WORD . . . Let's read a few more to toast our point (God's point) to a further crisp . . .

Isaiah 49:23 (NASB), *". . . Those who HOPEFULLY WAIT for Me will not be put to shame."*

This promise is repeated in Psalm 25:3 (NASB), *"Indeed, none of those who WAIT for You will be ashamed . . ."*

Isaiah 25:9, *"And it will be said in that day, "Behold, this is our God. We have waited for him, and He will save us. This is the Lord; We have waited for Him; We will be glad and rejoice in His salvation."*

Isaiah 64:4, *"For since the beginning of the world men have not heard not perceived by the ear, Nor has the eye seen any God besides You, Who acts for the one who waits for him."*

Isaiah 33:2, *"O LORD, be gracious to us; We have waited for You . . ."*

Hosea 12:6, *"So you by the help of your God, return, Observe mercy and justice, And wait on your God continually."*

Habakkuk 2:3, *"For the vision is YET for an appointed time, But at the end it will speak, and not lie. Though it tarries, WAIT for it; because it will surely come, It will not tarry."*

Luke 24:49 (GNT), *". . . But you must wait in the city until the power from above comes down upon you."*

Acts 1:4 (NASB), *"Gathering them together, He commanded them not to leave Jerusalem, but to WAIT for what the Father had promised, "Which," He said, "you heard of from me."*

Zephaniah 3:8, *"Therefore WAIT for Me", says the Lord . . ."*

CHAPTER SEVENTEEN

Promised You Some Science (Part I)

Not So Voodoo

Interesting fact . . . the first actual photo was taken in 1826. For the next couple of decades however, the idea of photography elicited fear and suspicion in many people. How could a picture be reproduced without someone physically drawing or painting it, skeptics wondered? Many couldn't fathom how light could capture and store images, so they feared and shunned it.

A few hundred years before that . . . in the 1300-1400s, well before photography as we know it was created, certain people began to figure out the basic principles of lenses and cameras. Using light, they could project an image on the wall or piece of paper, but no printing was possible at that time so recording the image was a lot harder than projecting it. The instrument used for processing pictures became known as the *Camera Obscura* (which is Latin for the darkroom). Historians believe many Renaissance artists used *Camera Obscura* as an aid in drawing, but few of them admitted to this for fear of being charged with association with occultism. An Italian scholar and nobleman was accused of sorcery in the 1500s for trying to promote this tool to other artists.

Let's leave this whole sorcery and occult accusation business alone to settle for a bit, we'll return to it with a point soon.

These days most of us take the whole idea of visual film and recorded sound for granted since our lives are so flooded with it, but when you stop to really think about it . . . how does a moving, living being get inside your TV screen and talk to you? Voodoo! Nah . . . of course not. The science of TV can be explained easily . . . light and sound are captured then turned into pulses of electricity that are transmitted from the television station in waves and are then received by your own TV. But none of this was even dreamed up a couple hundred years ago. If you could go back and describe cable news or Netflix to your great, great grandparents, perhaps they'd think you are crazy at best or at worst . . . partaking in some sort of witchery!

Quantum Physics is the study of the smallest things in the Universe . . . subatomic particles. It has taught us that a large part of our Universe is beyond what our 5 human senses can register; that physical matter is actually just energy in different states of vibration and those vibrations can change according to how they are influenced. The quantum world has taught scientists that life is more a flow of subatomic energy than a collection of solid things. While we cannot hear or see this quantum world, it is every bit as real as this book you are holding in your hands.

Science has barely scraped the surface of understanding these things, but the more that becomes known about the quantum world, the more the belief that our own words and thoughts have no influence over our wellbeing and circumstances becomes laughable. The Bible declares that words on our lips can bind and loose, even bring death and life, and the more science uncovers, the more it supports the scriptures.

> The more that becomes *known* about the quantum world, the more the belief that our own words and thoughts have no influence over our *wellbeing* and circumstances becomes laughable.

Some Christians want nothing to do with the merging of science and spirit. So-called "New Age or New Thought" philosophies regarding sound, light, and electricity, etc. are still considered taboo in much of Christian culture. When it comes to embracing them in our spiritual walk, well, just watch out . . . start sharing that you are pondering these things, and you might find yourself on the prayer chain quick-smart! "Can we pray for Clara? She's gone all New Age!"

So, let's return to the whole photography occult association we opened this chapter with and make our point. Like the first misunderstood photograph, these energy-based aspects of our world are often illogically feared and misunderstood.

We say . . . "Bring them on!"

God is the ultimate Scientist, the Author of the speed of light, the Creator of bone and sinew, the Genius who fashioned electrical impulses that run through our body at speeds we can barely comprehend. The Bible speaks of these wondrous mysteries (as we'll soon show), so why shouldn't we also? God is the One who created every subatomic particle, every quantum frequency and pulse, every crystal, quartz, and magnet that influence the flow of energy. While current science has barely tapped the surface of understanding these aspects of our Universe, God certainly understands them all since He created them with just a spoken Word.

> God is the One who *created* every *subatomic* particle, every quantum frequency and pulse, every crystal, quartz, and magnet that influence the flow of energy.

Why should we repeat history and be like those who were afraid of photography . . . scared and skeptical just because we don't yet understand all of these things? As modern science plays a tiny bit of catch-up, knowledge gained about this world only reveals more and more of God's astounding creative power and glory.

Anthony Leggett is a physicist at the University of Illinois at Urbana-Champaign. In 2003, he won a Nobel Prize in physics, the most prestigious award in his field. Leggett has helped develop ways to test quantum theory. Regarding the quantum world and our budding understanding of it, he wrote, "Things that right now seem fantastic will be possible." This lines right up with the Word, which tells us God is the God of the impossible and that His understanding knows no limits!

Hebrews 4:12 (ESV) tells us, *"For the word of God is living and active, sharper than any two-edged sword, piercing to the division of soul and of spirit, of joints and of marrow, and discerning the thoughts and intentions of the heart."* Man has learned how to delve a little into the quantum world and split the atom, but God's Word has been utilizing the division of atoms far before man even dreamed up the discovery of such a thing.

A Mighty Voice

Come with us back to the beginning, to Genesis 1:1, *"In the beginning, God created the heavens and the earth. The earth was without form and void, and darkness was over the face of the deep. And the Spirit of God was hovering over the face of the waters. And God **said,** "Let there be light," and there was light."*

> Can you *imagine* the VIBRATIONS caused by such a *voice?*

Can you imagine the VIBRATIONS caused by such a voice?

The power in the voice of the Word . . . the atom obeying vibrations at the sound of the voice of the WORD that created all that is! Just thinking about the awesomeness of this is spine-tingling!

What powerful explosive vibration must have come forth from His lips to bring the world into existence. John 1:1-3 tells us, *"All things were made through Him, and without Him nothing was made that was made."* Everything . . . you . . . us . . . the galaxies . . . all formed through the voice of the Word.

We started Chapter 1 of this book by telling you that your words have power. They absolutely do. But there is more power in God's Words than our own. There is creative power and healing power in God's Word. It is when we speak His Words that His true power can manifest in our lives. Look again at Proverbs 4:20-22 (BSB), *"My son, pay attention to my words; incline your ear to my sayings. Do not lose sight of them; keep them within your heart. For they are **life to those who find them, and health to the whole body.**"*

The Science of Sound

We'll get deeper into the science of how our thoughts and emotions affect us in the last leg of these *Promised You Some* Science chapters. For this first leg, let's focus on actual spoken words and how they affect us.

Science has now uncovered some of the mystery and quantum influence of sound. Right up until as late as the 1970s, it was thought that solid matter was still, but now science understands that couldn't be further from the truth. Physical matter, just like a musical note, is always quivering and always making sound.

We think of sound as something we hear—something that makes noise we can detect with our ears . . . but in pure physics terms, sound is simply vibration going through matter. Everything from the chair you are sitting on to all the parts of your body vibrates at its own frequency. Your phone next to you looks like a solid, unmoving thing unless you yourself pick and it up and move it, but on a quantum level, it is moving and vibrating by itself.

Every motion and emotion, every energy and element that exists and surrounds us, has its own vibration even if we can't see the movement with our eyes or hear the sounds with our ears.

Why are we sharing this? Because this means things are not as we thought they were, they are not finite, they are changeable, and quantum physics reveals that they change in response to things we say and do!

The whole Universe and everything in it is in a constant state of vibration. These vibrations produce sound whether we hear them all or not. Sure, we think of nature making noise just by what we can hear . . . the leaves rustle with the wind, the waves crash on the shore, the thunder cracks. But that's just surface, tip of the iceberg stuff. In reality, nature is talking and singing in millions of ways we can't pick up on with our senses. Look at how Psalm 19:1-3 (ESV) describes this wondrous phenomenon of creation, *"The heavens declare the glory of God, and the sky above proclaims his handiwork. Day to day*

> This means things are not as we *thought* they were, they are not finite, they are *changeable.*

pours out speech, and night to night reveals knowledge. There is no speech, nor are there words, whose voice is not heard."

In reference to how nature would take over praising Him if people ceased doing it, Jesus said in Luke 19:40, *". . . the stones would immediately cry out."* Likewise, Psalm 148:3-4, encourages nature to give praise to God. *"Praise him sun and moon, praise him all you shining stars. Praise him, you highest heavens and you waters above the skies."*

> We are living *unawares* of millions of ultrasonic songs being played by *nature* all around us.

If it sounds a little crazy for scripture to talk directly to nature like this . . . to literally encourage it to sing praises . . . scientifically speaking, it's quite sound . . . pun intended. It is right in step with cutting-edge science. Research in the field of bioacoustics has revealed that we are living unawares of millions of ultrasonic songs being played by nature all around us. Don Lincoln is an American physicist, author, and science communicator who conducts research in Particle Physics. In an online article titled, *The Good Vibrations of Quantum Field Theories,* he writes, "The entire Universe is made of fields playing a vast, subatomic symphony. Physicists are trying to understand the melody." So, once again, secular science is just beginning to glimpse some understanding of what the scriptures already knew . . . that we are living in a booming, vibrating, worshipping universe. Our human ears are just not picking up on it. Dog's ears are able to detect far more spectrums of sound from nature than we do . . . but even they don't hear it all.

In other news . . . plants talk! Well not exactly, but kinda. It was long thought that plants do not make sounds of their own. Although humans cannot perceive sound from plants, recent studies using small, highly sensitive sound receivers have demonstrated that plants do make spontaneous sounds and even release sound emissions from their xylem (their water transporting systems).

Consider that the electron shell of the carbon atom produces the same harmonic state as the Gregorian chant. The tiny hydrogen atom emits one hundred frequencies which are more musical than a grand piano, which only emits eighty-eight frequencies.

Just because we can't see or hear these things happening does not mean they aren't occurring, for they surely are!

Allow us to give you a couple examples of the effects of sound vibration on living things taking place beyond our awareness. Stay with us here . . . we're sharing all this nature sings, talks, and responds stuff to set the scene for another important forthcoming point (important in our minds anyway . . . you know we love the big dramatic point cliff-hangers).

An extremely interesting experiment was undertaken at MIT (Massachusetts Institute of Technology), which showed how the vibrations that form music could be reproduced by observing the leaves of a plant nearby. The scientists situated themselves in a soundproof room. They watched the leaves of the plant in another room vibrate through a high-speed camera. The MIT researchers on their high-tech cameras saw the plant leaves pulsing uniquely to the tones and the rhythm of the music. The plants were able to reproduce the melody being played without actually "hearing" it (at least through what we know as ears) themselves.

Many other experiments have been conducted using plants and music. Plants actually thrive when peaceful music (such as classical) is played compared to plants not in the presence of music. Peaceful music causes significantly larger growth, more chlorophyll, and bigger root systems. Interestingly, plants do not do well in the presence of jarring rock music. They have less growth and less effective rooting. Not making up any theology against rock music here . . . it was only aggressive, jarring rock music that did the damage, but we found that piece of info interesting. You can do a quick online search for these studies to see the pictures of the effect of music on plant growth for yourself . . . fascinating.

The *plants* were able to reproduce the melody being *played* without actually "hearing" it

So, why are we telling you about these plant studies? They demonstrate that sound vibration definitively affects all its surroundings. Plants do not have mouths and ears, of course; they do not possess any animal mechanism to make sounds, yet they do. Likewise, they do not possess any mechanism to hear sounds, but they do

. . . they simply sense the vibrations. When music is played, the sound waves travel through the air and are received by the protoplasm of the plant. The whole plant's vitality is then affected by whether these vibrations are beneficial or not to its well-being. Interestingly, fruit flies, snakes, and a tiny species of frog call the sooglosid frog, all also perceive sound without actual ears.

Scientists are currently working on sound technology to enhance the future of crop growth in place of chemical fertilizers. Considering that sound-treated tomato plants showed 13.2% increased yields compared with control plants, this approach to advancements in plant growth is showing remarkable potential. A 2018 PubMed article titled *Beyond Chemical Triggers: Evidence for Sound Evoked Reactions in Plants* presents much research on how sound can be used to enhance plant health for the future. In it, the authors state, *"We propose that sound is an emerging physical trigger in plants beyond chemical triggers, such as plant hormones and other immune activators which have been used to improve plant health."*

So, this brings us to our big point. Similar to these plant studies, scientific evidence in this field of research is also revealing that words are containers, and they too emit their own, unique vibrations. These vibrations in words transmit emotions entwined within them that deliver more than a message to the ear . . . they affect everything within their range, either positively or negatively on a cellular level.

> The *force* of our words should never be *underestimated.*

The force of our words should never be underestimated. Similar to the impact of various sounds on the overall health of plants, words impact our hormones, our immune systems, our length of days, and our quality of those length of days. There are words that carry love and words that carry hate, and those that carry every emotion in between. But this is old news to the scriptures, which already stated some three thousand years ago in Proverbs 12:18, *". . . the tongue of the wise promotes health."* Then again in Proverbs 18:21 (NIV) it tells us, *"The tongue has the power of life and death . . ."*

If we ever thought it rational to consider words as just words . . . we have to reconsider our stance. That notion is no longer feasible in light of current research.

Continuing to believe that may be harmful to our wellbeing. We need to change our thinking to match the Bible first and foremost, but also to match what science is now uncovering.

Sound Moves and Creates

Before it was known that all matter vibrates, it was first learned that sound vibrates. The science that focuses on the study of sound vibrations began in the 16th century and is called Cymatics from the Greek word *Kyma,* which means wave.

> If we ever thought it *rational* to consider words as just words . . . we have to *reconsider* our stance.

In the Eighteenth Century, Ernst Chladni, a German musician and scientist who became known as the Father of Acoustics, brought pictures to life through sound with a very simple demonstration. He drew his violin bow around the edge of a plate that was covered with fine sand, and the sand formed different geometric patterns depending on the sound he made.

Dr. Hans Jenny, a medical doctor and scientist, was the pioneer in this field in the 1900s and his work revealed actual pictures that sound makes through vibrations. Dr. Jenny made invisible sound shockingly visible to the eye. Using a bit more technology than the simple violin bow of Dr. Ernst Chladni, Jenny placed sand, fluid, and powders on metal plates. He then vibrated them with a special frequency generator and a speaker, and intricate, beautiful patterns formed that were different for each individual vibration. These pictures only remained visible as long as the sound pulsed through the sand and powders and collapsed when the sound was stopped.

Intricate pictures of visible sound producing form . . .

If simple notes can create such beautiful and intricate imagery through vibrations on a sub-atomic level, imagine the powerful, sub-atomic vibrations that formed when God said, *"Let there be light . . ."*

Look at some of the other descriptions of the power of God's voice in His Word:

Psalm 68:33, *"To Him who rides upon the highest heavens, which are from ancient times; Behold, He speaks forth with His voice, a mighty voice."*

Psalm 29:3-9 (NASB 1995), *"The voice of the LORD is upon the waters; The God of glory thunders, The LORD is over many waters. The voice of the LORD is powerful, The voice of the LORD is majestic. The voice of the LORD breaks the cedars; Yes, the LORD breaks in pieces the cedars of Lebanon. He makes Lebanon skip like a calf, And Sirion like a young wild ox. The voice of the LORD hews out flames of fire. The voice of the LORD shakes the wilderness; The LORD shakes the wilderness of Kadesh. The voice of the LORD makes the deer to calve And strips the forests bare; And in His temple everything says, "Glory!""*

Don't tell us subatomic activity isn't being commanded in major ways in these sorts of verses. You betcha' atoms shake and come under His authority at the sound of His Words!

Psalm 46:6 (NASB), *"The nations made an uproar, the kingdoms tottered; He raised His voice, the earth melted."*

Ezekiel 43:2 (NASB), *". . . and behold, the glory of the God of Israel was coming from the way of the east. And His voice was like the sound of many waters; and the earth shone with His glory."*

Speaking to the Waters

Think it is a stretch for us to say that just because sound waves can make patterns that words can powerfully affect our lives? Well, let's keep making the case. Cymatics has also explored the effect sound has on water and has proven that sound waves alter the inner structure of water cells and make water change its physical shape under a microscope. Dr. Masaru Emoto from Japan has conducted an extensive study on the power of sound and thoughts over water. His research indelibly proves that our thoughts and feelings expressed through spoken words (and music) change the structure of water.

Dr. Emoto developed a technique where he used a powerful microscope in a very cold room along with high-speed photography to capture the changes in water's expression when exposed to different sounds and thoughts. His photographs discovered that differing patterns of crystals form in frozen water depending on the concentrated words and thoughts directed to it. Water exposed to loving words and thoughts showed complex, brilliant, and colorful snowflake patterns. In contrast, samples exposed to negative communication formed incomplete, asymmetrical patterns with lifeless colors.

In another experiment, Dr. Emoto played classical music and folk songs from Japan and other countries, through speakers placed next to water samples and then froze them. He compared these crystalline structures to samples that had been exposed to chaotic, heavy metal music and the results were drastically opposing. Samples that were exposed to the beautiful music each formed their own unique, beautifully geometric crystal formations dependent on the different lovely musical pieces. The samples exposed to the discordant, clashing tones showed the water crystal's basic hexagonal structure to be shattered in pieces.

> Words *create* either beauty or ugliness around us or *within* us.

Just as certain sounds created certain forms, so too can our words create either beauty or ugliness around us or within us. (It is also important to note that babies grow in a sack of water within us. The words we speak help create either a beautiful haven of water for them to thrive in or something else entirely.)

Effects on Disease

The power of vibrations through sound and music has also been powerfully illustrated through the works of Fabien Maman, a French composer and bioenergetician, and biologist Helene Grimal. Their research together experimented with both healthy cells and cancer cells to observe their response to voice and various instruments. In *The Role of Music in the Twenty-First Century*, a book by Maman, he reports dramatic effects from sound and voice on cancer cells. Maman said certain musical notes (those sung by the human voice were most effective) actually exploded cancer cells.

There is even more exciting research emerging on sound and healing. A wealth of new studies shows benefits to mental health through singing and music. An analysis of 400 studies published in *Trends in Cognitive Sciences*, April 2013, found that music dramatically improves the body's immune system and reduces stress.

Listening to music was also found to be more effective than prescription drugs in reducing anxiety before surgery. The researchers found that listening to and playing music increases the body's production of the antibody immunoglobulin A and natural killer cells—these are our bodies defenses against invading viruses and diseases. Music also reduces levels of the stress and the fat-promoting hormone cortisol.

Researchers at Khoo Teck Puat Hospital in Singapore found that patients who took part in live music therapy sessions reported relief from persistent pain (*Progress in Palliative Care*, July 2013). Melanie Kwan, co-author of the study and President of the Association for Music Therapy said, "When their acute pain symptoms were relieved, patients were finally able to rest."

Music has also been shown to help with stroke recovery. One 2008 study published in the Oxford Academy *Brain* Journal enrolled 60 patients hospitalized for major strokes. All received standard stroke care. In addition, one-third of the patients listened to recorded music for at least one hour a day, another third listened to audiobooks, and the final group did not receive any auditory stimulation. After three months, verbal memory improved by 60% in the music listeners, compared with 20% to 30% in the audiobook group and the patients in the control group. In addition, the music listeners' ability to perform and control certain mental operations improved by close to 20%. The patients in the other two groups did not improve at all in this area.

> Music dramatically *improves* the body's immune system and *reduces* stress.

Lee Bartel, Ph.D., a music professor at the University of Toronto, has been studying whether sound vibrations absorbed through the body can help patients with Parkinson's disease, fibromyalgia, and depression. Known as vibroacoustic therapy, this involves using low-frequency sound—similar to a low rumble—to produce vibrations that are applied directly to the body. While more research is needed, many of the results are very promising. Two groups of Parkinson's patients were treated (20 with dominant tremor symptoms and 20 with slow/rigid movement symptoms) with five minutes of 30

> Whether you can't *sing* a note on key or whether you can belt notes out in spectacular fashion— it doesn't matter... singing will make you *healthier* and happier.

Hz vibration. Both groups showed improvements in all symptoms, including less rigidity and better walking speed with bigger steps and less tremors.

So, practical application . . . start singing! Whether you can't sing a note on key or whether you can belt notes out in spectacular fashion—it doesn't matter . . . singing will make you healthier and happier. A pilot study published in the *British Journal of Nursing* found that singing therapy could significantly reduce the anxiety and depression patients can experience following major surgery. The effect was strong enough that the authors suggested doctors prescribe singing therapy before trying antidepressants.

Sing positive songs; of course, the best ones would contain scriptures. But if you are not a Bible believer . . . sing anyway! Science is learning that singing allows release to what is locked up in our bodies . . . you can think of it like a cleanse.

And consider this . . . none of these studies looked at vibrations of the spoken or sung Word of God where we find our promise of healing through the finished work on the cross! If specific musical notes can smash cancer cells when sung, imagine what God's Word on our lips as songs or faith-filled prayers can do!

Want to know how many times the Bible encourages us to sing or mentions singing? Over 450 times! Fifty of those are direct commands to sing! Let's get to it! If we are ever at a red light and we look over and notice you belting it out over your steering wheel while you wait for the light to change . . . hey, big atta girl, high five from us! We'll hopefully be doing the same.

Speaking of music . . . we need to take a couple of wee paragraphs before we close up this chapter to talk about dancing since it pretty much always goes with music. We could list thousands of studies that show the health benefits of partaking in this holiest of jigs, but we'll refrain and just give a few for time's sake. Yes, you did just read the word . . . "holy!" Dancing is Biblical (we already talked about King David's dance through the streets). King Solomon, the wisest man who ever lived, stated that there is a time for dancing (Ecclesiastes 3:4).

Sadly, similar to how King David was sneered upon for his dancing, we're of the opinion that once again, this is something wrongly vilified by some church folk. Dancing is often looked down on by Christians, but in truth, we should be the dancingest folks of all! That joy God has put inside us that just can't help bubbling forth and get our bodies a grooving . . . it's natural! Sure, just like anything, dancing can be used for evil purposes, but that's not the sort of dancing we are talking about here.

> More than *any* other form of exercise, dancing significantly *reduces* Alzheimer's and dementia risk.

Of course, dancing is good for your cardiovascular and muscular health since it is a form of exercise but let's focus for a moment on how it heals in other ways and why, if you haven't before, you need to start getting your dance on!

Researchers have found that:

*More than any other form of exercise, dancing significantly reduces Alzheimer's and dementia risk. One paper published in 2017 even found through brain imaging scans that dancing can increase the amount of white matter in the brains of elderly adults.

*Dancing has proven to be a powerful combat to depression and anxiety. A slew of studies points to the fact that dance—like other physical exercise but even more so—increases serotonin (our "feel good" brain chemical) and helps develop new neural connections in the brain.

*It is incredible for the immune system! Dancing helps prevent and combat a host of diseases through its ability to lower cortisol, which in turn decreases inflammation and raises a healthy immune response.

You don't have to be a good dancer, just like you don't have to be a good singer. All you have to be is that girl who speaks life, sings life, and dances life as you go through life! Try it out . . . who cares if you are a bit rusty. See how good it makes you feel to do a little boogie shuffle right now. (Shameless plug for our Workins DVD's (or streaming version) but hey . . . when something works . . . we end almost all of the fun twenty-minute exercise sessions with a crazy dance!)

> All you *have* to be is that girl who speaks life, sings life, and dances *life* as you go through life!

You may have heard that faking a smile, literally forcing yourself to put on a smile (one that reaches your eyes, not a grimace) even if you don't feel like it, brings real healing and happiness to your body. Multiple studies have shown that the act of smiling produces chemical changes in brain activity that lower heart rate, boost immune defense, release dopamine and serotonin, and even promote longevity! Your brain is literally a sucker for a grin! Similarly, singing, dancing, and speaking positive words even in the midst of challenges, even when you don't want to . . . changes your brain space and consequently the health of your body. And of course, these things surely make huge changes in the unseen quantum world, too.

The Bible is Our Best Science and Health Manual

Does God heal through physical elements of His creation? We'd have to say a big, "Of course!" All healing ultimately comes from the Word, which is Christ and His redemption (remember scripture tells us He was slain before the foundation of the world, so even before the actual calendar date of the cross, all physical healing pointed to the forthcoming event). But Jesus Himself used elements of physical nature to manifest healing sometimes. He used His own saliva on three different occasions to heal. Once to heal a deaf man, another time to heal a blind man, and another time He mixed His spit with dirt to reverse another man's blindness.

In the Old Testament, King Hezekiah was terminally ill. He asked God to heal him. God told him through His prophet Isaiah to put a poultice of figs on his ailment. He became well and was granted another 15 years of robust health. God, through His prophet, told a man with leprosy to bathe seven times in a certain stream, and he was cured.

God being all-powerful, doesn't need to use His nature to heal, of course, but He more than occasionally does! The scriptures declare that herbs are for the service of man. So is sunlight, pure water, good food, negatively charged ions in the earth and oceans, and positive thoughts and emotions. And some of the things we've just mentioned like dancing, laughter, and singing.) Those are just a few; the list of physical healing elements goes on and on. They are all here to service us just as you take your car to be serviced to keep it running well.

These things, such as the healthy food we can taste and the sunlight we can feel . . . we can detect them with our senses, but they are just the tip of the grand scope of things. Think of them as a small island poking out of the ocean. That little island is actually just the top of a huge mountain, most of which is covered by water and undetected by our eyes. The Quantum Universe may not be in our sight, but it is far larger, much more powerful, and has an even greater ability to heal or to destroy than what we can see. Yet, you can influence it. You can speak into it, sing into it, and dance your way into shifting it for your good.

> God being all-powerful, doesn't need to use His *nature* to heal, of course, but He *more* than occasionally does!

CHAPTER EIGHTEEN

Promised You Some Science (Part II)

What the Rice!

More about the science of words here in this chapter. Now on to a biggie . . . an experiment that has mystified the scientific world for decades. Dr. Emoto's most well-known experiment (we talked about him and his sound and water experiments in the last chapter) is one where he took three sterilized beakers, put the same amount of rice and water in each one, and left them for thirty days. Each day he spoke to two of the jars with strong emotions backing his words. To one, he spoke LOVE, and to the other, he spoke HATE. He would say "thank you" or other words of appreciation to the first and things like "you're an idiot" to the other. The third beaker of rice and water he simply ignored.

The beaker that was the recipient of loving words and emotions never rotted. It stayed clean and white for the full 30 days. The rice water inflicted with hateful words and emotions grew huge black splotches of ugly mold, and the beaker that was ignored just simply rotted. Many people have tried this experiment at home and have amazingly experienced the same results. Again, we urge . . . go Google it, and you'll see result after result online.

Our own children did this experiment as part of a homeschooling science experiment, and astoundingly got these very same results. The rice and water they spoke love to did not rot while the one that had hate-filled words spoken over it did . . . disgustingly! We shared the results of this study on one of our weekly Trim Healthy Podcasts and encouraged others to do it to see if they got similar results. We have heard back from so many and have seen their online pictures of their jars of rice after 30 days . . . results just like ours! These and many other experiments are published in Dr. Emoto's book *The Hidden Messages In Water.* A simply astounding video, *The Secret of Water,* which shows his ice crystal experiment, can be viewed online as well, if you need to see it to believe it.

We Are 70% Water

These experiments are compelling when we remember that our bodies average around 70% water. What we speak over ourselves and others around us really does matter! It is scripture . . . it is science. They match up! Look at what Proverbs 16:24 says, *"Pleasant words are like a honeycomb, Sweetness to the soul and health to the bones."* And what are the most pleasant of words? The 26th verse of Proverbs 15 tells us, *". . . the words of the pure are pleasant . . ."*

We can learn to train our tongue in the truth of God's Word to build up and beautify, or we can let it run amuck and tear down and destroy. A study that helps reveal how our words have the physical power to either bless or curse our own bodies was published in an article titled *Patient Knows Best* in a 1991 issue of *Reader's Digest.* More than 2,800 men and women 65 years and older were asked to rate their health as being excellent, good, fair, or poor. Their answer to this question remarkably predicted who would live and die over the next four years. After the question was posed, their actual health was also assessed. The study revealed that those who rated their health as poor were four to five times more likely to die than those who rated it as excellent. But get this . . . it didn't matter what their health actually was according to their medical examinations. People with actual poor health who stated that they had good health were part of the group who lived longer! The results were literally astounding and, of course, back up the Word of God like science

> We can *learn* to train our tongue in the truth of God's Word to build up and beautify, or we can let it run *amuck* and tear down and destroy.

ends up doing time and again. Proverbs 15:23 tells us that *"A man has joy by the answer of his mouth."*

This study about answering positively or negatively is not just a one-off study. According to Ellen Idler, a sociologist at Rutgers University (1985-2009), these findings are backed up by a review of five other extensive studies that involved 23,000 people. A very recent *John Hopkins* study about heart disease published, and it reaches similar conclusions. People with a family history of heart disease who also had a positive outlook were one-third less likely to have a heart attack or other cardiovascular event within 5 to 25 years than those with a more negative outlook. This finding held even for people who had the most risk factors for coronary artery disease.

The Bible Backs Up the Science

Science only shadows what the Bible has already laid out and encouraged as bedrock foundation truth for LIFE. As an example, think of the verse, *"Do all things without complaining . . ."* (Philippians 2:14). Research shows that most people complain once a minute during a typical conversation. Yikes!

God does not want us to complain for so many reasons, but surely one of the foremost being He knows it is awful for our health. When you complain, your body releases the stress hormone cortisol. Cortisol directs oxygen, blood, and energy away from everything but the systems that are essential to immediate survival. One effect of cortisol, for example, is that it raises both your blood pressure and blood sugar.

When you *complain,* your body releases the stress hormone *cortisol.*

All this extra cortisol released by frequent complaining greatly impairs your immune system. It makes you more susceptible to whatever colds and flus are going around, not to mention high cholesterol, diabetes, heart disease, and obesity. It even makes the brain more vulnerable to strokes!

Complaining literally *shrinks* your *brain*!

Complaining literally shrinks your brain! Yep, a study from Stanford University has shown that complaining shrinks the hippocampus—an area of the brain that's critical to problem-solving and intelligent thought. Damage to the hippocampus is serious, especially when you consider that it's one of the primary brain areas destroyed by Alzheimer's.

Even complaining about the weather is not good for your health! Let's be that girl who is not part of the norm, complaining at least once per minute. Let's pull complaining entirely out of our speech!

What is the opposite of complaining? Gratitude! Psalm 92:1 tells us, *"It is a good thing to give thanks . . ."* There is not just one, but hundreds of places in the Bible encouraging us to be thankful, and once again, science thoroughly agrees. Gratitude, rather than shrinking the brain as complaining does, enhances it. A study published in a 2015 edition of *Frontiers in Psychology* showed that people who express and feel gratitude have a higher volume of grey matter in the right inferior temporal gyrus (sciency speak for the right part of the brain).

Gratitude also activates and regulates an area of the brain called the hypothalamus. A 2009 series of studies using MRI's of brains showed the limbic system in general, of which the hypothalamus is a part of, is activated during gratitude. This, in turn, regulates all kinds of bodily functions, including hunger, sleep, body temperature, and metabolism.

People who express and feel *gratitude* have a *higher* volume of grey matter.

Yet another method shown to be as effective (if not more so) as medication for depression? You guessed it . . . gratitude. In one study, scientists asked participants to write a few sentences each week, focusing on particular topics. One group wrote about things they were grateful for that had occurred during the week. A second group wrote about daily irritations or things that had frustrated them, and the third wrote about events that had affected them (with no emphasis on them being positive or negative).

After 10 weeks, those who wrote about gratitude were significantly more optimistic and felt better about their lives. And get this . . . they also had fewer visits to physicians than those who focused on sources of aggravation.

Robert Emmons, Ph.D., professor of psychology at UC Davis and leading scientific expert on the science of gratitude, says this: "The practice of gratitude can have dramatic and lasting effects in a person's life. It can lower blood pressure, improve immune function, and facilitate more efficient sleep. Gratitude reduces lifetime risk for depression, anxiety and substance abuse disorders, and is a key resiliency factor in the prevention of suicide."

> Gratitude reduces *lifetime* risk for *depression,* anxiety and substance abuse disorders.

But gratitude doesn't just positively affect your health; let's have a quick wee look at what gratitude can do for your marriage! Focusing on everything that's wrong with your partner, i.e., complaining in your mind or out loud, is a quick and easy way to be miserable. There's a growing body of research that shows words and actions of gratitude in marriage are crucial to success. One new study published in the *Journal of Social and Personal Relationships* found that expressions of spousal gratitude were a significant predictor of marital quality. The data is in . . . gratitude-focused couples are less likely to seek divorce.

> Words and *actions* of gratitude in marriage are crucial to *success.*

Drop and Give Me Three!

It is all well and good to encourage gratitude. But how, when it is not yet a well practiced habit? One method that has been a huge help for us is what we call the "drop and give me three."

In the wonderful book, *Mini Habits*, Stephen Guise encourages small goals rather than large. His goal of just one pushup a day eventually led to a daily habit of many more. This ability to achieve small goals rather than feeling overwhelmed by large ones spurred him on to accomplish many life achievements one little bite at a time. Anyone can do just one pushup a day!

We took Stephen's general advice and applied it to gratitude . . . mini step by mini step. As soon as we noticed ourselves using complaining words or thinking dark, gloomy and ungrateful thoughts, we reminded ourselves to "drop and give me three." Anyone can think of three things to be grateful for, even when it seems like everything is going wrong. In fact, when things are going wrong is the best time to exercise our gratitude muscle. In the same way that a soldier is trained for battle and is told to drop and do push ups by his commander when he or she is out of line, we began to strengthen our gratitude muscles by basically dropping (in other words instantly stopping the complaining or self pity) and directing ourselves to be thankful for three things. We discovered that three usually leads to more!

Here are just a few verses from the Word that come to mind on the importance of choosing and using our words carefully.

Proverbs 31:26 (NLT), *"When she speaks, her words are wise, and she gives instructions with kindness."*

Matthew 15:18 (NASB), *"But the things that come out of the mouth come from the heart, and those things defile the person."*

Ephesians 4:29 (NIV), *"Do not let any unwholesome talk come out of your mouths, but only what is helpful for building others up according to their needs, that it may benefit those who listen."*

James 3:10 (NLT), *"And so blessing and cursing come pouring out of the same mouth. Surely, my brothers and sisters, this is not right!"*

1 Peter 3:10 (NLT), *"If you want to enjoy life and see many happy days, keep your tongue from speaking evil and your lips from telling lies."*

The Danger of Ignoring

One of the interesting results of Dr. Emoto's rice water experiments we talked about earlier was the beaker that was ignored. It rotted!! It didn't develop the dense ugly patches of black mold like the beaker of rice water that was hated, but it rotted slowly, nonetheless.

Most of us probably grew up with the saying, "If you don't have anything nice to say then don't say anything at all!" It's a good saying, and we have reminded our children of this a time or two . . . (or more like a thousand times or two). It is an especially needful caution in this day and age of knee-jerk and hurtful social media comments. But in the real world, it isn't the best approach . . . it's just not the worst.

To ignore something or someone still does damage. We have to get creative in thinking of good things to SAY even about our enemies!!!!! Say what???!!?? Yup, it's scripture. Matthew 5:44 (KJV) tells us, *"But I say unto you, Love your enemies, bless them that curse you, do good to them that hate you, and pray for them which despitefully use you, and persecute you."* Romans 12:14 (YLT) tells us, *"Bless those persecuting you; bless, and curse not."*

> We have to get *creative* in thinking of good things to SAY even about our enemies!!!!!

The Dark Side of Silence

There is definitely a time for silence, especially when we haven't yet gained control over our tongue. But silence is not always the perfect choice, and it never builds up! In fact, studies have shown it can harm the brain.

Charles Nelson is a professor of pediatrics at Harvard Medical School and Boston Children's Hospital. After more than a decade of research on this subject, he said, "Neglect is awful for the brain." His studies show that being raised without someone who is a reliable source of attention, affection, and stimulation is detrimental to the brain, and in his own words, ". . . the wiring of the brain goes awry."

Nelson visited Romanian orphanages in 1999 and saw toddlers rocking back and forth alone in their cribs, desperate for attention. Their odd behaviors, delayed language, and other symptoms suggested stunted brain development. He and some other colleagues began studying these children using a technology called electroencephalography (EEG), which measures electrical activity in the brain. Many of the orphans showed dramatically reduced brain activity, and in Nelson's words, "Instead of a 100-watt light bulb, it was a 40-watt light bulb." As the children

Too much *silence* and not enough life building words literally stunted their *brain* growth.

grew older, he could study their brains using an MRI and found that their brains were actually physically smaller.

There was no malnutrition found in these children and the orphanages and children were kept clean, but there was an even worse deprivation, the void of attention. There was nobody to coo and sing over them or whisper sweet words into their little ears. Too much silence and not enough life building words literally stunted their brain growth.

This has to make us think of our current culture's dilemma. The screens (phones/devices) that are used (even around the dinner table) avert our focus from one another, hinder life building words spoken, and prevent important eye contact with our spouses and children. We are challenged to make sure that our children are not just fed and bathed but above all are loved with THOUGHTS, HEART, WORDS, and DEEDS. Attention is the new superfood. It nourishes brains, souls, and bodies!

The more encouraging *words* are spoken to a child at an early age, the fewer problems they will have with their *identity* and purpose for life

Words Affect Our Children

While on the subject of children and our words, or lack of them, a groundbreaking study by Betty Hart and Todd Risley coined *The Early Catastrophe* proves once again the power we have in our mouths. Their research shows that the words we speak to our children between birth to age four greatly impacts their future. Their study revealed that the more encouraging words are spoken to a child at an early age, the fewer problems they will have with their identity and purpose for life as an adult.

Remember, we are "that girl" who is not orphaned. Our God is our ultimate example of a parent. He is our Daddy and is attentive towards us. He even sings over us! The beautiful words of Zephaniah 3:17 (ESV) plays its lullaby through our minds, *"The LORD your God is in your midst, a mighty one who will save; he will rejoice over you with gladness; he will quiet you by his love; he will exult over you with loud singing."* How beautiful is that scripture! And notice it is **loud** singing even . . . God's love for us is so great; He can't help but sing loudly over us!

We are not ignored. The Bible says His thoughts are vast towards us. Look . . . Psalm 139:17 (ESV), *"How precious to me are your thoughts, O God! How vast is the sum of them!"* These are thoughts of LOVE, and Jeremiah 29:11 (KJV) describes them, *"For I know the thoughts that I think toward you, saith the LORD, thoughts of peace, and not of evil, to give you an expected end."*

Speak to Ya' Waters, Mate!

Back to the topic of the water experiments . . . we have a saying between the two of us which our families on the Hilltop have all picked up on now. We frequently say . . . "Speak to ya' waters, mate!". Yes, this is spoken with a bit of Down Under, "sister lingo" slang, because that is how we relate to each other, so please excuse the improper English. But if we ever hear each other say, "I'm stressed!" or "I'm overwhelmed.", or if we notice other words like, "can't", "tired", "sick", or "awful" we remind each other that our bodies are made of living water and that the words we say affect the structure of our cells which use this water.

These days we only really have to give each other a "waters" look. Then inevitably, we realize we've misspoken and say . . . "Oops . . . I'm speaking to me waters, aren't I?" Then we change our speech to speak words that build up rather than tear down.

> We remind each other that our *bodies* are made of living water and that the words we say affect the structure of our *cells* which use this water.

Sometimes we will catch each other saying uplifting things when circumstances are hard, and we'll encourage with, "Speaking to ya' waters, aren't ya', mate? Good on ya!". At other times when the old negative slip-ups creep in, such as, "I'm just feeling really rundown," we might sarcastically say with a lifted eyebrow, "Oh . . . just speaking to ya' waters, are ya', matesies?"

It was after we heard of Dr. Emoto's experiments that we birthed this phrase, and you can adopt it, too, if it will help you keep your mind and tongue from eroding LIFE and LOVE from you and those around you. The scripture in 1 Thessalonians 5:11 (ESV) comes to mind, *"Therefore encourage one another and build one another up, just as you are doing."* We'll let you leave the "mate" part out if it feels too weird.

God Spoke to the Waters

In thinking of how thoughts and intentions wrapped up in our words affect the water within and around us, we can't help but think back to the beginning. On the first page of the Bible in Genesis 1:1-3 (ESV), we read, *"In the beginning God created the heavens and the earth. The earth was formless and empty, and darkness covered the deep waters. And the Spirit of God was hovering over the surface of the waters. Then God said, "Let there be light: and there was light."* Wow . . . God spoke to the waters!!!!!!!!!!

If you go back and read the scripture verses on page (174) under the heading *A Mighty Voice*, you will see how often the word "waters" is associated with His voice.

The experiments and scientific discoveries showing the impact of positive emotions, words, and music on water is all just kiddy pool stuff compared to the power of the Word of God in our hearts and on our lips. If mere earthly, loving words can prevent rice water from rotting, then what happens when the WORD of God who is LOVE itself is spoken over the waters . . . especially the troubled waters of our life???

If we really want to dive deep into the river of healing, then we'll be that girl who swims in the Word . . . who washes in the deluge of His supernatural voice, who drinks of cell flooding, body, mind, and spirit hydration that can't help but overflow healing all around us.

God has spiritual water that is beyond the purest and most refreshing on this earth. He wants to pour it out on us, so we can then be a conduit and pour it out on others. In John 7:37-38, Jesus stood up and cried out, *"If anyone thirsts, let him come to me and drink. Whoever believes in me, as the Scripture has said, 'Out of his heart will flow rivers of living water'."*

We can be "that girl" whose heart is the cistern of Living Water, so that it flows out and irrigates the dry world around us. Isaiah 50:4 (ESV) tell us, *"The Lord God has given me the tongue of those who are taught, that I may know how to sustain with a word him who is weary."* We can, through Christ, be that girl who pulses with the POWERFUL, healing vibrations of the Word and is flooded with the Living Waters of the WORD.

If mere earthly, *loving* words can prevent rice water from rotting, then what happens when the WORD of God who is LOVE itself is *spoken* over the waters . . . especially the troubled waters of our life???

Speak HIS WORD Over the Troubled Waters of Life

Look at these verses and be encouraged to get the WORD into your mouth. These scriptures can run through your mind and spill out of your mouth as that girl who swims in the powerful WORD of His LOVE during troubled times.

Psalm 40:1-3 (NIV), *". . . I waited patiently for the LORD; he turned to me and heard my cry. He lifted me out of the slimy pit, out of the mud and mire; he set my feet on a rock and gave me a firm place to stand. He put a new song in my mouth, a hymn of praise to our God. Many will see and fear the LORD and put their trust in him."*

Psalm 3:3 (NLT), *"But you, O LORD, are a shield around me; you are my glory, the one who holds my head high."*

Psalm 42:11 (KJV), *"Why art thou cast down, O my soul? and why art thou disquieted within me? hope thou in God: for I shall yet praise him, who is the health of my countenance, and my God."*

John 16:33, *"These things I have spoken unto you, that in me ye might have peace. In the world ye shall have tribulation: but be of good cheer; I have overcome the world."*

Psalm 34:17 (ESV), *"When the righteous cry for help, the LORD hears and delivers them out of all their troubles."*

Romans 8:38-39 (NIV), *"For I am convinced that neither death nor life, neither angels nor demons, neither the present nor the future, nor any powers, neither height nor depth, nor anything else in all creation, will be able to separate us from the love of God that is in Christ Jesus our Lord."*

2 Corinthians 1:3-4 (NIV), *"Praise be to the God and Father of our Lord Jesus Christ, the Father of compassion and the God of all comfort, who comforts us in all our troubles, so that we can comfort those in any trouble with the comfort we ourselves receive from God."*

Isaiah 41:10 (NLT), *"Don't be afraid, for I am with you. Don't be discouraged, for I am your God. I will strengthen you and help you. I will hold you up with my victorious right hand."*

Held Together by HIS WORD

Remember back in the last chapter when we talked about how Dr. Jenny displayed visible sound through his experiments with sand on metal plates? His research concluded that the formations could not be held together without the vibrations . . . when the notes of music stopped, the formations eroded. The Bible says we are held together by JESUS THE WORD, who SPOKE all things into existence. Colossians 1:16-17 (NIV), tells us, *"For in him all things were created: things in heaven and on earth, visible and invisible, whether thrones or powers or rulers or authorities; all things have been created through him and for him. He is before all things, and **in him all things hold together**."*

The very thing that *holds* our bodies together is in the form of a *cross*.

He is the LOGOS, the SPOKEN WORD. He is our Savior who redeemed us back to Himself through the cross. THE CROSS HOLDS US TOGETHER. We are undone without the cross! This is scripture, and now here is some interesting science to muse upon.

In our bodies, there is something called "laminin", which is a cell adhesion molecule. It is literally the stuff that holds the membranes of our bodies together. You can learn about laminin in a few seconds on Wikipedia. Incredibly, the very thing that holds our bodies together is in the form of a cross. (Well, the general form of a cross, some look more perfectly cross like than others). But scientific sites, without any relation to Christianity write about its formation as the shape of a cross and refer to the "two short arms" and one "long arm" of it.

This is beyond fascinating when we look again at this verse in Colossians 1:17 (NIV), *"He is before all things, and in him **all things hold together.**"* His voice spoke us and this world into being, and that voice and its mighty vibrations continue to uphold all things. Science is just tapping into the surface of His handiwork and getting a little glimpse of the wonder! We are truly that girl who is the child of the LIVING GOD whose words, just like those beautiful sand patterns, hold everything in formation.

Scientific diagram of laminin

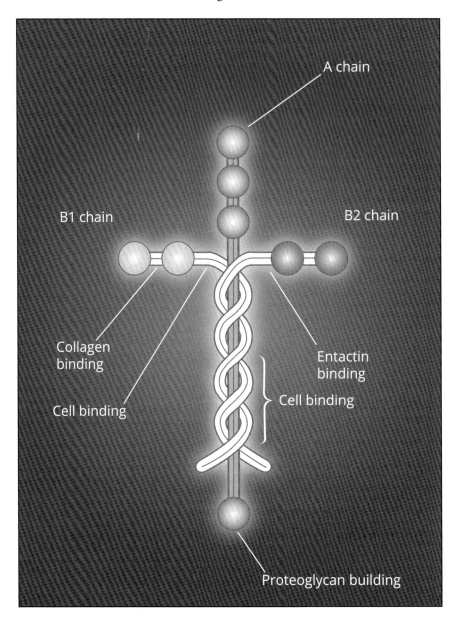

Laminin under a microscope. Original image source unknown.
Taken from online image search results.

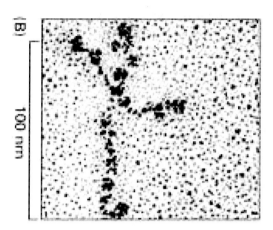

Note—We are not trying to make a theology out of showing laminin like this . . . it is just interesting to ponder. And we realize there are a few who believe the cross Jesus died on may have been a one-stake post rather than a two-beamed cross. We looked deeply into this. It would take a whole chapter to trace the history of crucifixions, but needless to say, if you want to be a study nerd like us, you can historically narrow down the style of cross used at the time and place of Jesus' death. It almost undeniably points to the shape most of us think of as a traditional cross. When you put that together with certain scriptures, there is little doubt that it was a traditional cross. Remember when Doubting Thomas said he wouldn't believe it was Jesus "*. . . Unless I see in His hands the imprint of the nails . . .*" (John 20:25 NASB). This was nails plural. Thomas would have said "nail" if Christ was killed on a singular pole/stake. But if two nails were used, it would mean one for each arm stretched out rather than one through both hands held above his head on a singular pole.

CHAPTER NINETEEN

Promised You Some Science (Part III)

Mind Over Matter

Seat belts on . . . you're entering another long chapter zone here . . . but eyes on the road (no heads nodding off or any *"Are we there?" yets)* 'cause this is important stuff. Time to look at what science has discovered about our thoughts and their ability to either heal or destroy.

The word "worry" in the dictionary is derived from an old English word that literally means to strangle or choke. This is the truth of how something that we would typically think of as safely boxed up within our minds can actually strangle the life out of our bodies. Worry and anxiety, when left to seed in the mind can greatly affect the physicality of the body. There is much research that shows that our complete selves . . . body, mind, and soul can either be torn down or built up through our thought life.

Please note . . . in this chapter we'll be sharing some studies that reveal thought patterns can have even more sway over depression markers than medications. This does not mean we are against medication or that if you are taking antidepressants you should stop. Sometimes meds are vitally important and effective. But antidepressants and anti-anxiety prescription fills are rising alarmingly. In the last 15 years, the use of these meds has spiked more than 65%. New data reveals diagnosis of major depression is at an all-time high and continues rising dramatically among all age groups (but especially younger people).

But the question needs posing: Is medication really always the answer to this epidemic? Or is it too often an expensive Band-Aid, covering up a problem that requires lasting healing through trained, healthy thought patterns rather than a temporary and often only partial chemical fix? We've already discovered that simple things like singing and dancing can effectively combat brain depression. Could free-of-charge thought and attitude adjustments be an even more effective medicine for your mind and consequently for your body?

Let's find out.

Dangerous Conversations

What are we talking to ourselves about, and how does that affect our mental health? This is what Dr. Aaron Beck, one of the early theorists on the subject of treating depression by changing a patient's self-talk, wanted to study. He designed an extremely telling experiment by recruiting a large group of people with similar levels of depression and divided them into two groups. For twelve weeks, the first group was treated with anti-depressant medication, while the second group was treated with no meds, only therapy that focused on changing their self-talk.

The results were astounding. The medication group showed only 20% of the subjects with complete recovery, and 33% dropped out of the study before completing the twelve weeks. The "positive self-talkers" who all were medication-free showed a whopping 75% that achieved complete recovery. Only 10% of the group either failed to show improvement or dropped out before completion. A follow-up by the doctor after a year showed the improvement gained by both groups to be maintained.

A much larger and more recent meta-analysis 2016 study published in *JAMA Psychiatry* rocked the world of psychiatry when it found that patients with depression undergoing MBCT (Mindfulness-Based Cognitive Therapy) were significantly less likely to relapse into depression than those taking antidepressants. Rather than implementing a Buddhist approach to mindfulness, this study used mind training that was entirely secular. Professor Kuyken, an Oxford University

The *"positive* self-talkers" who all were medication-free showed a whopping 75% that achieved *complete* recovery.

clinical psychologist, said, "It's about training the mind so people can see negative thoughts, negative feelings, the early signs of a depressive relapse, and learn the skills to respond to those in a way that makes them more resilient."

A woman in one of his classes would start to have thoughts such as, "I'm no good, I'm not a very good mother, I'm going to mess up my children and they are going to suffer from depression as I do", he said. Through training, Professor Kuyken said the woman was "able to recognize her negative thoughts as negative thoughts, not facts, and not engage with them as much."

Don't mind us if we inject a little hand on hip "told you so" moment here. Remember back in the *Journey into Your Secret World* chapter on thoughts where we talked about Ed? Yeah, he's that eating disorder inner voice (or what we know Biblically to actually be the accuser) who speaks lies into people's minds. Now, here we have another secular professor acknowledging that not all our thoughts should be embraced. Some of them are completely WRONGO! Just like the Bible advises . . . science is now agreeing that there are voices in our heads that are not our own, and they should not be entertained.

Science is now *agreeing* that there are voices in our *heads* that are not our own.

Thoughts Making You Sick?

Neuroscientists have also revealed that untrained thoughts make people very sick! They are not harmless little airy fairies floating around in our minds. Toxic thoughts create the conditions that seed and fertilize illness. Partner with them, and they become matter . . . they dig roots into our physicality and become pathways to death. Excuse the drama here, but science actually agrees.

One simple, fearful thought is not so simple or innocent as we may have let ourselves believe. Researchers have discovered that with no help from other destructive emotions or forces, just one single fearful thought triggers more than 1,400 known physical and chemical responses and activates more than 30 different hormones.

Now for a more in-depth explanation of how this happens.

We're All Allergic!

For some, it is peanuts. Others react to gluten. But there's something every single human is allergic to . . . fear. And when we stress or worry, we fear. They are all one and the same; they just go by different names.

Just one single fearful thought **triggers** *more than 1,400 known physical and chemical* **responses.**

To understand what fear does to us, we need a basic understanding of the autonomic nervous system. Autonomic basically means automatic. This system is a pretty big deal because it is in charge of what we don't consciously decide. It automatically regulates our bodies by turning on different electrical signals. Think of hormone secretion, body temperature, immune function, heart rate, blood sugar levels, digestion . . . there's a heap more but they are all the responsibility of your autonomic nervous system. You don't consciously tell them what to do . . . they just do.

This autonomic nervous system has two components . . . the SYMPATHETIC and the PARASYMPATHETIC nervous systems.

The sympathetic is all go and rev and grrrr. It functions like the gas pedal of a car. It triggers the fight or flight response, cutting off all energy from repair and protection of our health for a burst of adrenaline to be able to handle any perceived danger.

The parasympathetic nervous system, on the other hand, acts like the brake. It's more, "Take a chill pill, dude!" It is like a refreshing deep breath and an, "Aaaaahh-hhhh she'll be alright, mate!" It is also called the REST AND DIGEST SYSTEM. It calms our bodies down.

So, to recap . . . sympathetic equals . . . grrr. parasympathetic equals . . . ahh.

Your sympathetic (grrrr) is awesome when used only for what it is designed to be used for. You need to jump out of the way of a moving car? Burst of adrenaline . . . heartbeat up . . . MOVE!!! NOW!!!! It saves you!

But when your sympathetic chums up with fear, it's a bad friendship. The sort of unhealthy relationship your parents would have warned you against. Normally, after that car speeds off and you realize you are fine, then your parasympathetic (ahhh) floods in and puts a brake on the stress. But fearful thoughts don't speed off on their own. Fear breeds more fear; it only grows.

When stress (fear) is still detected after initial adrenalin and epinephrine surges subside, the hypothalamus (the command center of your brain) gets the impression that more grrr action is needed. It thinks danger is still looming, so it has to bring in the second guns . . . the big ones! This is a three-artillery deal called the HPA axis—your hypothalamus, your pituitary gland, and your adrenal glands. They all gang up together to force your sympathetic to keep the pedal to the metal. And like anything else, your sympathetic nervous system gets more proficient with practice . . . to the point where your stress response ends up almost always firing. This is known as chronic stress, and it keeps this HPA axis activated like a motor that is idling too high for too long. But inevitably, the engine burns out.

Fear breeds more fear; it only *grows.*

This burnout occurs because when we nest fear or stress and worry, our parasympathetic (ahhh) cannot come flooding in as it usually would to slam the brakes on (grrr) and bring the chill pill our bodies need. In other words, we can't two-time. We can't date grrr and ahhh at the same time and take them both out for a spin. Our body only allows one at a time.

So, we need to frequently remind ourselves . . . ask ourselves this question . . . what bodily state are we causing by our thoughts; sympathetic or parasympathetic? Those of us who are allergic to peanuts or gluten don't go chowing down on them. Likewise, we gotta stop nibbling on fear girls! So long as we're entertaining fear, ahhh is simply not a state our bodies can reach. But we need . . . no . . . we *REALLY NEEEEEED* ahhh! We need to digest our food. (Gut problems, anyone?) We need to rest our adrenals. (Adrenal Fatigue, anyone?) And we

We can't date *grrr* and *ahhh* at the same time and *take* them both out for a spin.

need our pituitary gland to focus on hormone secretion for our sexual and reproductive organs rather than just for fight and flight hormones.

Our parasympathetic nervous system ensures that we metabolize, digest, assimilate, excrete, detoxify, heal, protect, and reproduce. It also deals with viruses; it is in charge of our immune system. Fear, on the other hand, IMMOBILIZES AND PARALYZES our white blood cells, which are our body's disease and infection-fighting army. It disengages our body's T cells which are our Navy Seal immune fighters, the best and most elite of our immune system. But that's just the tip of the iceberg of our body's sympathetic reaction to fear.

Full Blown Allergic Reaction

The studies are piling up, and they show fearful thoughts affect our physical health in the following ways:

- They cause weight gain by raising cortisol, depleting serotonin, and lowering metabolism.
- They cause gastrointestinal problems such as ulcers and irritable bowel syndrome.
- They decrease fertility.
- They lead to accelerated aging.
- They impair memory and cause damage to the hippocampus of the brain.
- They interrupt processes in our brains that regulate emotions and normal decision making.
- They cause fatigue, clinical depression, and PTSD.
- They raise blood pressure.
- They promote the formation of artery-clogging deposits, raising the risk of heart attacks and strokes.

Our Daddy God, who knows best, tells us through His Word to NOT FEAR 365 times. Isn't that awesome? That's a warning for every day of the year. While we are designed to get ourselves out of harm's way, we are not designed for FEAR. It is a rogue emotion; it is part of our fallen nature. It must be uprooted. We are designed for LOVE because God is love, and love created us. When we choose peace . . . true peace . . . not the world's peace, depending on our circumstances, but peace based upon the promises in God's Word, then we open ourselves up to love . . . real love. And 1 John 4:18 tells us, *". . . perfect love casts out fear . . ."*

The Bad Crowd

It's not just fear. There are a bunch more loser types you want to avoid keeping company within your mind. Latest neuroscience research reveals that other negative thoughts such as bitterness cause ill health in the body too. Cancer, diabetes, asthma, allergies, skin problems (just for a start) can be furnaced by the toxic waste from negative thoughts all piled up and poisoning us from the inside out. Dr. Caroline Leaf, a neuroscientist who has studied the mind, body connection for decades, says, "There are intellectual and MEDICAL reasons to FORGIVE!"

We are *not* designed *for* FEAR.

Once again, the Bible proves itself to be our best health manual. As the One who created our bodies and minds, God is the ultimate expert on how to take care of them. Ephesians 4:31-32 (NIV) advises, *"Get rid of all **bitterness**, rage and anger, brawling and slander, along with every form of malice. Be kind and compassionate to one another, forgiving each other, just as Christ forgave you."*

Allowing God to work His character and nature inside of us is HEALTHY for our bodies!!!! Hebrews 12:15 (ESV) instructs, *"See to it that no one fails to obtain the grace of God; that no **root of bitterness** springs up and causes trouble, and by it many become defiled."* And of course, Proverbs 17:22 again, let's look at it in the (HCSB) version summing it all up, *"A joyful heart is good medicine, but a broken spirit dries up the bones."*

Negative *thoughts* such as bitterness *cause* ill health in the body

Stinkin' Thinkin' Equals Compromised Immune System

The brain is connected to the entire body through the nervous system, which means a healthy, clean running brain equals a healthy, clean running body. Likewise, a toxic, polluted brain means a toxic and polluted body. We revealed how fearful thoughts pull down your immune system . . . other members of the bad crowd do it, too. Negative thoughts such as sadness or anger are also associated with higher levels of inflammation in the body. Inflammation affects the ability of your white blood cells to create antibodies and T Killer cells (which, as we mentioned are your body's "Navy Seal" immune fighters). Negative thinking causes them to become less effective.

Researchers at Penn State recently published a study in the journal *Brain, Behavior, and Immunity*. They found that negative mood measured multiple times a day (via blood testing) resulted in higher levels of inflammatory biomarkers. Chronic inflammation contributes to numerous common diseases, including cardiovascular health, diabetes, and some cancers.

This builds upon prior research linking depressive and hostile thinking to a compromised immune system. A 2003 study led by Richard Davidson at the University of Wisconsin studied the prefrontal cortex (PFC) of the brain. People who had the greatest activity in the right PFC when asked to dwell on distressing episodes in their life had markedly lower antibody levels. In contrast, those who were asked to recall happy times and showed exceptional activity in the left PFC when recalling these events developed high antibody levels. Davidson concluded that thoughts and emotions play an important role in regulating systems in the body.

Thoughts such as sadness or anger are also associated with higher *levels* of inflammation in the body.

If junky, funky thinking depresses your immune system, the opposite has also been shown to be scientifically true. *"Lovely"* thinking described in Philippians 4:8 (you know . . . that verse that tells us to think on things that are lovely, good, pure, and honest, etc.) make your white blood cells so powerful they can even destroy cancer cells! Dr. O. Simonton, a renowned oncologist, noticed that patients given the same dose of radiation for similar cancers had vastly different outcomes. When he looked into why, he concluded that people who had a more positive attitude, generally lived longer and had fewer side effects.

He began to study this phenomenon, and in his book, *Getting Well Again*, he describes a study on a group of patients diagnosed with terminal diseases with less than a year to live. Along with their regular medical treatments, he gave them the task of visualizing in their minds their white blood cells being a powerful, aggressive force against the foe of their disease. He encouraged the cancer patients to imagine scenes like their white blood cells becoming knights, riding on magnificent stallions, and defending the invading hordes of evil. He also encouraged them to think of other battalions of white blood cells coming alongside and cleaning all the dead carcasses of defeated foe from off the battlefield. It didn't matter if they made up their own "mind movie" as long as their own white blood cells were the victors.

> People who had a more *positive* attitude, generally lived *longer* and had fewer side effects.

Simply Put . . . Thoughts Change Everything

The results from Dr. Simonton's study were astounding. Complete healing was seen in many and others with only months to live, outlived their prognosis by years. It didn't matter what the disease was, be it debilitating arthritis, asthma, cancer, or other painful diseases; the power and simplicity of thoughts changed everything.

Dr. David Bressler Hess of the UCLA Pain Clinic put the same idea to work in his practice dealing with people who suffer chronic pain. When his clients imagined an image of their pain and projected it reducing in size and intensity, the pain would follow suit and reduce dramatically.

Dr. David Stoop, author of *You Are What You Think*, works with many people who have weight problems. One of his most important treatments is having his patients visualize themselves thin. He writes, *"The degree of difficulty in ridding the body of excess weight is related to the difficulty they have creating that mental image of themselves fifty or one hundred pounds thinner."*

Of course, thinking yourself thin doesn't miraculously happen while eating burgers and fries and drinking sugary shakes, but allowing yourself to visualize success means you'll be more able to make and stick to the habits necessary to get there. Your mind is powerfully capable of physically manifesting its beliefs. Once again, it all stems back to what we choose to think.

> Allowing yourself to *visualize* success means you'll be more able to make and *stick* to the habits necessary to get there.

Thoughts Affect Physical Matter

Your mind indisputably does have influence over your matter. Dr. David Stoop, in his book *You Are What You Think,* tells a sad but true story of a man that well illustrates the danger of worry. This man had a mother who died of cancer, and from the day of the funeral onwards, he feared that it would be his story to die of cancer, just like his mother. He went to many doctors convinced that he had cancerous tumors because of the fatigue and pain he began to feel all through his body. The doctors couldn't find anything and told him it was just in his mind. In fact, this was precisely where it was and where it began to germinate.

He wouldn't give up his quest to prove to the doctors that he had cancer and continued to worry and make appointments for check-ups. A tumor was found eventually where there had been only healthy tissue before, and within a year, he was dead and buried beside his mother.

Dr. David Stoop tells another story that reveals the ability of our thoughts to command our body. A young man was in the habit of sneaking rides on freight trains. One night he climbed into what he thought was a regular box car and shut the door. The door locked behind him, and when his eyes became adjusted to his surroundings, he realized that he was in a refrigerated boxcar. He started to scream for someone to rescue him, but he soon gave up and lay on the floor trying to fight off the freezing cold that he thought was agonizingly attacking his body.

He started to scratch a message on the boxcar floor, which he never finished. The next day, when the repair men came to fix the broken-down freezer box, they found the man dead. His body showed every sign of hypothermia. He had frozen to death, even though the temperature of the boxcar did not get below fifty degrees all night. The cooling systems were not working, but this man's mind sure was. It was working against him and convinced his body that he was dying of the cold, which is what he did.

A study done a few years ago in the mountains of Italy reveals similar findings. Researchers took 120 people on a trip and spread a rumor among 25% of the group that the thin mountain air at such high elevations could cause debilitating migraines. That same 25% of the group reported the worst headaches of all of the 120 study subjects. Not only that, blood testing revealed that an enzyme in their blood associated with headaches also spiked in that one group.

A Japanese study from the 1960s gathered together a group of 13 people known to be highly allergic to poison ivy. Each subject had one arm rubbed with a harmless leaf but was told it was poison ivy. Their other arm was rubbed with real poison ivy itself, but they were told it was a harmless leaf. All 13 arms reacted to the non-poison ivy leaf! Yup, every single one of them. Only 2 of the test subjects reacted to poison ivy itself; makes you go hmmmm.

Once Again Science Plays Catch Up

Modern research shows every system of the body is affected by thoughts. But the Bible revealed this first. Proverbs 23:7 tells us that as someone thinks within himself, he (or she, of course) actually is. Some skeptics of positive belief and confession argue that this verse is often interpreted the wrong way. Well, our skeptic friends do have a point. Usually only part of this verse is quoted and if you read the context of this passage in Proverbs, it is not about someone thinking a certain positive thing and suddenly attaining it. More accurately, it is about a selfish man pretending to be generous. So, we freely admit they are correct on that part. But the verse actually proves the point well for those of us who understand that inner thoughts depict who we really are versus who we pretend to be to others. Let's look at both verses 6 and 7 to get the full meaning . . .

"Do not eat the bread of a miser, Nor desire his delicacies; For as he thinks in his heart, so is he. "Eat and drink!" he says to you, But his heart is not with you."

Your inner thoughts decide your real truth and the above passage only cements that. The Bible also says in Deuteronomy 30:19 (NLT), *"Today I have given you the choice between life and death, between blessings and curses. Now I call on heaven and earth to witness the choice you make. Oh, that you would choose life, so that you and your descendants might live!"* We can bless our body by choosing thoughts of PEACE and Joy. These choices decide who we will truly become mentally and physically. If we don't make the choice to think these "blessing" thoughts, then we are by default choosing thoughts that curse. Our minds are our most powerful tool to build up or tear down our bodies. Let's be that girl who harnesses our mind power to wield LIFE!

> We can *bless* our body by *choosing* thoughts of peace and joy.

I Have a Gut Feeling . . . Now Science!

Healthy thoughts, which are again *"lovely"* thoughts, allow proper digestion to take place. The gut is now scientifically known to have a brain of its own and the old saying, "I have a gut feeling", has become established science. A well-wired gut brain sends the right messages to orchestrate a harmonized body.

Speaking of harmony, nothing seems to get along without sweetly tuned hormones. Healthy thoughts help keep a tuned-up hormonal symbiosis. Every other bodily system is affected by hormones. Even our fertility can be affected by our thought life. Skin, too. Our skin is affected by the way we choose to think. Skin is our first line of immune defense and the largest organ in our body. Beautiful thinking radiates through your skin and can help make it radiant and glowing. How? Choosing *"lovely"* thoughts boosts the entire cardiovascular system, which affects circulation and blood flow to the skin.

Our bodies have an electromagnetic rhythm and harmony that is orchestrated by the heart, which can only work properly when there is proper communication between the mini-brain (the gut) and the skull brain. Healthy thinking promotes those proper messages and signaling. Rotten thoughts promote hypertension. Good thoughts support the vascular system and help to lower constricted blood flow.

CHAPTER TWENTY

Promised You Some Science (Part IV)

Prune Wisely

If you've been stuck in negative thought patterns, don't think you have to stay there. Neuroscience has coined a saying that goes like this, "Neurons that fire together wire together." This cute little one-liner simply means that the more a neuro-circuit fires up and runs in your brain, the more that neuro-circuit is strengthened and established. It's the ol' "practice makes perfect" adage, and the mind is no exception.

Healthy thinking catches on! A healthy thought links with another healthy thought and they marry and have healthy thought babies, and soon your mind and brain and body are alive with a vivacious and flourishing healthy thought forest that literally clears the air around you.

Your Brain Has Gardeners

The science of how your thought life can get healthier is explained through gardening. Neuroscientists have found that our brain has amazing abilities to clean, organize, declutter and build itself with the help of certain cells called "glial" cells. Glial cells manage the garden of your brain that is responsible for growing nice and healthy neuron connections between synapses. These glial cells are master gardeners and work to water and oxygenate the connections that are marked as prized or "super important."

The glial gardeners know which brain pathways to nurture by which brain circuits are the most rehearsed. The pathways that are not used enough get cut off. It is only well-rehearsed circuits that don't get the "karate chop" from the glial gardeners.

All this pruning of the brain by glial cells is done while you are asleep, and that is why your mind is so much clearer first thing in the morning or after a little power nap. Your brain literally has sleep shift gardeners to "fix the place up," so to speak, for a new day.

What does this mean for us?

We Gotta Take Thought of Our Thoughts!

We have to be that girl who decides to think *"lovely"* thoughts while we are awake, so we'll grow stronger and harvest more *"lovely"* thoughts. We also have to make sure our neural gardeners take the axe to "ugly" thoughts. We do this by cutting them off during the day so that when we sleep, they won't be tended to and fertilized . . . they'll be removed from our prized neural pathways and won't be able to cause their destruction to the rest of our body. We can't allow worry weeds to choke and strangle all of the beautiful flowers in our mind, and we simply do this by not giving them the time of day!

> We have to be *that girl* who decides to think *"lovely"* thoughts while we are awake, so we'll *grow* stronger and harvest more *"lovely"* thoughts.

Nurturing healthy thoughts is not only about avoiding illness; it actually causes your brain to grow, science tells us. You literally get brainier. Wow! Think of a car. If you fill it with old junky gas, it performs poorly and dies sooner. But when you put in the right stuff, it runs smoothly and powerfully. Toxic thinking (which can be described as thoughts that have not been filtered through the WORD OF GOD) is the sludgy, polluted, stanky gas that makes you sputter out really quick into ruin. You become dull-minded and sick. There is just no nicer way to put it. Just like in the case of complaining . . . your brain actually shrinks!

The WORD Is Our Sludge Filter

Here is just a sampling of the Word that we can filter depressed and oppressive negative thoughts through. After running the sludge of darkness through the WORD, we'll have clean gas for our minds. Yes, the following are all repeat scriptures from chapter 18 but if you're like us, you need to hear them over and over again until they set up shop inside you.

Psalm 40:1-3 (NIV), *". . . I waited patiently for the LORD; he turned to me and heard my cry. He lifted me out of the slimy pit, out of the mud and mire; he set my feet on a rock and gave me a firm place to stand. He put a new song in my mouth, a hymn of praise to our God. Many will see and fear the LORD and put their trust in him."*

Psalm 3:3 (NLT), *"But you, O LORD, are a shield around me; you are my glory, the one who holds my head high."*

Psalm 42:11, *"Why are you cast down, O my soul? And why are you disquieted within me? Hope in God; For I shall yet praise him, The health of my countenance, and my God."*

1 Peter 5:6-7 (NIV), *"Humble yourselves, therefore, under God's mighty hand, that he may lift you up in due time. Cast all your anxiety on him because he cares for you."*

John 16:33, *"These things I have spoken unto you, that in me you may have peace. In the world you willl have tribulation: but be of good cheer; I have overcome the world."*

Psalm 34:17 (ESV), *"When the righteous cry for help, the LORD hears and delivers them out of all their troubles."*

Romans 8:38-39 (NIV), *"For I am convinced that neither death nor life, neither angels nor demons, neither the present nor the future, nor any powers, neither height nor depth, nor anything else in all creation, will be able to separate us from the love of God that is in Christ Jesus our Lord."*

2 Corinthians 1:3-4 (NIV), *"Praise be to the God and Father of our Lord Jesus Christ, the Father of compassion and the God of all comfort, who comforts us in all our troubles, so that we can comfort those in any trouble with the comfort we ourselves receive from God."*

V Stands for Vagus

Now for our favorite bit of science . . . saving it for the final science chapter here so we can end with a doozy. There is a nerve in your body which is actually more like a muscle in that the more you use it, the stronger it becomes. Meet your vagus nerve. You and Vagy (nicknames remember) need to become the best of friends, if your goal is to live a healthy, long life.

This nerve is the literal link between your mind and body. Think of it as a big power line that runs from your brain to your gut, constantly passing information between the two. When activated, the vagus regulates all aspects of your body, including heartbeat, blood pressure, digestion, endocrine function, pain levels, immune defense, and even the health and length of your telmerones (your cells that determine how swiftly or slowly you age). It even prevents and undoes the damaging effects of chronic inflammation and organ damage. Remember earlier in this chapter how we talked about your parasympathetic nervous system? The one that makes your body go, "Ahhh"? Well, Vagy turns that on.

Notice we said, "When activated." You're the one who does this activating. In a similar way to how you have control over the glial gardeners of your brain and which thought patterns they will either fertilize or cut down during the night while you sleep, you can also influence your vagus nerve to do wonderful things for your health.

Dr. Jeffrey Rediger, in his ground-breaking book *Cured,* has this to say about the vagus nerve, "*. . . the more you use it, the better you get at using it, and the more health benefits you reap.*"

> When activated, the *vagus* regulates all aspects of your body, including heartbeat, blood pressure, digestion, endocrine function, pain levels, immune defense, and even the *health* and length of your telmerones

So how do we activate this nerve? Well, now that the scientific and medical world is learning how huge a part it can play in improving health, they, of course, are trying to harness its power. Studies are currently underway exploring how stimulating this nerve can prevent or reverse conditions such as arthritis, colitis, epilepsy, congestive heart failure, Crohn's disease, headaches, depression, diabetes, and many more. Currently there are clinical trials using electronic pulses to stimulate the vagus in order to help people with chronic pain, and they're showing much promise.

But you don't need to involve yourself in a clinical trial. There are other, much more available, and natural ways to stimulate your Vagy. Slowing your breathing, in for 5 seconds, hold, out 5 seconds. This can turn vagus power on in your body. In fact, that long breath out is the one that stimulates this nerve more than the breath in.

Here's an interesting hack to stimulate your Vagy . . . gargle . . . yes, do it twice a day after brushing your teeth night and morning. Not only does it help stimulate your vagus nerve, but it tones the muscles in your soft palate, which helps prevent snoring and other problems as you age.

Dispelling stressful thoughts and focusing calmly on positive ones is a vagus stimulator. But simply doing what is known as "meditating" is not that great for your vagus. One interesting 2013 study published in *Psychological Science* revealed that it was only when participants cleared stressful thoughts from their minds and then purposefully thought good thoughts about people in their lives (what the study actually called loving-kindness thoughts) and positive thoughts about their lives, in general, did their vagus nerve get stimulated. So, a blank mind doesn't do much for Vagy, but a mind filled with thinking *"lovely"* thoughts as the Bible instructs us to think . . . that does much!

> Dispelling *stressful* thoughts and focusing calmly on *positive* ones is a vagus stimulator.

Singing turns this nerve on, too. Actually, singing at the top of your lungs turns it on far more thoroughly. Singing with a group of people . . . (church, anyone?) does it powerfully. Hugging turns your vagus nerve on, too. Actually though . . . a strong hug is what studies have shown to be more effective at raising vagal tone than a weak hug. So, hug your loved ones! If you're married . . . lean in and linger. Quickie hugs should be saved for only the times when you or he is rushing out the door, late for something. "Longy" hugs are what we should practice.

If you're a nursing mama, you are in a blessed season. A 2017 *PubMed* study revealed that breastfeeding women had significantly higher vagal tone than non-nursing women.

> People who *laugh* more often also have higher numbers of *T cells* in their blood.

Gratitude turns it on. Just think, when you teach your children to be thankful . . . to say, "please and thank you" and mean it . . . you are not only teaching them good manners . . . you are teaching them a positive health practice for life!

Smiling turns it on, but laughing turns it on even more! Studies show immune system function is increased through laughter. A 2003 study published in *Alternative Therapies in Health and Medicine* looked at natural killer cell activity in response to laughter. The study found that people who laugh more often also have higher numbers of T cells in their blood. These are the cells that boost the immune system and fend off disease. The researchers concluded with this, "Low NK cell activity is linked to decreased disease resistance and increased morbidity in persons with cancer and HIV disease, laughter may be a useful cognitive-behavioral intervention."

Notice a theme here? We've already talked about many other health benefits of basic human behaviors like gratitude, laughter, singing, etc. Our loving Daddy God designed us to thrive expressing these. But we get to be adults, and so many times we forget to do these things. We allow stress and the seriousness of life to take over, and we stop living by design. Keeping your vagus nerve on is just one more reason to live as our Daddy created us.

But here's the best part we've been saving for last regarding you and your Vagy. New research has revealed that perhaps the most powerful way to turn your vagus nerve on is through . . . wait for it . . . LOVE! In his book *Cured*, Dr. Jeffrey Rediger says, "When you experience feelings of love and connection it's like playing a whole song for your vagus nerve."

We are not merely talking about the "fall in love" aspect of love here, although that too can stimulate your vagus. We're talking about the small moments of love you cultivate throughout the day with your husband, friend, child, coworker, or even a stranger. These moments of connection . . . of caring . . . of engagement . . . of conscious, heartfelt giving and receiving from someone in your home or on the street are considered some of the most powerful vagus stimulators.

You don't have to go around saying, "Oh, how I love you" to everyone . . . although let's do that a lot to our loved ones. But it is these sorts of moments: a caring smile, kind eyes as you open the door for someone, or a stop and chat with a mother and her baby, an authentic listening ear for a co-worker, etc. These moments of warmth, connection, and openness to others fan the powerfully healing flame of vagus power.

Perhaps the most *powerful* way to turn your vagus nerve on is through . . . wait for it . . . LOVE !

You might have guessed by now, but yep, as we did with our "speak to your waters" one-liners, we've also cultivated a way of encouraging one another in all things vagus here on the Hilltop. "My Vagy has been getting a workout," we tell each other when we're excited about how we've been learning to practice deeper and more frequent micro-moments of love with our families or strangers. Or when we notice each other distancing ourselves from people . . . "Forgetting about your Vagy, are ya', mate?" we caution. Of course, you don't need to be as weird as we are with all this . . . but you can, if you want!

Created for Love

So, what have we learned? Essentially love is your disease-busting, anti-aging, total health miracle pill! If you think that sounds like we're selling some sort of "too good to be true" snake oil . . . according to new discoveries in science, it is spot on and once again backs up the scriptures, which exhort us over and over again to love one another.

Love is your disease-busting, anti-aging, total health *miracle* pill!

Of course, becoming more skilled in this love practice should not be taken as a formula . . . love more and you'll never ever get sick. We're certainly not promising that. But, just as how we should eat smartly and wisely move our bodies in order to prevent and heal illnesses, loving others more consciously and more often can do the same . . . in fact, it can probably do a lot more! In *Cured*, Dr. Jeffrey Rediger writes that if you, "*. . . rearrange your life to more frequently experience those higher states of love and other positive emotions, you can "inoculate" yourself against chronic flight-or-fight response as surely as you can get vaccinated against tuberculosis or the flu.*"

Barbara Fredrickson Ph.D. has studied the vagus nerve and how emotions impact our health for over two decades. In an article titled *The Science of Love*, she puts it this way, "*Just as your body was designed to extract oxygen from the Earth's atmosphere, and nutrients from the foods you ingest, your body was designed to love. Love—like taking a deep breath or eating an orange when you're depleted and thirsty— not only feels great but is also life-giving, an indispensable source of energy, sustenance, and health.*" She goes on to say, "*In describing love like this, I'm not just taking poetic license, but drawing on science: new science that illuminates for the first time how love, and its absence, fundamentally alters the biochemicals in which your body is steeped. They, in turn, can alter the very ways your DNA gets expressed within your cells.*"

Big wow for all that, right? Well, there's a bigger wow coming. These micro-moments of love with others are obviously fantastic, but we realized there's a far greater piece of the picture here.

Get this . . . if giving and receiving love with others helps our health so immensely, just think of what a love relationship with God does. The scriptures describe God as love itself.

Love Is a Person.

Our Father is the Author of love, the ultimate source of it. Let's look at 1 John 4:7-8 for greater clarity, "*. . . for love is of God; and everyone who loves is born of God* *and knows God. He who does not love does not know God, for God is love."* And now science tells us love heals? Well, it is no wonder God's name is Jehovah Rapha which means, "I Am Healer".

Science tells us love *heals*.

His love for us is so vast and so true that John 3:16, tells us, *"God so loved the world, he gave his only son . . .".*

We can bask in this love all day and all-night long. It is constantly on tap. The Word tells us that He *"loved us first"* (1 John 4:19).

His love is *"perfect,"* and it is what *"casts out fear,"* (1 John 4:18) the same fear that keeps our "grrrr" sympathetic nervous system on . . . there's an answer for it . . . yay!

It *"never ceases,"* (Lamentations 3:22). It has been *"lavished upon us,"* (1 John 3:1). It is *"everlasting"* (Jeremiah 31:3). It is *"great"* (Ephesians 2:4). Nothing *"can separate us from it,"* (Romans 8:39). It has been *"poured into our hearts"* (Romans 5:5). It *"endures forever"* (Psalm 136:26). It is *"unfailing"* (Psalm 107:8). It *"covers our sins"* (1 Peter 4:8). It *"compels us"* (2 Corinthians 5:14). He *"quiets us with his love"* (Zephaniah 3:17). It is his *"banner over us"* (Song of Songs 2:4). The earth is *"filled with it"* (Psalm 119:64).

The scriptures go on and on and on describing God's love. We've barely scratched the surface of them here.

We are that girl who can open up to receive God's incredible love and let it sink into every pore in our body. We can then practice loving Him back with every fiber of our being . . . and let the overflow pour out to others. On our bed at night . . . let's ponder His love. When we wake in the morning . . . let's immerse our minds with it . . . throughout the day let's ruminate on how incredible it is! We do this not just to reap the scientifically proved health benefits, of course . . . we do it because we're in a love relationship with Him. But, hey . . . the health benefits are good gravy!

So, let's:

TAKE THE AXE TO FEAR

CUT OFF EVERY ROOT OF BITTERNESS

FORGIVE

THINK ON EVERYTHING LOVELY

STOP COMPLAINING

BE GRATEFUL

TAKE OUR JOY MEDICINE EVERYDAY

USE OUR IMAGINATION FOR LIFE

CHOOSE HEALTHY THOUGHTS FOR A HEALTHY BODY

PRACTICE HAPPY THOUGHTS . . . PRACTICE MAKES PERFECT

KILL NEGATIVE THOUGHTS BY IGNORING THEM . . . DON'T MAKE THEM INTO A NEST

RUN OUR THOUGHTS THROUGH THE FILTER OF THE WORD

PURPOSEFULLY SHOW LOVE TO OTHERS OFTEN AND WHOLEHEARTEDLY

BATHE IN GOD'S NEVER ENDING, ALWAYS ON TAP, INCREDIBLE LOVE!!!!

Sides

No meal is complete without a substantive side. Relish these deep declarations of the most important kind. Take your time with them. Read them, mull over them, speak them, live them!

CHAPTER TWENTY-ONE

I'm That Girl Who Deletes Fear

I refuse fear a place at my table, for I don't negotiate with terrorists.

I won't sit down and have a cup of tea and a chat like fear
is my friend. I will not listen to one word of fear's lies. Not
one foul whisper of its deception will I agree with.

I delete fear from the hard drive of my mind and from the power of my tongue.
I turn my back on it. Fear is a stranger's voice to me. Its words are not my own.

Fear may try for me, but it only propels me into the arms of my Father.

Strong arms.

Safe arms.

Fear cannot touch me here.

It is my Father's voice I seek. His voice is filled with faith and
belief. It is the voice I give all of my agreement to.

His voice is familiar.

It is kind.

He tells me over and over to not fear.

I am lifted into love by His words. This perfect love
casts out all fear. It rips it out by the root.

Fear no longer grows in my heart, for love has overtaken.

I am bursting with it.

MY FATHER'S VOICE

Isaiah 41:13, *"For I, the LORD your God, will hold your right hand, Saying to you, 'Fear not, I will help you'."*

Isaiah 41:10, *"Fear not, for I am with you; Be not dismayed, for I am your God. I will strengthen you, Yes, I will help you, I will uphold you with My righteous right hand'."*

Isaiah 43:1, *". . . Fear not, for I have redeemed you; I have called you by your name: You are Mine."*

Lamentations 3:57 (ESV), *"You came near when I called on you; you said, "Do not fear!"*

Matthew 10:31, *"Do not fear therefore; you are of more value than many sparrows."*

Luke 12:32, *"Do not fear, little flock, for it is your Father's good pleasure to give you the kingdom."*

2 Timothy 1:7, *"For God has not given us a spirit of fear, but of power and of love and of a sound mind."*

Hebrews 13:6, *"So we may boldly say: 'The LORD is my helper; I will not fear. What can man do to me?'."*

1 John 4:18, *"There is no fear in love; but perfect love casts out fear, because fear involves torment. But he who fears has not been made perfect in love."*

Psalm 91:4-5, *"He shall cover you with His feathers, And under His wings you shall take refuge; His truth shall be your shield and buckler. You shall not be afraid of the terror by night, Nor of the arrow that flies by day."*

Psalm 34: 4-5, *"I sought the LORD, and He heard me, And delivered me from all my fears. They looked to Him and were radiant, And their faces were not ashamed."*

Psalm 23:4 (ESV), *"Even though I walk through the valley of the shadow of death, I will fear no evil, for you are with me; your rod and your staff, they comfort me."*

Psalm 27:1, *"The Lord is my light and my salvation: whom shall I fear? The Lord is the stronghold of my life; of whom shall I be afraid."*

For more scriptures to help delete fear, see page 372.

DECLARATIONS—I WILL CONFIDENTLY SAY:

I'M THAT GIRL WHO NO LONGER LISTENS TO FEAR

I'M THAT GIRL WHO NO LONGER AGREES WITH FEAR

I'M THAT GIRL WHO DOESN'T ALLOW THE
WORDS "I FEAR" OUT OF MY MOUTH

I'M THAT GIRL WHO RESTS IN PERFECT LOVE

I'M THAT GIRL WHO PUTS OFF FEAR AND PUTS ON FAITH

I'M THAT GIRL WITH THE SOUND MIND

I'M THAT GIRL WITH A NEW NAME . . . FEARLESS!

CHAPTER TWENTY-TWO

I'm That Girl Who Defies Anxiety

No longer do I call this "my anxiety" for I refuse to claim ownership of it.

I dive into peace. I leap from the narrow, shaky plank of anxious thoughts into its deep warmth.

My Shepherd, the Prince of Peace, catches my trembling body and brings me to His chest. I feel His heart and love for me, and I am soothed.

This peace is boundless.

Unfathomable.

My body obeys His voice and calms.

This sort of peace passes all my understanding. It drowns the storm that rages. It leads me beside the still waters. My heart, mind, and body begin to swim in it. I stretch out each limb within its tranquil force.

I bathe.

I bask.

I let it wash me.

I let all tension slip away. I stay here . . . carried and loved. I was made for this peace.

I return all my love to my Shepherd, my Prince of Peace. I breathe Him in . . . fill my lungs to capacity. He's more satisfying than oxygen. He holds me like a baby, and I give Him total trust.

He soothes me with His lullaby. His voice is tender.

I start to hum along.

MY FATHER'S VOICE:

Jeremiah 29:11, *"For I know the thoughts that I think toward you, says the Lord, thoughts of peace and not of evil, to give you a future and a hope."*

Isaiah 35:4 (ESV), *"Say to those who have an anxious heart, "Be strong; fear not! Behold, your God will come with vengeance, with the recompense of God. He will come and save you."*

Philippians 4:6-7 *"Be anxious for nothing, but in everything by prayer and supplication, with thanksgiving, let your requests be made known to God; and the peace of God, which surpasses all understanding, will guard your hearts and minds through Christ Jesus."*

John 14:27, *"Peace I leave with you, My peace I give to you; not as the world gives do I give to you. Let not your heart be troubled, neither let it be afraid."*

Psalm 55:18, *"He has redeemed my soul in peace from the battle that was against me . . ."*

John 16:33, *"These things I have spoken to you, that in Me you may have peace. In the world you may have tribulation; but be of good cheer, I have overcome the world."*

Isaiah 9:6, *"For unto us a child is born, unto us a Son is given; and the government will be upon his shoulder. And his name will be called Wonderful, Counselor, Mighty God, Everlasting Father, Prince of Peace."*

Isaiah 26:3, *"You will keep him in perfect peace, Whose mind is stayed on You, Because he trusts in You."*

Psalm 4:8, *"I will both lie down in peace, and sleep; For You alone, O Lord, make me dwell in safety."*

Romans 16:20, *"And the God of Peace will crush Satan under your feet shortly. The grace of our Lord Jesus Christ be with you. Amen."*

Ephesians 2:14, *"For He Himself is our peace, who has made both one, and has broken down the middle wall of separation."*

Numbers 6:26, *"The Lord lift up His countenance upon you, and give you peace."*

1 Corinthians 14:33, *"For God is not the author of confusion but of peace . . ."*

For more scriptures to help defy anxiety see page 373.

DECLARATIONS—I WILL CONFIDENTLY SAY:

I'M THAT GIRL WHO HAS A DEEP RELATIONSHIP WITH PEACE

I'M THAT GIRL WHO DOESN'T NEST ANXIOUS THOUGHTS

I'M THAT GIRL WHO LETS GO OF ALL TENSION

I'M THAT GIRL WHO LIVES, WALKS AND
BREATHES IN A CALM YET STRONG BODY

I'M THAT GIRL WHO IS MATURING INTO DEEP SOUL REST

I'M THAT GIRL WHO IS SOOTHED BY LOVE'S SONG

I'M THAT GIRL WITH A NEW NAME . . . PEACEFUL!

CHAPTER TWENTY-THREE

I'm That Girl Who Sheds Depression

I refuse to wear this dark and heavy mental cloak.

I shed it, for it no longer fits me. I burn it with a spark of joy. I breathe in thankfulness, exhale heartfelt praise and remind myself that He is the lifter of my head.

It's a fresh wind that I awake inside of me, and it blows on my offering of gratitude until it is a blazing wildfire.

Choosing to burn my clothes of despair is an easy choice.

My only choice.

All depression and oppression and every lurking shadow around me is turned to ashes by this flame of ignited gratefulness for all my Father has given to me.

I defiantly hum my thanks. I raise my voice and sing it louder. As my discarded clothes of gloom burn, I ***put*** on joy like a festive sweater. I wear it with confidence because it was gifted to me.

It is mine.

My Father paid a high price for it. He delights in my choice to wear it every day.

No matter my circumstances.

And when I wear my Father's gifts, I look more like Him and I can hear His voice more clearly.

MY FATHER'S VOICE:

Psalm 34:17-18 (NIV), *"The righteous cry out, and the LORD hears them: he delivers them from all their troubles. The Lord is close to the brokenhearted and saves though who are crushed in spirit."*

Psalm 30:11, *"You have turned for me my mourning into dancing; You have put off my sackcloth and clothed me with gladness."*

Psalm 3:3, (ESV), *"But you, O LORD, are a shield about me, my glory, and the lifter of my head."*

Galatians 5:1, *"Stand fast therefore in the liberty by which Christ has made us free, and do not be entangled again with a yoke of bondage."*

Psalm 42:11 (ESV), *"Why are you cast down, O my soul, and why are you in turmoil within me? Hope in God; for I shall again praise him, my salvation and my God.*

2 Corinthians 4:8, *"We are hard-pressed on every side, yet not crushed; we are perplexed, but not in despair."*

Proverbs 12:25, *"Anxiety in the heart of man causes depression, But a good word makes it glad."*

Isaiah 61:3 (NASB), *"To grant those who mourn in Zion, giving them a garland instead of ashes, the oil of gladness instead of mourning, the cloak of praise instead of a disheartened spirit. So they will be called oak of righteousness, the planting of the Lord, that He May be glorified."*

Psalm 40:2-3 (NIV), *"He lifted me out of the slimy pit, out of the mud and mire; he set my feet on a rock and gave me a firm place to stand. He put a new song in my mouth, a song of praise to our God. Many will see and hear and put their trust in the Lord."*

Ephesians 6:11, *"Put on the whole armor of God, that you may be able to stand against the wiles of the devil."*

James 4:7 (ESV), *"Submit yourselves therefore to God. Resist the devil and he will flee from you."*

For more scriptures to help shed depression, see page 374.

I WILL CONFIDENTLY SAY:

I'M THAT GIRL WHO HAS OUTGROWN ALL
OF HER OLD CLOTHES OF DESPAIR

I'M THAT GIRL WHO CHOOSES TO WEAR THE GIFT OF JOY

I'M THAT GIRL WHO KNOWS THAT A THANKFUL HEART
AND WORSHIP WILL DESTROY DEPRESSION

I'M THAT GIRL WHO TELLS THE SPIRIT OF DARKNESS TO "RACK
OFF" (flee) THROUGH THE AUTHORITY OF THE NAME OF JESUS

I'M THAT GIRL WHO DEFIANTLY SINGS, SMILES, LAUGHS, AND
EVEN DANCES WHEN DEPRESSION TRIES TO STEAL MY JOY

I'M THAT GIRL WITH A NEW NAME . . . HAPPY!

CHAPTER TWENTY-FOUR

I'm That Girl Who Banishes Bad Moods

Moping when things don't go my way is not my true nature.
"I'm just in a bad mood" was the line I used to say.

No more.

My mood is not dependent on whether things are easy or tough.

I was reborn to be in a good . . . calm . . . unphased . . . rock
steady mood . . . even when things don't go my way.

I'm that good mood girl. How? Christ is that Way and He gave me His mind.

Time spent in a bad mood has never paid off. It only ever took from
me. It's only reward . . . a looming spider web of bad thoughts and
words which only ever led to bad choices and bad results.

Bad moods stunted my mind, butchered my hope, hurt
my body, and paralyzed my ability to love.

Now I take the axe to pity and pouting. I reject all melancholy,
all negativity, and every persuasive draft of the doldrums.

They don't even suit me. I thought they were my
color, but they were oh so wrong for me.

I will not be swayed by foul winds of emotion. I will dwell up
here in the mountain of joy and set my spirit free to hum the
tune of good cheer that I hear upon the heights. No whimpering
whisper from the bottomlands will drag me down.

I have life to live abundantly . . . life to share extravagantly.

This is my new color. It's so me.

MY FATHER'S VOICE:

Philippians 2:5, *"Let this mind be in you which was also in Christ Jesus."*

Proverbs 3:17, *"Her ways are ways of pleasantness, And all her paths are peace."*

Psalm 57:7, *"My heart is steadfast, O God, my heart is steadfast; I will sing and give praise."*

Proverbs 29:11, *"A fool vents all his feelings, But a wise man holds them back."*

Proverbs 25:28, *"Whoever has no rule over his own spirit Is like a city broken down, without walls."*

Ecclesiastes 11:10, *"Therefore remove sorrow from your heart, And put away evil from your flesh, For childhood and youth are vanity."*

Psalm 62:2, *"He only is my rock and my salvation; He is my defense; I shall not be greatly moved."*

Ecclesiastes 7:9, *"Do not hasten in your spirit to be angry, For anger rests in the bosom of fools."*

Proverbs 12:14, *"A man will be satisfied with good by the fruit of his mouth . . ."*

Colossians 3:8, *"But now you yourselves are to **put off** all these: anger, wrath, malice, blasphemy, filthy language out of your mouth."*

Romans 7:5, *"For when we were in the flesh, the sinful passions which were aroused by the law were at work in our members to bear fruit to death."*

Psalm 26:2, *"Examine me, O Lord, and prove me; Try my mind and my heart."*

3 John 1:11, *"Beloved, do not imitate what is evil, but what is good. He who does good is of God, but he who does evil has not seen God."*

Isaiah 26:4 (ASV), *"Trust ye in Jehovah for ever; for in Jehovah, [even] Jehovah, is an everlasting rock."*

2 Samuel 22:32 *"For who is God, except the Lord? And who is a rock, except our God?"*

Ephesians 4:23, *"And be renewed in the spirit of your mind."*

1 John 1:5, *"This is the message which we have heard from Him and declare to you, that God is light and in Him is no darkness at all."*

Proverbs 17:22, *"A merry heart does good, like medicine, But a broken spirit dries the bones."*

For more scriptures to help banish bad moods, see page 375.

I WILL CONFIDENTLY SAY:

I'M THAT GIRL WHO RENEWS HER MIND
BY THE WASHING OF THE WORD

I'M THAT GIRL WHO HAS HARDWIRED A "BAD MOOD
ALERT" INTO HER MIND, WHEN THE BUZZER RINGS,
THE GLOOMIES GET IMMEDIATELY CANNED

I'M THAT GIRL WHO IS BECOMING NATURALLY POSITIVE

I'M THAT GIRL WHO IS INTENTIONAL TO
BE STEADY, AND SOLID OF MIND

I'M THAT GIRL WHO WATCHES THE WEATHER . . . NO
BLEAK RAINY DAYS INSIDE OR STORMS UNDER THE
ROOF AND DEFINITELY NO TORNADOES UPSTAIRS

I'M THAT GIRL WITH A NEW NAME . . . STABLE!

CHAPTER TWENTY-FIVE

I'm That Girl Who Grabs Joy

I am attracted to joy. I crave it. I hunt it.

I light upon it like a stealth winged bird to a shiny treasure. I train
the eyes of my heart to search it out. Then I never let it get away.
When I bring it to my bosom, I drain every drop of its essence.

I am a joy grabber.

I grab it in the mundane tasks of life. I grab it in the rain . . . in the sun . . .
in the snow . . . in the wind. I grab it when others only see flaws and faults. I
grab it in the rocky valleys of life. Joy lights my way through the darkness.

Joy is my portion. It is my spirit food. It is my strength. I awake to live in it.

I must. The alternative to joy is poison to my flesh.

Joy has a voice. I lean in to listen. The Author of
joy speaks to me, and I echo His call.

This joy knows no bounds. It makes me dance when
my circumstances show no reason.

I see it now. Even through the camouflage. I catch it. I
grab it . . . again and again . . . and I share it.

This joy, now mine, will be contagious.

MY FATHER'S VOICE:

John 15:11 (NIV), *"I have told you this that my joy may be in you and that your joy may be complete."*

Jeremiah 15:16 (NIV), *"When your words came, I ate them; they were my joy and my heart's delight, for I bear your name. LORD God Almighty."*

Psalm 16:11, *"You will show me the path of life; In Your presence is fullness of joy; At Your right hand are pleasures forevermore."*

Romans 15:13 (NIV), *"May the God of Hope fill you with all joy and peace as you trust in him, so that you may overflow with hope by the power of the Holy Spirit."*

John 16:24, *"Until now you have asked nothing in My name. Ask, and you will receive, that your joy may be full."*

Psalm 71:23, *"My lips shall greatly rejoice when I sing to You, And my soul, which You have redeemed."*

Acts 2:28, *"You have made known to me the ways of life; You will make me full of joy in Your presence."*

Proverbs 10:28 (NIV), *"The prospect of the righteous is joy, but the hopes of the wicked come to nothing."*

Philippians 4:4, *"Rejoice in the Lord always. Again I will say, rejoice!"*

1 Peter 1:8-9 (ESV), *"Though you have not seen him, you love him. Though you do not now see him, you believe in him and REJOICE with JOY that is inexpressible and filled with glory, the outcome of your faith, the salvation of your souls."*

Nehemiah 8:10, *". . . Do not sorrow, for the joy of the LORD is your strength."*

1 Thessalonians 5:16-18, *"Rejoice always, pray without ceasing, in everything give thanks; for this is the will of God in Christ Jesus for you."*

2 Corinthians 6:10, *"As sorrowful, yet always rejoicing; as poor, yet making many rich; as having nothing, and yet possessing all things."*

Isaiah 55:12, *"For you shall go out with joy, And be led out with peace; The mountains and the hills Shall break forth into singing before you, And all the trees of the field shall clap their hands."*

For more scriptures to help grab joy, see page 379.

I WILL CONFIDENTLY SAY:

I'M THAT GIRL WHO HUNTS JOY

I'M THAT GIRL WHO NEVER LETS JOY OUT OF HER SIGHT

I'M THAT GIRL WHO LOOKS FOR JOY IN
THE UNLIKELIEST OF PLACES

I'M THAT GIRL WHO KNOWS THAT "JOY" HAS BEEN BOUGHT,
PAID FOR, AND GIVEN . . . AND IT RUNS OVER IN MY LIFE

I'M THAT GIRL WITH A NEW NAME . . . JOY GRABBER!

CHAPTER TWENTY-SIX

I'm That Girl Who Only Looks Back to Give Thanks

I am free from hurts in my past.

So, I will only look back to give thanks.

Thankfulness for lessons learned, and healing wounds rather than permanent scars.

My time for mourning has ceased. Comfort has been promised me.

I capture only the beauty of my yesterdays, to crown the present. This is not denial. This is my deliverance.

I refuse to dwell on the shadows of my past. Dragging them up over and over again only makes today a graveyard. I will no longer make shrines in my mind for the corpses of yesterday . . . to burn through time bestowed me for life today on past hardships.

My redeemed now is worth my full attention.

I let go.

I open my clenched fists that have been clinging to a rotting, stopped clock in my past. I free my hands for the work of today . . . to forgive . . . to love . . . to laugh . . . to give . . . to serve . . . to create . . . to build . . . to heal.

I release the clutches of my mind from clinging to ugliness in my past and cling only to the beautiful.

No more broken records. I sing a new song for a new day.

MY FATHER'S VOICE:

2 Corinthians 5:17, *"Therefore, if anyone is in Christ, he is a NEW creation. Old things have passed away; Behold, all things have become new."*

Romans 6:4, *"Therefore we were buried with Him through baptism into death, so that just as Christ was raised from the dead by the glory of the Father, even so we also should walk in NEWNESS OF LIFE."*

Psalm 30:5, *". . . weeping may endure for a night, But JOY COMES with the MORNING."*

Matthew 5:4, *"Blessed are those who mourn, For they shall be comforted."*

Isaiah 43:18-19, *"Do not remember the former things, Nor consider the things of old. Behold, I will do a NEW thing; now it shall spring forth; Shall you not know it? I will even make a road in the wilderness and rivers in the desert."*

Ephesians 4:22-24, *"That you put off, concerning your former conduct, the old man which grows corrupt according to the deceitful lusts, and be RENEWED in the spirit of your mind, and that you put on the NEW MAN which was created according to God, in true righteousness and holiness."*

Philippians 3:13-14, *"Brethren, I do not count myself to have apprehended; but one thing I do, forgetting those things which are behind and REACHING FORWARD to those things which are AHEAD, I press toward the goal for the prize of the upward call of God in Christ Jesus."*

Psalm 118:24, *"**This** is the day the Lord has made; We will rejoice and be glad in it."*

Ezekiel 36:25-27, *"Then I will sprinkle clean water on you, and you shall be clean; I will cleanse you from all your filthiness and from all your idols. I will give you a NEW heart and put a NEW spirit within you; I will take the heart of stone out of your flesh and give you a heart of flesh. I will put my Spirit within you and cause you to walk in my statutes, and you will keep MY judgments and do them."*

For more scriptures to help with only looking back to give thanks, see page 381.

I WILL CONFIDENTLY SAY:

I'M THAT GIRL WHOSE SLATE IS CLEAN EVERY MORNING

I'M THAT GIRL WHO IS COMFORTED

I'M THAT GIRL WHO IS PRESENT IN THE NOW

I'M THAT GIRL WHOSE TOMORROW
DOESN'T STINK OF YESTERDAY

I'M THAT GIRL WHO MEDITATES ON BEAUTY

I'M THAT GIRL WHO SETS HER SIGHTS FOR-
WARD AND NEVER TURNS BACK

I'M THAT GIRL WITH A NEW NAME . . . FREE!

CHAPTER TWENTY-SEVEN

I'm That Girl Who Walks in Healing

I'm a cross girl.

I believe it was on that cross where Christ died for both the forgiveness of my sins and for the healing of my body.

It is a finished and perfect work.

This is not just a nonchalant mental assent "belief," a Sunday School story, or a fairy tale. No, this is a wholehearted, spirit and soul, bedrock belief because the Word tells me it is so.

This is my truth . . .

THE truth.

By His stripes I am healed. BY HIS STRIPES I AM HEALED.

I do not deny that I may feel sick, but I certainly deny the right of sickness to attach itself to me. It has no authority. Christ became the curse, so the curse of sickness has no claim on me. It must leave.

I speak to my body and tell it to align itself to the Word of God and to the TRUTH that sets me free. My body is blood-bought and sickness must bow its knee to my Redeemer Jesus, Whose Name is above every name. That Name that is above cancer, diabetes, fibromyalgia, Hashimoto's, PCOS, arthritis, or any earthly ailment.

All sickness must bow to my Healer, my Jehovah Rapha, the God who heals and completely restores, mentally, emotionally, and physically.

I deny the voice of sickness that continually whispers of my weakness. Away with its sly, seducing, and sniveling lies. Let the weak say, "I am strong."

I'm that girl who is strong.

MY FATHER'S VOICE:

Isaiah 53:5, *"But he was wounded for our transgressions, He was bruised for our iniquities; the chastisement for our peace was upon Him, and by His stripes we are healed."*

Psalm 107:20, *"He sent His word and healed them, and delivered them from their destructions."*

Psalm 103:2-4 (NIV), *"Praise the Lord, my soul, and forget not all his benefits—who forgives all your sins and heals all your diseases, who redeems your life from the pit and crowns you with love and compassion."*

Jeremiah 17:14, *"Heal me, O Lord, and I shall be healed; SAVE me, and I shall be saved, for You are my praise."*

Psalm 147:3, *"He heals the brokenhearted and binds up their wounds."*

Mark 9:23, *"Jesus said to him, if you can believe, all things are possible to him who believes."*

Mark 5:34 (NIV), *"He said to her, "Daughter, your faith has healed you. Go in peace and be freed from your suffering."*

Romans 10:17, *"Faith comes from hearing and hearing from the word of God."*

Psalm 41:2-3 (NIV), *"The LORD protects and preserves them—they are counted among the blessed in the land—he does not give them over to the desire of their foes. The Lord sustains them on their sick bed and restores them from their bed of illness."*

Romans 8:11, *"But if the Spirit of Him who raised Jesus from the dead dwells in you, He who raised Christ from the dead will also give life to your mortal bodies through His Spirit who dwells in you."*

Luke 8:50, *"But when Jesus heard it, He answered him, saying, "Do not be afraid; only believe, and she will be made well."*

Mark 10:52, *"Then Jesus said to him, 'Go your way; your faith has made you well.' And immediately he received his sight and followed Jesus on the road."*

James 5:14-15, *"Is anyone among you sick? Let him call for the elders of the church, and let them pray over him, anointing him with oil in the name of the Lord. And the prayer of faith will save the sick, and the Lord will raise him up. And if he has committed sins he will be forgiven."*

For more scriptures to help walk in healing, see page 384.

I WILL CONFIDENTLY SAY:

I'M THAT GIRL WHO DAILY RECEIVES MY HEALING

I'M THAT GIRL WHO WALKS OUT OF SICKNESS
ARMED WITH THE TRUTH OF HIS WORD

I'M THAT GIRL WHO DOESN'T TRUST HER SENSES
BUT TRUSTS UNASHAMEDLY IN THE CROSS

I'M THAT GIRL WHO REFUSES TO SIGN FOR ANY
SICKNESS PACKAGE. IT IS NOT MINE!

I'M THAT GIRL WHO DOESN'T WALK INTO SICK-
NESS THROUGH MY OWN WORDS BUT WALKS OUT
OF SICKNESS THROUGH MY SAVIOR'S WORDS.

I'M THAT GIRL WITH A NEW NAME . . . HEALED!

CHAPTER TWENTY-EIGHT

I'm That Girl Who Gets Her Hopes Up . . . Way Up!

I refuse to listen to false wisdom that encourages "don't get your hopes up."

It's a trap.

It only keeps me stuck in the doldrums and the lackluster land of impossibilities. There is no encouragement in murdered dreams. So, I won't be consoled by compulsory defeat.

Keeping my hopes strapped down by the heavy weights of "what if's" and "probably not's" is no way to truly live.

I will not let the airplane of my life, which is designed to soar in the sky, never feel the thrill of flight through advice to "stay safe on the tarmac". Fear of failure will not dissuade me from feeling the wind.

Dismissing the impossible is not "safe," it is death before life gets a chance to bud.

The slayer of my hope is the assassin of my potential. I dare to defy this naysayer!

I will have the grit to defend my God given right to believe against all odds. Doubt wears like a too tight shoe and I won't be crippled.

God is my greatest advocate for peculiar hope. He told me he *"takes pleasure"* when I hope and when I am persuaded in the reality of that which doesn't even yet exist.

He created me for crazy stories and crazy good faith.

I'm designed to believe.

MY FATHER'S VOICE:

2 Corinthians 3:12, *"Therefore, since we have such hope, we use great boldness of speech."*

1 Peter 1:3, *"Blessed be the God and Father of our Lord Jesus Christ, who according to His abundant mercy has begotten us again to a living hope through the resurrection of Jesus Christ from the dead."*

Psalm 71:14, *"But I will hope continually, And will praise You yet more and more."*

Psalm 71:5, *"For You are my hope, O Lord God; You are my trust from my youth."*

Psalm 25:5 (NIV), *"Guide me in Your truth and teach me, for You are God my Savior, and my hope is in you all day long."*

Ephesians 1:18, *"The eyes of your understanding being enlightened; that you may know what is the hope of His calling, what are the riches of the glory of His inheritance in the saints."*

Psalm 147:11, *"The Lord takes pleasure in those who fear Him, In those who hope in His mercy."*

Romans 15:13, *"Now may the God of hope fill you with all joy and peace in believing, that you may abound in hope by the power of the Holy Spirit."*

Romans 8:24, *"For we were saved in this hope, but hope that is seen is not hope; for why does one still hope for what he sees?"*

Romans 8:25, *"But if we hope for what we do not see, we eagerly wait for it with perseverance."*

Micah 7:7 (AMP), *"But as for me, I will look expectantly for the Lord and with confidence in Him I will keep watch: I will wait (with confident expectation) for the God of my salvation. My God will hear me."*

Hebrews 11:1, *"Now faith is the substance of things hoped for, the evidence of things not seen."*

Mark 9:23, *"Jesus said to him, 'If you can believe, all things are possible to him who believes'."*

For more scriptures to help get your hopes up, see page 386.

I WILL CONFIDENTLY SAY:

I'M THAT GIRL WHO CLINGS TIGHTLY TO HOPE

I'M THAT GIRL WHO IS UNASHAMED OF CRAZY
HOPE (hope that looks foolish to man)

I'M THAT GIRL WHO TALKS HOPE, DREAMS
HOPE, AND PROJECTS HOPE

I'M THAT GIRL WHO BUILDS HOPE IN OTHERS

I'M THAT GIRL WHO ABANDONS THE
TARMAC OF DOUBT AND DEFEAT

I'M THAT GIRL WITH A NEW NAME . . . HOPEFUL!

CHAPTER TWENTY-NINE

I'm That Girl Who Heals Her Home

I am a life-giver.

I breathe a current of life and love into the atmosphere of my home.

I come alive when I love.

And when I love, I look like Him . . . the Healer. As I imitate the One Who mends the broken, I myself become whole.

I feed the hungry, nurture the weak, and wake to serve. I am not a doormat. I *choose* to serve. I am a love slave who has given my life to this work. This is my true identity, even if I never fully realized it or if I sadly forgot. This is the very essence that my Creator stirred within my matrix.

It is who I am because it is Who He is.

I have been given great responsibility to set the thermostat of the atmosphere in my home. My face and my words reflect this love in me. My tone and my expressions heal rather than harm. I may weep, but I will laugh, I will smile . . . even in the hardest of times.

I will keep the fire of joy burning bright to warm the souls that gather near and to help repair the breeches in any deflated family member's heart.

I am not a coward who cannot say "I'm sorry" when I've wronged others . . . in my home or in my life. I will use it often. It will be one of my favorite phrases . . . until it feels effortless on my lips.

I live to build. I will enlarge the vision, confidence, courage, and health of those entrusted to my devotion. I will zealously work to bolster . . . to batten up . . . to bind together any place of brokenness. This will be my favorite work. I am made in the image of the Great Physician. Healing is my destiny.

MY FATHER'S VOICE:

Isaiah 58:12, *"Those from among you shall build the old waste places; You shall raise up the foundations of many generations; And you shall be called the Repairer of the Breach, The Restorer of Streets to Dwell In."*

Isaiah 61:1, *"The Spirit of the Lord God is upon Me, Because the Lord has anointed Me To preach good tidings to the poor; He has sent Me to heal the broken-hearted, To proclaim liberty to the captives, And the opening of the prison to those who are bound."*

Proverbs 24:3-4, *"Through wisdom a house is built, And by understanding it is established; By knowledge the rooms are filled With all precious and pleasant riches."*

Proverbs 14:1, *"The wise woman builds her house, But the foolish pulls it down with her hands."*

Joshua 24:15, *". . . But as for me and my house, we will serve the Lord."*

Luke 6:48, *"He is like a man building a house, who dug deep and laid the foundation on the rock. And when the flood arose, the stream beat vehemently against that house, and could not shake it, for it was founded on the rock."*

Ephesians 4:29, *"Let no corrupt word proceed out of your mouth, but what is good for necessary edification, that it may impart grace to the hearers."*

Acts 20:35, *"I have shown you in every way, by laboring like this, that you must support the weak. And remember the words of the Lord Jesus, that He said, 'It is more blessed to give than to receive'."*

Colossians 2:2, *"That their hearts may be encouraged, being knit together in love, and attaining to all riches of the full assurance of understanding, to the knowledge of the mystery of God, both of the Father and of Christ."*

Galatians 6:2, *"Bear one another's burdens, and so fulfill the law of Christ."*

Isaiah 28:16, *"Therefore thus says the Lord God: "Behold, I lay in Zion a stone for a foundation, A tried stone, a precious cornerstone, a sure foundation . . ."*

Hebrews 13:2, *"Do not forget to entertain strangers, for by so doing some have unwittingly entertained angels."*

For more scriptures to help heal your home, see page 389.

I WILL CONFIDENTLY SAY:

I'M THAT GIRL WHO SETS A THERMO-
STAT OF PEACE AND JOY IN HER HOME

I'M THAT GIRL WHOSE MOUTH SPILLS OUT
RIVERS OF LIFE-GIVING WORDS

I'M THAT GIRL WHOSE MOOD LIFTS THE SPIR-
ITS OF THOSE AROUND ME

I'M THAT GIRL WHOSE ARMS ARE EAGER TO HUG AND SERVE

I'M THAT GIRL WHO FORGIVES SO THAT THE DAM THAT
HOLDS BACK HEALING CAN BREAK OPEN AROUND ME

I'M THAT GIRL WITH A NEW NAME . . . HEALER!

CHAPTER THIRTY

I'm That Girl Who Has Chosen Faith

I have decided the path for me.

I have chosen to walk the faith track. It is a choice set firmly into the framework of my mind, soul, and spirit.

I do not bend or warp when a wind of question comes whistling through the rafters. I do not crack or splinter when a wrecking ball of human reasoning forces its blow.

I stand.

Strong.

Straight.

Stalwart.

Like a soldier guarding the most precious and valuable asset needed for victory.

Faith is my strongest weapon against all enemy attacks. I do not let unfulfilled dreams, lethargic thinking, the muck of confusion, physical symptoms, reluctant hope, and injurious uncertainty anywhere near my decision of faith.

My mind is made up, and no situational curveball will change my resolute and unflinching loyalty to faith. I choose uncompromising allegiance to the truth . . . the Word of God.

Every promise of God and every Word from scripture is mine to have and to hold and to love and to cherish. They are not intangible and distant, but intimate, substantial, near, and personal.

Through the currency of faith, I can exchange all that is the Word of God into experience.

MY FATHER'S VOICE:

Psalm 119:30, *"I have chosen the way of truth; Your judgments I have laid before me."*

1 Corinthians 16:13 (NIV), *"Be on your guard; stand firm in the faith; be courageous; be strong."*

Hebrews 3:14 (NIV), *"We have come to share in Christ, if indeed we hold our original conviction firmly to the very end."*

1 Corinthians 2:5, *"That your faith should not be in the wisdom of men but in the power of God."*

Hebrews 11:6, *"But without faith it is impossible to please Him, for he who comes to God must believe that He is, and that He is a rewarder of those who diligently seek Him."*

Hebrews 11:11 (NIV), *"And by faith even Sarah, who was past childbearing age, was enabled to bear children because she considered him faithful who had made the promise."*

James 1:5-8, *"If any of you lacks wisdom, let him ask of God, who gives to all liberally and without reproach, and it will be given to him. But let him ask in faith, with no doubting, for he who doubts is like a wave of the sea driven and tossed by the wind. For let not that man suppose that he will receive anything from the Lord; he is a double-minded man, unstable in all his ways."*

Mark 9:23 (NIV), *"If you can?" said Jesus. "Everything is possible for one who believes."*

John 20:29 (NIV), *"Then Jesus told him, ‹Because you have seen me, you have believed; blessed are those who have not seen and yet have believed'."*

2 Corinthians 5:7, *"For we walk by faith, not by sight."*

Romans 10:11, *"For the Scripture says, 'Whoever believes on Him will not be put to shame'."*

Matthew 21:21-22, *"So Jesus answered and said to them, "Assuredly, I say to you, if you have faith and do not doubt, you will not only do what was done to the fig tree, but also if you say to this mountain, 'Be removed and be cast into the sea,' it will be done. And whatever things you ask in prayer, believing, you will receive."*

For more scriptures to help choose faith, see page 392.

I WILL CONFIDENTLY SAY:

I'M THAT GIRL WHO REJECTS HUMAN REASON-
ING AS THE CAPTAIN OF HER MIND

I'M THAT GIRL WHO DARES HER SOUL TO SEE
WHAT HER EYES CANNOT YET SEE

I'M THAT GIRL WHO SEIZES EVERY PROM-
ISE AS HER PERSONAL GIFT TO OPEN

I'M THAT GIRL WHO DOESN'T WAIVER IN HER BELIEF
. . . I REMAIN STEADFAST UNTIL THE END

I'M THAT GIRL WHO UNDERSTANDS THE POWER
OF THE WORD OF GOD ON HER LIPS

I'M THAT GIRL WITH A NEW NAME . . . FAITHFUL!

Desserts

Fun, and delicious . . . bite into these lighthearted life changers!

CHAPTER THIRTY-ONE

I'm That Girl Who's Jolly Fantastic!

From Pearl . . .

Several years ago, if you knew me and greeted me with a "How are you doing?" my response would have been entirely different than it is today. Always wanting to be honest about my not-so-easy life, I would come back with, "I'm okay, thanks." or "Getting by." or "Not too bad." Or what about this one . . . "Not as good as some, but better than others." I heard someone say that once and liked it, so I used it sometimes.

These responses were my way of being authentic. I didn't want to lie when asked about the state of my wellbeing. In my mind, things weren't perfect . . . many days were tough, so why would I automatically say, "Great, thanks!"?

We were discussing responses to greetings on a recent Trim Healthy Podcast (aka The Poddy), and I mentioned that for most of my life, I had taken the super honest approach and answered "How are you's" with a subdued and what I considered a truthful response. Our co-producer Lesley looked at me in astonishment. She'd worked for us for three years at that point. We had spoken on the phone almost every workday, and after saying, "Hello," she'd always ask how I'm doing. For three years, I had told her how great or jolly fantastic I was . . . and meant it! Not all days in those three years had been easy . . . she knew that because she is both a close friend and an integral part of our business. She said, "I just can't imagine you as that other person."

I'm not that girl anymore because focusing on all the things to be grateful for in my life . . . all the many blessings is why I *am* jolly fantastic. No matter the challenges I may be facing, when I tell others how fantastic I am, I am speaking it into both the physical and spiritual world. My body hears me and gets in line with my words. The spirit world hears me, and I believe it does the same. You bet . . . even on the hardest of days, I'm that girl who is beyond blessed. Of course, I can still share my struggles. I am fortunate to have an amazing family and community of people who I can ask to pray for me when needed. But even on my hardest days . . . I am GOOD because God is GOOD. I am BLESSED . . . because He has showered His blessings upon me, starting with a cleansed heart and new mercies with the new sun every morning. I'm reminded of 2 Corinthians 3:12, *"Therefore, since we have such hope, we use great boldness of speech."* Yeah, we do!!!! Bold Baby Bold! This is how we need to roll!

> No matter the *challenges* I may be facing, when I tell others how fantastic I am, I am *speaking* it into both the physical and spiritual world.

Perhaps it is not your jive to tell anyone you are "jolly fantastic," but how about having a blast practicing some of these responses and releasing their power into the physical and spiritual world. When asked how you're doing, how about . . .

"Soooo great!"

"Incredibly blessed."

"Shockingly good."

"Full of fabulousness."

"Couldn't be better."

"Particularly well."

"Happy and grateful."

I WILL CONFIDENTLY SAY:

I'M THAT GIRL WHOSE LIFE IS SHOWERED WITH BLESSINGS.

I'M THAT GIRL WHO IS MUCH MORE THAN FINE.

I'M THAT GIRL WHOSE VOICE DECLARES
THE GOODNESS OF THE LORD.

I'M THAT GIRL WHOSE BODY LISTENS AND RESPONDS
EVERY TIME I PRONOUNCE MYSELF "DOING WELL."

I'M THAT GIRL WHOSE CUP RUNS OVER AND
I'M NOT ASHAMED TO SHARE IT.

I'M THAT GIRL WHO LOOKS FOR HER BLESS-
INGS AND NEVER FORGETS THEM.

CHAPTER THIRTY-TWO

I'm That Girl Who Remembers How to Laugh

From Serene . . .

Who doesn't love the giggles of little children?! Their cheek-busting, belly-rolling, throat-bursting laughter is what makes children so spectacularly unadulter-ated and uncomplicated. Their innocence explodes into uncontainable joy at the simplest of stimuli. The sight of a ball in flight, an ear flop of a puppy, a crazy face pulled by a sibling, or an odd noise repeated over and over is utter hilarity to them. It is worth all the energy they can muster to honor the moment with a stupendous and outrageous guffaw.

Watching my children and grandchildren react to life with boundless humor is refreshing and inspiring to me. Sometimes I will even look up babies laughing on YouTube for a good half hour, for a full intensive reset back to the liberation of taking life more playfully and knocking myself out of my dirge straight jacket.

I don't know when I stopped laughing freely and started racking up serious sighs as my preferred vocal outlet. I am aware that it happened though. Many times, my first reaction to my children getting all rambunctious and giggling up a storm has been to scold them back to seriousness. "Inside voices, please!", "You all need to settle down!", "Stop the crazy silliness in there!" But these days when I catch myself responding like this, I am putting a stop to such big ol', boring sad-ness. Why should they put a cap on their joy? Why should they act like adults who are mostly all "et up" with stodgy sobriety?

Yes, there is a time for children to learn to be quiet and not disturb others with their noise. But the truth is I don't want them to turn into that dull, drab, me who was telling them to shush. I want to join them . . . to become that girl who remembers how to laugh again. I want to get a bit nonsensical again . . . maybe a tad wacky . . . even a might kooky. It has become my goal to join my children's "cracky uppy" club.

At the start of this recent endeavor to get "cracky uppy" again, it was quite a challenge to keep up. *Oh, no! We are laughing again . . . alright . . . got to get all lighthearted and free again, I guess. Man, what hard work!* Dirge . . . blah . . . sigh . . . fish twisted face . . . that was me as I wrestled to break through all my layers of adult seriousness. But, now . . . forgive me for boasting, but I'm getting quite good at this. Or at least I am riding with the help of training wheels. Don't get me wrong. I try not to laugh at poo-poo, bum-bum, fart stink humor too much . . . it's a mom's job to keep things a little on the polite side. Children find bodily functions so funny. But I can't say I don't either, so it is hard not to giggle along with them sometimes when someone in the family lets out a ripper. But I do draw the line at misguided, immature laughter centered around the poor fortune of others.

> I want to *join* them . . . to become that girl who remembers how to *laugh* again.

The important thing is . . . I'm actually riding this merry-go-round of peppy splendor . . . and it's ultimately a better ride than my old popped tire bike. My life has greatly improved by being childlike. God always knew this was the better way to live. Many times over, the Bible repeats our need to become like a child if we want to enter into the Kingdom of Heaven.

I'm sure that God has a great laugh. As I am thinking about what it might be like right now, I am super pumped to get to hear it audibly one day. Got a feeling it is not some lemony little snicker wickle. I bet it is very grand indeed . . . a full-throated guffaw me thinks that would beat any Santa Claus's HO-HO-HO hands down.

Laughter is not the only thing I seemed to forget about, though. I used to sing all day long. I would hum and croon and even belt it out occasionally, even while grocery shopping. I guess it was a gradual decline, but every year that I became more adultly refined, I somehow became pristinely polished out of habits that bred joy.

My children sing all day. They sing while washing the dishes or sweeping the floor. They even let their bodies follow their groove with a few gorgeous little trendy side steps or whole arm, snake-like, cool dude dance waves. The broom will even become their microphone. But when I sweep? Oh, I mean business. The air is full of flying dust, and I suppose, if I am honest, it is mingled with murmurs and astonished exclamations of why the filth of the earth could so rudely occupy territory on my floor.

I know who looks and feels happier when they clean, and I am inspired to remember how to sing around the house again. I have a lot of children . . . more than 10 if you're counting, so sometimes the noise of many children singing at once in close proximity, often chanting out different songs, can be quite overwhelming. It is a mean ol' mom to shut them up, I know. So, I reckon if you can't beat 'em you join 'em, like the famous old adage. Lately, instead of suffering through noise overload, I've just been adding to it. I jump on board with my best pick of their songs, and my nerves seem to find a lovely homeostasis with my decision to join the choir. It's crazy, 'cuz there's more noise, but it works, and we are all happy Kumbaya campers.

I was recently on a vacay with my cousin Melissa, and as we were walking together along the streets or beaches, I would often hear the soft, sweet humming of a song. Her singing would catch me off guard because I don't find it a common practice among most of us serious, boring adults. It was a peaceful, contented sound and held the glory of a happy inner space that seemed to float up and out on wings. I was convicted again in a gentle, inspiring way to remember how to sing again. What I really mean by this is the natural habit and joy of singing just because. If I really need a reason . . . what about just because I am happy to be alive . . . just because I am saturated to overflowing with the love of my Heavenly Daddy . . . or just because I am super blessed by the wonder and charm of music or just because I have learned it births a well of joy inside of me and heals my body?

You may not have children all around you singing and laughing or friends who haven't forgotten these enchanted, whimsical arts. Maybe you haven't realized that you have lost these gratifying and satisfying habits of old . . . or may I say . . . of young. And that's their remarkable side effect. Laughing and singing around in life keeps us young. As we more thoroughly mentioned somewhere in those science chapters, it is scientifically proven that laughter is an effective therapy for disease, pain, and depression. It boosts the immune system, perks up the heart, exercises the lungs, and heals the brain. A quick internet search will fill your head with pages of verified data on the why's and how's.

Dr. William Fry, a Stanford University psychiatrist, has noted in his research that children laugh more than four hundred times a day, compared to adults who, on average, only laugh about a dozen times a day. Sadly, I think a dozen times is actually a generous stretch for some of us . . . I probably scored on the low side of that on many days. In his book, *Anatomy of an Illness: As Perceived by the Patient,* Norman Cousins has termed laughter as "inner jogging" because a good-hearted belly laugh gives every system of the body a workout.

> Laughter is an effective *therapy* for disease, pain, and depression. It boosts the immune system, perks up the heart, exercises the lungs, and *heals* the brain.

As a health and fitness nut, I was excited to hear that singing is also classed as an aerobic activity by the extra amounts of oxygen delivered to the brain. Singing also slashes cortisol, our hormone that surges in times of stress. My ambition to become a singing star within the walls of my house and my fenced-in yard was all fired up when I learned that singing heals and prevents the decaying of the brain. It has been found as an effective treatment for neurological issues, from stuttering, Parkinson's disease, acquired brain injury, and even helps children with autism. The best news is that the research shows even out-of-tune singing carries the same amazing benefits. So, let's let it rip, aye? Hear me belt . . . "Let it go . . . Let it go . . . You can't hold me back anymore!!!"

I WILL CONFIDENTLY SAY:

I'M THAT GIRL WHO'S A BELLY LAUGHER

I'M THAT GIRL WHO JOINS THE FUN INSTEAD OF POO HOO'ING

I'M THAT GIRL WHO MAKES AN ADDICTION OUT OF SINGING

I'M THAT GIRL WHO FEELS SO YOUNG INSIDE BECAUSE
SHE REMEMBERS HOW TO BE CHILDLIKE

I'M THAT GIRL IN THE "CRACKY UPPY" CLUB

CHAPTER THIRTY-THREE

I'm That Girl Who Waits for Her Reward

From Pearl . . .

A few years back I was sitting in the passenger seat as my husband drove through a fast food joint and placed the order for himself and the children. He looked at me . . . waiting for me to tell him what I wanted. It was snack time, not mealtime. In about 20 minutes we'd be home, and I had planned on a healthy and yummy snack once home. I'd been thinking about it . . . Ahhh . . . a creamy coffee with a couple of healthy and blood sugar friendly muffins I'd made the day before . . . so delicious! But now fast food beckoned . . . the easy . . . the quick . . . the "I get to eat NOW!!!"

I don't despise fast food; I rarely eat it these days. But there are times in my life, even now, when I decide to enjoy it as part of my "food freedom/refuse to be chained down to legalism in any way" approach to life. But up until that drive-thru moment, if the family ordered fast food, I would have felt left out and deprived if I didn't join in and place my order.

By this time, I'd just started grasping the concepts of "I'm That Girl," and was in the beginning stages of realizing the power of choosing an overcoming path through the way I directed myself to think and talk. It hit me . . . I'm that girl who loves to wait for her reward! I wouldn't be deprived waiting 20 more minutes for my snack at home . . . I'd be empowered. That was me . . . that girl who *could* wait . . . who actually enjoyed waiting . . . who would anticipate her snack on the ride home, enjoy it when I got home, digest it well, then feel fantastic after eating it. "I'm good," I told my husband, then smiled . . . truly smiled as I realized that I was

281

> Our world is geared for *instant* gratification. Waiting is a *lost* art . . . but a much-needed one.

good . . . I was not deprived at all. I was, in fact, the excellent waiter . . . the fun anticipator . . . the girl completely opposite to deprived . . . the girl flooded with good things, and a couple of those good things were waiting to get in my belly when I got home.

Our world is geared for instant gratification. Waiting is a lost art . . . but a much-needed one. The truth is . . . waiting needn't be tedious . . . it can be a load of fun. We can practice enjoying rather than despising the wait . . . that girl who waits for her delayed package without getting upset . . . that girl who waits until proper mealtime or snack time without grazing and nibbling at will . . . that girl who waits (and who gives enormous amounts of patience) for loved ones who are struggling with communication and behavioral skills . . . that girl who waits in line without allowing a buildup of frustration or resentment toward the person taking waaaaaay too long at the counter . . . that girl who, once they're finally done

> We can *practice* enjoying rather than *despising* the wait.

and walk past us on the way out, can smile and wish them a good day.

That's us . . . girls who **put** on patience . . . who respect it as an art form and understand how much practice any art form takes. We're the girls who wear patience as our identity . . . the ones who cast off frustration and any old nature demands for instant gratification and wait . . . we graciously and joyously wait.

I WILL CONFIDENTLY SAY:

I'M THAT GIRL WHO ENJOYS ANTICIPATION

I'M THAT GIRL WHO IS EMPOWERED BY THE WAIT

I'M THAT GIRL WHO DOESN'T DEMAND "NOW"

I'M THAT GIRL WHO **PUTS** ON PATIENCE

I'M THAT GIRL WHO PRACTICES PATIENCE

I'M THAT GIRL WITH EXCELLENT WAITING SKILLS

CHAPTER THIRTY-FOUR

I'm That Girl Who Doesn't Stress Her Figs

(What the dickens are you talking about? Don't worry I'll explain.)

From Serene . . .

I never used to understand the resting and the receiving of healing. Somehow, I thought I had to work and sweat and worry and swat at it manically in desperation. With all my frantic "work", I forgot about the actual FAITH part. I had it upside down. Now through God's grace, He has shown me how to BELIEVE and in my believing how to REST and in my resting how to show my faith through ACTIONS.

Psalm 103:2-3 has become a verse I continually speak over my life, *"Bless the Lord, O my soul, And forget not all His benefits: Who forgives all your iniquities and, Who heals all your diseases."* So, as I walk as one receiving this healing promise, I endeavor to behave as one who is continually getting this healing. My choices and actions need to agree with my stand of faith. I believe God's gifts of healthy food as medicine and His herbs and plants are part of my natural daily walk into healing. So, too, are divinely inspired inventions and medical advancements. They can all carry within their matrix the glorious redemption of the cross. The curse is broken so even the humble weeds can impart God's healing. Who says technology can't be part of it too? Not me. All of these things can be positioned through the cross to be a conduit of all of its healing victory.

So back to the odd title of this "I'm That Girl" declaration. What does it mean to be that girl who doesn't stress figs? I mean, figs aren't common in every backyard for foraging. By "figs," I am talking about the category of anything we might use from this natural world to harmonize with and facilitate health and healing.

I started calling them this after I read the story in the Bible in Isaiah 38:21 (NIV) where the prophet said, *"Prepare a poultice of figs and apply it to the boil and he will recover."* This was an inspired idea from God. The same God who in other stories used mud, rivers, or even spit to perform a miracle. And yes, the same God who didn't need any earthly help and zapped many supernaturally from Heaven, and they were instantly healed. With just a word or a simple touch of His hand, when He walked here in the flesh, people were made completely whole.

> My *choices* and actions need to agree with my stand of *faith.*

Why sometimes figs? Why sometimes not? I don't know. But I do know God is super-duper creative and often loves to choose to work through His creation of herbs and human hands. I do know, though, that it is only through Him that healing originates. I am fully persuaded that it is only through His shed blood for me that I can now receive this gift of health, walk in it, and find deep soul rest within its crimson covering. The Old Testament pointed towards the cross, and in the 21st century, we point back . . . but it was the moment of the cross that has allowed for healing in all ages by all manners.

I'm sure I'm not the only one who has struggled with feeling like a faith failure for using natural remedies or perhaps even conventional medicine while at the same time praying for healing. But I now realize that I can use these "figs" without feeling that I am not in faith. God made the figs, right? It was by His perfect ingenuity and design that they house healing properties. Herbs, plants, body honoring medicine, and surgeries must come from God if they furnish true healing. How can they be from the accuser since he has only come to steal, kill, and destroy? (Note that I am not talking about dangerous, addictive pharmaceuticals that mask symptoms, bring excessive levels of toxicity, and destroy the body at a cellular level.)

There were many times in my anxious past when I got derailed because I put my trust and confidence in the "figs" only. But they don't deserve that reverence or reliance. They may be chosen as a tool of the Healer, but they are not the Healer. Back then, if I felt like I didn't have money in our budget for special "figs," I felt vulnerable and stressed. If I didn't know in the whole haystack of "figgy" options which one might be beneficial to me, I would get totally overwhelmed and spiral down into an internet meltdown from the constant study and research. If I missed a dose of a "fig," . . . agh!!!! My health was running down.

I refuse to walk in such health-degrading misery any longer!!!! I'm becoming that girl who can have faith while also taking natural action without choosing between the two and without stressing. My health is sustained by my Father, whose promise of healing is mine. I lean into Him and ask for an open door or some special insight or confirmation if He wants me to pick up a few "figs" that might help beyond eating a wholesome diet. I love to say that verse to myself found in 2 Peter 1:3, *"As His divine power has given to us all things that pertain to LIFE and GODLINESS, through the knowledge of Him who called us by glory and virtue."* I am assured that the Holy Spirit will lead me to everything I need for LIFE and for living like Him. He knows the perfect "fig" amongst ALL the "figs" for me. No more restless study. I study without obsession now and with a heart resting and leaning in towards His whisper.

> I'm becoming that girl who can have faith while also taking natural *action* without *choosing* between the two and without stressing.

If I don't have the money for the "fig" I've found . . . no worries, mate. If He wants to use it to help heal me or a family member heal, then He will provide. After all, He is the Great Physician. He owns the cattle on a thousand hills and has enough dough to furnish the medicine for His treatments.

I used to think it was all about me and how much I tried. Oh, the brain and body trauma of endlessly trying without connecting to the anchor of something soooo much bigger than myself. I was missing the refuge of real hope, where I could get all warm and delightfully cozy and fully snuggle with peace and take shelter. I was getting sicker every day that I tried to get better because my figs and my efforts had become my god. Ouch! I can only see it looking back now. But that is the cold hard truth.

Watching my oldest son walk through Stage 4 Lymphoma (lymphatic cancer) brought amazing faith lessons to me. His body became basically a shell of his former self . . . wasting away in a trauma ward with giant tumors taking over his face and neck . . . not even able to breathe properly. I was faced with a choice. I could believe, or I could despair. Sometimes I failed; I'd slump into fear and into "plan B's" and "what if's" and worry about what the harsh chemotherapy would do to him. But through it all, God taught me how to stand and how to rest in that stand. My son is now strapping and strong. God's healing power supernaturally and through both medical and natural "figs" have sustained him. I stand in belief that they will continue to do so.

Now, I no longer run from disease like a scared, electrocuted cat. I am not in fear of viruses. I don't lie awake and worry about strange symptoms like I used to, or anguish over what diseases may befall my family. I live free. 5G cell towers, depleted soils, or an accidental ingestion of a GMO corn chip isn't going to strip me of my health or my serenity (ha-ha . . . my name). He created me for such a time as this. He placed my family perfectly in this timeline . . . for this year and beyond. He holds the world in His hands. Nothing folds till He makes the call. Colossians 1:17 says, *"He is before all things, and in Him all things hold together."* I am encouraged by Acts 17:28, where it tells me, *"For in Him we live and move and exist . . ."* Job 33:4 shuts up my puny fears, *"The Spirit of God has made me, And the breath of the Almighty gives me LIFE."*

The Bible is timeless and just as relevant for today as ever. I read in there that God wants me to prosper and be in good health . . . that's good health now . . . all in the midst of the crazy health concerns we cannot control. Ultimately our health is a

> 5G cell towers, *depleted* soils, or an accidental ingestion of a GMO corn chip isn't going to strip me of my *health* or my serenity.

gift from Him, and He will sustain it. Of course, He wants us to honor our bodies and to choose life on our plates. He might even want us to pick up one of His "figs", but He sure won't want us picking it up with anxiety and with the weight of the world added to it. His "figs" are best paired with joy, and a large glass of crimson peace . . . peace that was pressed out at the foot of the cross.

This wonderful unwinding in the arms of Jehovah Rapha (the God who fully restores) is such a splendid way to live. His timing is perfect, His methods are perfect, and His promise of healing is tried and true. I love to dwell on Psalm 12:6, *"The words of the Lord are pure words, Like silver tried in a furnace of earth, Purified seven times."*

I WILL CONFIDENTLY SAY:

I'M THAT GIRL WHO PURSUES HEALTH WITHOUT OBSESSION

I'M THAT GIRL WHO PUTS HER TRUST IN GOD, NOT GOODS

I'M THAT GIRL WHOSE FAITH IS DA' BOSS AND NOT HER WORKS

I'M THAT GIRL WHO LEARNS A FIG OR TWO (ha-ha)

CHAPTER THIRTY-FIVE

I'm That Girl Who's a Bed Maker

From Pearl . . .

My whole life, I couldn't see the point of making my bed. Please don't blame my mother. She tried her best to instill bedmaking in me, but it didn't take. The way I looked at it was I'd just climb back in bed that night and mess it up again, so why make it in the first place? The result of that thinking was more than 40 years of, at best . . . rare bedmaking. I'd only do it on days when I'd look around my bedroom and couldn't deal with the horror of the mess one minute longer.

I grew to realize that on those nights after my room was picked up . . . getting into a made bed was actually something pretty special. I felt more peace in a picked up room . . . just walking past my made bed brought satisfaction and a calming presence to my life. So, about 5 years ago I made the decision . . . I wanted to live in a room where the bed was made.

I tried to become a bedmaker. I'd do okay for a few days . . . even a couple of weeks. Then, life would hit. I'd get too busy or I'd forget. Or I would just put it off until later in the day and then never get back to it. All the trying in the world didn't seem to help me. I resigned myself to not being naturally talented at it. My identity was "Pearl, the Struggling Bedmaker." Other people? Well, it came easy for them. I was good at some things . . . regular bedmaking was not one of them. Perhaps I should just be okay with that.

So I gave up. Back to months of no bedmaking because I knew if I tried again, I'd just fail again. Then one day, we recorded a Poddy with our co-host Danny Valdes. Danny talked of how he grew up fatherless . . . well, he had a series of stepfathers and his mom's live-in boyfriends . . . one after the other . . . most who treated him terribly. Once he became a husband and father himself, he had no anchor, no role models to emulate. He struggled to want to come home to his family and be the father and husband they needed. That was until he realized it wasn't him that was broken . . . it was his identity. *"What if you could, Danny?"*, he asked himself. *"What if you could be that father and husband your family needs and deserves?"*

He started doing the things a good father would do, saying the things a good father would say . . . telling himself he was that guy . . . that present father . . . that loving husband. Years later, he is that dad . . . that husband. His beautiful family of 4 children and a gorgeous loving wife is intact and thriving. He believed, practiced, and acted his way into it. (Get Danny's book . . . *"What If You Could?"* to read his whole story.)

He *believed,* practiced, and *acted* his way into it.

"What if I could be a bedmaker?", I asked myself. What would a bedmaker do? What would a bedmaker think? How would she act? She certainly wouldn't have struggling thoughts over it . . . thoughts of failure. A bedmaker would enjoy making her bed. She'd see an unmade bed and think . . . "Oh, that's not me. Let's make that bed!" So, I started calling myself a bedmaker . . . thinking of myself as one. I was a natural at it . . . bedmaking wasn't hard or foreign to me; it was part of who I am. *"I live a bedmaking life,"* I told myself.

Years later now, as I sit here writing this . . . you bet I'm a bedmaker. If you walked into my room right now, you'd see a made bed . . . not perfectly . . . I'm not going to win any bedmaking competitions, but it is done! My room is not spic and span, but it is picked up, and it works for me . . . it gives me peace . . . it is my resting place. But here's the thing . . . there are still days when I don't make my bed. That used to derail me . . . I felt like a failure . . . *look at me, not making my bed again* . . . shame . . . defeat. Not now. I'm a bedmaker whether my bed gets made or not. It is intrinsically who I am. Natural bed makers don't give up bed making. It is ingrained in their matrix. So, I naturally return to it after a day or several days when life gets away from me.

"Pearl, the Bedmaker." If I can do it, you can, too. But perhaps for you it is not bedmaking. Perhaps it is something else you'd love to stick at, but you've failed at over and over again. Take a page from Danny and believe, practice, and act your way into it. You're not that struggling girl with the soda addiction and the one who can never pass on the fries. You're the naturally health minded girl . . . you live and think and speak and act like someone gifted in this talent. Put on your identity and "what if you could it" until you're "coulding" it for realz.

I WILL CONFIDENTLY SAY:

I'M THAT GIRL WHO BRINGS ORDER AND BEAUTY TO HER HOME

I'M THAT GIRL WHO ASSIGNS HIGH VALUE TO SMALL TASKS

I'M THAT GIRL WHO DOESN'T DESPISE THE FEW
MINUTES IT TAKES TO SET THINGS RIGHT

I'M THAT GIRL WHO PICKS UP RATHER THAN STEPS OVER

I'M THAT GIRL WHO'S BECOMING A NATURAL AT
WHAT SHE USED TO FIND CHALLENGING

I'M THAT GIRL WHO WEARS AN IDENTITY OF SUCCESS
NO MATTER HOW MANY FACE PLANTS SHE TAKES

CHAPTER THIRTY-SIX

I'm That Girl Who Crowns and Anchors Her Meals

From Serene . . .

Me hungry . . . me eat now . . . me eat anything . . . me not think through . . . me just grab and swallow . . . me food monster! There is so much wisdom in the third chapter of Ecclesiastes, where it talks about a time for everything. There may have been a time in our lives when shoving anything and everything in any order into our mouths was the general approach. But there comes a different time . . . one of maturity and responsibility, where wisdom, forethought, intelligence, understanding, and creativity are required when it comes to food.

Don't worry . . . I'm not insisting you become a detailed meal planner here. Personally, I am not much of one . . . at least not when it comes to pre-planning two weeks' worth of dinners and having them all lined up for perfect rotation. More power to you if you are; you keep being you! By jingoes, though, I do have a simple plan that overarches every meal and snack (unless I decide to throw in a cheat treat occasionally). You could say it is more like a motto or a mission statement that is formed into a question. When I ask this simple yet inspiring question, my answer becomes my meal success.

What is anchoring and crowning my meal?

Asking this question will allow you to achieve incredible diet success (and I don't mean "diet" diet . . . but just wise eating) whether you're a meal planner or a winger. Wingers . . . well, we can get ourselves in a lot of free-spirited trouble. This question can make the winging life a successful one. But even if you're a planner . . . sometimes planners are just not able to plan . . . am I right? Or you're thrown off your plan, and bad things happen! This question can save you, too.

Let's start with the first part of this powerful question. Every meal needs an anchor. An anchor will stabilize your energy, allowing for a firm meal foundation to set up sustained fuel burning. Anchors allow you to stay solid and satisfied for 3 to 4 hours. There is no "rush and crash" response when you have put down your anchor. There is no wacky snacky behavior when the anchor is set. Protein is your anchor that fuels "Steady Eddy" post-meal behavior.

When I anchor my breakfast oatmeal with Creamy Dreamy Plant Protein (shameless shout-out to one of my favorite THM Focus Foods), I am answering this empowering question. When I anchor morning sautéed veggies with a couple of golden eggs, I am answering this empowering question. When I anchor my fresh lunch salad with a salmon filet, grilled chicken, or sachet of tuna, I am answering this empowering question. Or I can anchor salad with a full cup of black beans from the plant anchor kingdom for a change-up. When I anchor a large smoothie for an on-the-go lunch with some whey protein I am answering this empowering question.

Every *meal* needs an *anchor*.

Maybe I choose to answer it by putting a spoonful of collagen in my afternoon hot tea or coffee that I enjoy with a handful of raw walnuts. For dinner, I might throw down the anchor with some crumbled grass-fed beef tossed amidst some purple cabbage and a delicious sprinkling of spices. Sometimes I enjoy lentil soup for dinner. Lentils are rich in protein so they're an anchor all on their own but perhaps I feel like making the anchor even a little steadier with a small addition of pulled chicken breast. I anchor with a celebration of both animal and plant proteins in my diet, and I combine them together sometimes when they need a little help from each other.

No matter my choice of anchor, I always answer my question, or I don't put my fork to my mouth . . . or better yet . . . I answer it before putting anything in the pan or the toaster. Speaking of toaster . . . I anchor my whole grain sourdough or sprouted toast with egg whites then pile on the sautéed veggies, or I anchor toast with low-fat cottage cheese, then top with peaches and cinnamon or fresh tomatoes and black pepper. Or I anchor a toasted sandwich with lean turkey, then pile with veggies and mustard or salsa.

The second part of my question for success is . . . what is crowning my meal? Practically every meal needs a crown. Food is elevated to something way more than just a tummy filler when you put a crown on it. A crown nourishes your cells and fills in and tops up nutrient deficiencies. It balances your meal, making it not too heavy and all sorts of just right. It usually comes in deep, rich, or bright colors. It makes sense when your think of the royal gems embedded within a crown . . . jewels like emeralds and rubies. No meal or snack should be stripped of this royalty and splendor. I place a crown on every meal unless I choose without shame to go peasant and plain while traveling or just 'cuz it's my once in a while "no crown meal" . . . that's okay here and there.

These crowns I speak of are found in the plant kingdom. Your first go-to crown should be deeply pigmented greens; yep, those vitamin and mineral packed non-starchy leaves and other veggies. Never be stingy with these leafy and other veggie crowns . . . pile them as high as you want as they enlarge the volume of your meal and boost health. Coming in at a tie for the win are berries and vibrant colored fruits.

> Food is *elevated* to something way more than just a tummy filler when you put a *crown* on it.

Superfood green powders such as spirulina, moringa, and matcha also have their crowning place . . . especially if you're not eating the leaf form in your meal. Let's not leave out antioxidant-rich baobab powder or mushroom extracts like chaga. You can even dust your crown with extra credit crown dust with super spices and herbs like cinnamon, ginger, turmeric, oregano, and even black pepper. I am leaving so many out, but you get the gist.

I know what some of you might want to ask here . . . can beloved cocoa and coffee be crowns, too? Aren't they from the plant kingdom, and aren't they rich in antioxidants, flavonoids, and polyphenols? Well . . . 'tis true that Americans get more antioxidants from coffee than any other source. But guess why? Because they're not eating enough of all the other crowns. Coffee and cocoa need not be deprived of their crown status . . . they make the grade but be sure you're pulling more crowns into your meals than just a cup of coffee or stevia-sweetened hot chocolate.

So, let's get practical and look at how this plays out in real life. I might have my anchor figured out . . . maybe it is chicken. But I can't just have a chicken breast and brown rice. I have to crown it! This way, my body is treated like royalty. I will answer the question of "Where is my crown?" by choosing a nice pile of deeply pigmented broccoli.

Maybe it is afternoon snack time, and I am in afternoon shake or smoothie mood. I am anchoring it around a combination of a half scoop each of whey and collagen. Sounds all wonderful, but it AIN'T that wonderful until I crown it! I will answer my crowning question by throwing in a handful of spinach which won't detract from the flavor, or ¾ cup of frozen okra, which will bless my whole body, especially my gut and waistline, and I'll barely know it is in my shake. Or perhaps I just go with a teaspoon or two of dark green moringa and spirulina powders or a little matcha blended into the mix.

I crown my oatmeal with cinnamon and crown my lunch with dark salad greens. I crown my desserts, snacks, and salads with deep purple and rich red berries, and I crown my tilapia fillet with a fresh mango and cilantro salsa. My steak is crowned with a line of asparagus soldiers, and my fried eggs are crowned with garden zucchini or golden squash hash.

This question becomes fun. It's rather addicting.

You get the picture, right? This question becomes fun. It's rather addicting. I crown my All-Day Sipper drink with turmeric, and I crown my pot roast with creamed organic spinach. I crown the afternoon picnic with dazzling pink watermelon, and I crown my tuna fish sprouted grain wrap with finely chopped cucumber and onion and a side of pickled ruby red beets. You can crown with kale and crown with the jewels of bright purple cabbage or onion . . . here a crown, there a crown, everywhere you go a crown.

So, there you have it . . . your two special questions that can change your health and diet success from mediocre to amazing. Remember them . . . "What is my anchor?" and "What is my crown?" Love it? Good!

I'm that girl who literally adores asking these questions, and I have been feeling the benefits for years. That old season where it was just . . . anything goes on my plate hodgepodge . . . it's over, girlfriend! I feel better than I did at 18 because at 18 I never asked myself these "new season" questions. There is a time for everything, remember? And it is now time to experience the amazing benefits of anchors and crowns.

I WILL CONFIDENTLY SAY:

I'M THAT GIRL WHO IS A "THINK IT THROUGH" EATER

I'M THAT GIRL WHO REMEMBERS TO ANCHOR HER MEALS

I'M THAT GIRL WHO CROWNS HER MEALS BECAUSE SHE IS ROYALTY

I'M THAT GIRL WHO UNDERSTANDS THIS IS HER SEASON FOR WISDOM EATING

I'M THAT GIRL WHO GETS CREATIVE WITH DIFFERENT ANCHORS, BOTH PLANT AND ANIMAL

I'M THAT GIRL WHO LOVES TO EXPLORE, UNCOVER, AND BRING TO HER PLATE AND CUP THE VAST WORLD OF BEAUTIFUL CROWNS

CHAPTER THIRTY-SEVEN

I'm That Girl Who Trains Her Resting Face

From Pearl . . .

You know you have one, right? I discovered mine by noticing it in the mirror as I passed and happened to see myself mid-stride. I also noticed it (in a scary way) on my phone selfie . . . nothing like catching yourself there for a reality check . . . am I right? Sadly . . . it was also brought to my attention from comments from my children. "Why are you sad, mom?" Or even worse, "Why are you stressed, mom?"

"I'm not," I would answer, but my face told a truer tale. There were many years when I felt worn down by life's troubles, and my face learned to wear that stress, worry, and too often, pity for myself. Unknowingly I had lived with these thoughts so much, their expressions had taken over.

You've probably seen this in others. Some end up with a pinched, bitter look on their face from years of resentment and feelings of anger toward others. Some end up with a downtrodden look on their face from a sense of victimhood over issues they couldn't get over. Some end up looking so eaten up with life that their resting face displays a world of pain.

"What is your resting face?" It is a good question to ask ourselves.

Mine wasn't pretty. I feel I am an okay-looking person. My sweet husband calls me perfect and beautiful, but that is love speaking. I'm sure not a supermodel or a Miss Universe, but I do my best with what I've been given, and I look after my face and body. I'm happy with my looks, and as I get older, I only get more comfortable with them. But all of that is wasted with a sour or dour resting face.

Imagine if the hint of a smile became our *resting* expression.

I'm on a journey to train mine into a smile or at least into a peaceful, calm look.

Science tells us that a smile can help heal our bodies. Imagine if the hint of a smile became our resting expression. No, I'm not talking about a constant, huge, fake grin because that would just be weird . . . but a composure of peace, of calm, and deeply entrenched happiness. A smile whenever I see my husband . . . when I see a stranger . . . when I see my children. A smile for myself. A smile for God. That is what I am in training for. Wanna join me?

I WILL CONFIDENTLY SAY:

I"M THAT GIRL WHOSE MOUTH CORNERS ARE
NATURALLY UP RATHER THAN DOWN

I'M THAT GIRL WHOSE FACE LIGHTS UP A ROOM

I'M THAT GIRL WHOSE EYES AND MOUTH
SPARKLE WITH LOVE AND JOY

I'M THAT GIRL WHO CHECKS FOR SOUR, DOUR
EXPRESSIONS AND REMOVES THEM

I'M THAT GIRL WITH THE PEACEFUL RESTING FACE

CHAPTER THIRTY-EIGHT

I'm That Girl Who Doesn't Eat Chemicals

From Pearl . . .

While sitting at our boarding gate at the airport recently, I was people watching and enjoying my preflight snack from Starbucks of Egg White Bites and an Americano coffee with just the right amount of some creamy half and half poured in. Oh, egg white bites . . . I gotta give them a shout-out, the red pepper ones specifically. They're yummy, savory, protein-rich morsels of delightfulness, and nobody's even paying me to say that. But I digress . . . the story continues that I was not feeling deprived in the least as I love seeking out healthier options at cafés and restaurants . . . a fun hobby of mine.

But then a lady came down and sat right across from me. She pulled out a package of Doritos and started crunching while scrolling on her phone. Crunchy things . . . they're my favorite! I thought of that zesty, cheesy taste of Doritos and suddenly wondered why I had to be all egg whitey when she could be all Doritoey. It didn't seem fair.

I looked around . . . I couldn't spy any Trim Healthy Mamas . . . they'd be aghast if they spied me eating Doritos. "Why not, though?" I thought, feeling rather sorry for myself in my no Dorito dilemma. "Why shouldn't I get to chomp on Doritos every now and then, too?"

But then I started to think about what Doritos actually are . . . sure, the corn base was once food from the earth, but the finished product is far from it. Yes, I could go get a bag and secretly binge on them, but would I be better off? How would I feel afterward and for the rest of the day? Did I really want to eat those chemicals? The answer was easy. No, of course I didn't.

"I'm That Girl Who Doesn't Eat Chemicals," I told myself. "You know yourself, Pearl," I said inside my head. "Chemicals are not what you put in your body . . . it's not that you are caught up in legalism and are a super stricty food Nazi . . . it's just that eating chemicals is not who you are!"

> Would I be *better* off?
> How would I feel *afterward* and for the rest of the day?

I stopped feeling deprived and actually began to feel empowered. I smiled at the lady across from me, hopefully not in a superior "I know best" way, but I was just glad she was enjoying her snack. I didn't need her snack; I had eaten my own snack and now felt settled that my decision was a wise one for me.

"Comparison is the thief of joy." That's what our mom always told us kids growing up and it rang true that day. I was happy until I compared snacks. But I'm on a different path with different goals, which means my food choices will look different

> I'm on a different *path* with different goals, which means my food *choices* will look different from others.

from others. If I'm to be a healthy mother to my adult children, grandmother to my grandkids, and healthy and passionate wife to my husband . . . then . . . you bet . . . I DON'T EAT CHEMICALS! Yeah . . . a chemical may slide in here and there . . . I'm not obsessive about it, but on the whole, they're not what I put in my mouth.

When temptation for foods that are processed to barely recognizable beckon . . . you know the ones . . . full of dyes and chemicals or sugar and trans fats, remember it is what you tell yourself that will prevent you from constantly caving. Summoning all sorts of self-control, yet still feeling deprived due to our HARD choice only leaves us with a sad, diet-wounded feeling. You can tell I'm speaking from experience here. An "I can't have that" mentality is powerless. It takes all our authority away. But "I don't have that!" Oh, it brings back all our power. It puts us back in charge, and we can steer our bodies to better, healthier places.

I WILL CONFIDENTLY SAY:

I'M THAT GIRL WHO EATS FOODS FROM THE EARTH

I'M THAT GIRL WHO IS EMPOWERED BY HER HEALTHY CHOICES

I'M THAT GIRL WHO DOESN'T PLAY FOOD COMPARISON WITH OTHERS

I'M THAT GIRL WHO, WHEN FACED WITH TEMPTA-TION, ASKS HERSELF HOW SHE'LL FEEL AFTERWARD

I'M THAT GIRL WHO SAYS, "I DON'T" RATHER THAN, "I CAN'T"

Another reason to stand straight (shoulders over hips over heels) is because it protects our whole pelvic floor. Many female issues such as prolapse, incontinence, and diastasis recti (when the stomach muscles split and separate) are often caused and worsened by poor posture. Muscles that are given loads to bear are more able to hold up and stay strong through the years . . . it is when they are not given work that they atrophy. If I slouch, this throws my weight off the muscles that are supposed to hold me straight . . . my all-important back chain of muscles . . . my glutes, lower back, and back of thighs. They stay engaged and toned when I give them my body weight to balance through a straight stance. They also speak to my pelvic floor . . . holding all my female insides together as they should be held. Slouching takes my weight off them and throws it, giving the weight to muscles that weren't created to hold me up. So, while standing and sitting aligned makes me look better on the outside, it is also doing wondrous things for me on the inside.

Now when I catch myself slouching, I don't chide myself for it . . . I just remember who I am and naturally come into line. Queens don't slouch.

> Slouching *decreases* lung capacity, impairs blood flow, increases pain and inflammation, decreases brain function, causes mineral bone loss . . . the list goes on and on.

I WILL CONFIDENTLY SAY:

I'M THAT GIRL WHO REPRESENTS THE ROYAL FAMILY

I'M THAT GIRL BESTOWED WITH GRACE AND POISE

I'M THAT GIRL WHO PROTECTS HER INSIDES BY ALIGNING HER OUTSIDES

I'M THAT GIRL WHO GIVES HERSELF QUEENLY POSTURE CHECKS

CHAPTER FORTY

I'm That Girl Who Knows When to Go to Bed

From Serene . . .

I didn't always have the prowess and prudence to know how to lure myself to the final destination of the day. Sometimes I still don't know how to efficiently land the plane, but on the whole, my identity of late is that girl who is earlier to bed and earlier to rise, rather than late to bed and a drag the next day.

This overarching, new banner I now wear has been doing wonders. One of the problems with being up too late . . . and you'll probably relate to this . . . I tend to turn into a munchie monster the moment the clock strikes a minute past 9:30 pm. If I'm not into my off-to-bed routine, well, suddenly I'm ferociously hungry . . . and not for sane food. Just give me a jar of peanut butter and a spoon! Give me hearty chunks of bread and thick pieces of cheese . . . TOGETHAAA!!! I'm not much for craving junk food, but even healthy foods like these shoveled without sane thought into a tired human is usually not the wisest decision at the end of the day. I'm only hungry because my body is trying to gain energy for the marathon of staying awake past wisdom.

Cortisol (our stress hormone) is likely to surge after 10:30 at night. Overproduction of cortisol puts weight on the belly and burns up adrenals. While that one surges, another one sinks. Our human growth hormone, responsible for repair and youth and a trim, svelte body is pretty much turned off if we don't go to sleep at a reasonable time. That's not what we want . . . we want it churning all night

. . . repairing and preventing accelerated aging. Wise sleep times are what keeps it turned on.

You'd think with this choir of chirping knowledge in my head for all these years I would have been a sleepy nigh-nigh angel face at wise hours, but no . . . I was often the one still raiding the fridge and holding my eyelids open at 11:00 pm on a weeknight. But I hadn't yet learned to change my identity from peanut butter nighttime victim to champion of the 9:30 pm pillow.

Deciding that I AM ONE OF THOSE sensible bedtime folks has been the thing to finally do the trick. I tell myself that I love to go to bed at a time that captures all of sleep's benefits. I tell myself that retiring to my peaceful boudoir, where I can decompress in its dim chamber of womb-like calm is my 9:30 spa-scapade. As the hour closes in before that, I'm that girl preparing for her getaway. Nursing babies are sometimes with me, but aloneness is not what I need . . . it is the stillness.

Your sane hour of sleep sensibility might be an hour or so later or earlier than mine, and of course, everyone is different, but you know when you have passed the threshold when your body is still awake, but your brain has left the premises. I understand some of us don't have a choice . . . there are evening work hours and even overnight shifts for some of us. I believe God can sustain us through crazy sleep hours if we have no choice in the matter. But when we have a choice, a bedtime by 10:30 pm makes the most health sense.

> I tell myself that I love to go to *bed* at a time that *captures* all of sleep's benefits.

To be totally transparent, before this "I'm a Wise Bedtime Girl" mindset, I had tried at other times in my life to get to bed earlier. I knew the perils of staying up too late, so I got super vigilant about getting more sleep. I became the sergeant major of my bedtime . . . and got myself a ridiculous sleep schedule. At the time, I had burned out adrenals from stress and struggle. I had not yet walked into any "I'm That Girl" understanding or victory. So, I gave myself an 8 o'clock bedtime and became super vigilant about it.

That only worked against me. My early bedtimes, my special sleep mask, and my "Do Not Disturb Mom" demands on my family didn't heal my adrenals because now I just stressed about getting enough sleep. I'd go to bed and start analyzing and obsessing about my health or lack of it while it was still light outside in the summer . . . my children still wanting to play in the warm, summer evening, and here I am frowning myself off to bed. The whole attempt was miserable, and I was no fun for several months . . . constantly obsessing over counting my sleep hours.

My new identity of now being a sensible sleeper is just that . . . sensible. I don't count my sleep hours. I am not that girl who doesn't know how to stay up on the weekend with the family and place the final crowning pieces on the jigsaw puzzle over laughter and hot chocolate well after my bedtime. I ain't the girl who doesn't know how to leave the sleep rules at home (for the most part) when she goes on a vacay. I am not that girl who freaks out and gets bitter and anxious over lost sleep through seasons of crying babies or tough life curveball seasons. I'm not that girl who doesn't know how to choose to feel as fabulous as possible on three hours or less if that's all she can possibly and honestly grab. But I sure am that girl who has made a lifestyle of honoring 9:30 pm and heralding my natural affection for it. That girl who sustainably retires early.

I love being a sleep dork . . . except for a weekend night here and there when my party-animal, pajama-loon self takes her rightful turn. Retiring early has not only curbed the snacking frenzy of late-night deranged food choices, but it has also made me capable of waking up early and getting a head start to my day before the whole household erupts in joyful chaos. By the time I am serving my family breakfast, I feel like my day has been founded well and off to an exciting and positive start. Energy is up because I already feel ahead and not behind.

Yeah, I'm that girl who manages her days well by supervising her pillow date the night before.

"Serene, off to bed with you, girl!" I lovingly tell myself.

I WILL CONFIDENTLY SAY:

I'M THAT GIRL WHO KNOWS HOW TO CREATE A SLEEP-INDUCING ENVIRONMENT

I'M THAT GIRL WHO OWNS THE AWESOME ABIL-
ITY TO TURN OFF THE LIGHTS

I'M THAT GIRL WHO GIVES MY BODY A BREAK
FROM FOOD BY GOING TO BED

I'M THAT GIRL WHO LOVES GOING TO BED EARLY BECAUSE
IT MAKES HER MORNINGS MORE PRODUCTIVE

I'M THAT GIRL WHO DOESN'T BECOME BEDTIME OBSESSED

I'M THAT GIRL WHO MAKES WISE BEDTIMES
A DELIGHTFUL, SUSTAINABLE HABIT

CHAPTER FORTY-ONE

I'm That Girl Who Never Gives Up!!!

From Serene . . .

There is a part to this particular identity that actually came naturally to me. I was born a passionate wolverine. I hated to let go of something even when the going got tough. I found a weird sort of fulfillment and pleasure from digging in my heels and trudging through the sludge of a project because hard meant it probably was good for me . . . right?

Well, I learned the hard way that being a girl that never gives up is only a positive identity when it's for things in life actually worth fighting for. I held onto crazy, unsustainable diets for years even when my body was screaming, "THERE IS SOMETHING WRONG WITH THIS ONE!!!" I dug deep tent pegs of dogmatic opinions into the ground of my youth and then grew older, only to realize that life would have been better lived had I let some of them go. But just because there are things in life that aren't worth contending for (such as becoming a raw food vegan and not letting one bit of cooked food touch my lips for seven whole years) doesn't mean there aren't things that gut grit, impassioned sense of duty, ardent zeal, and committed courage, weren't created to defend.

I think of lasting love and beautifully aged marriages. These don't happen without some grit and daring audacity against human impulses to choose forgiveness rather than offense and patient hope rather than present doubt. An enduring marriage is a thing to dig in and fight for . . . the epic grandeur of united hearts with a lifetime of matching memories. You bet I'm that girl who will dig in and cling and not give up on this.

Perseverance in uncompromising faith is something else I'm not giving up on. If God said it, then I'm gonna believe it, no matter if my experiences and earthly sight screams the opposite. The Bible calls me blessed for believing without seeing. I'm going to hold on with every breath and every heartbeat. Wild horses can't drag me from the soundness and truth of scripture.

Hope and belief for my children . . . you can't budge me on this. Children may turn prodigal or have emotional, mental, or physical conditions that test every fiber of our strength. But girls . . . we keep holding onto hope, to love, to life, to our commitment to see them through to a better day. Ten thousand chariots can't pull us from our post of prayer and pivot of action.

Choosing *life* on my plate! Yes, that's me. I'm that girl who does it *over and over* again.

Holding onto my health . . . cultivating then continuing in habits that heal and maintain my well-being are worth defending to the end. Choosing life on my plate! Yes, that's me. I'm that girl who does it over and over again. I'm not boasting here. I'm proclaiming it, and I want you to do the same. I'm never throwing in the towel on sustainable, life-giving exercise. God made our bodies to move and process foods from the earth. These are worth digging our heels in over.

I have much room to mature in this "finisher" identity still. I have projects I started months ago, some paintings and sewing that I intended to finish and give to others as blessings. I haven't finished them yet, and the accuser wants me to believe I never will . . . that I might as well give up because I'm a starter, not a finisher when it comes to my crafts. Too bad for him, as I am determined to be that girl who will follow through until the gift is on their lap with shiny ribbon and tape. Even if I can only carve out 10 minutes every week to work on them, I will just plod along until my plodding gets the job done. A "finisher" is the kind of girl I am . . . well, at least I'll start with sharing her identity until it's truly mine . . . mine . . . mine.

Many of us have personal dreams and visions that are worth holding onto, right until it is clear God decides otherwise. I have recently miscarried three babies, and knowing I am 44 and not 24, I have this deep desire to finish strong with another life in my arms. I am contending for this dream and speaking life into it. I actually talk to my womb. I try not to do it in public areas like airport bathrooms, but I may have slipped up a time or two. "You are not done yet . . . you precious womb . . . you are primed for life." I declare fertility and fruitfulness over it. It's actually fun and addictive stuff, this talking to your body. You could try it risk-free for thirty days, sanity back guaranteed if ya' want. If I'm being too spooky for you . . . just put this on the shelf!

A "*finisher*" is the kind of *girl* I am.

Along with speaking over my body, I am eating as nurturing as I can and taking my whole food prenatal vitamins. I have put some time into researching fertility-boosting super-foods, downing the smoothies choc-full of them, and daydreaming about future baby names. If you promise not to tell, I have also (TMI) elevated my legs post "Foxy Mama" stuff to give the little swimmers a leg up with their swim upstream. Now you can delete this sentence from your mind . . . pretty please. My main reason in sharing all of this vulnerability is to show you my tenacious refusal to give up this close to the end. It would be different if I didn't have the dream. I know it seems more logical to enjoy the large crop of children we have raised and take a final breather from pregnancy, babies, and all that comes with them. But I still have this longing inside of me, and I don't think it is upsetting to God, so I am holding on until God shows me otherwise. If His sovereign hand decides another story, then I will praise Him and rejoice that He knows best. This way, I can rest confidently that it wasn't by my words, deflated hope, negativity, or lack of courage to fight that my womb never bore life again. He may have another future for me and I'm determined to delight in whatever it is. But for now . . . I'm still baby making and hoping!

This is just one area of contending in my story. It might pale compared to the things you have contended and fought for . . . are still fighting for. Don't give up, you hear? These chords within our soul that lasso dreams and hold on for dear life are meant to play on long after their first sounding. Let's let them echo and ascend into a crescendo in the heavens where their melody dances above us in the night sky. When we look up and get our face out of the dust of fear and failure, we will see they are still very much alive.

Some women I know are my heroes. They have had to fight for intimacy in marriages where one has become wheelchair-bound or when both have simply lost sexual function. They have chosen to not just give up without staging a big push back on something so precious as their "oneness". Their intimacy may not look easy like it does with young sexually primed adults, but oh, the preciousness of it!

Others I know have had debilitating accidents and have had to fight for every syllable voiced, step taken, and hand raised. I know a woman who was seriously burned in an outdoor barbecue accident where her flowing skirt caught fire, and her whole body burst into flames within seconds. Recovery was extremely intense. Her husband wished he could just give in and spoon feed her as the simple task of her trying to feed herself was beyond tortuous. But they both knew that if she didn't move her arms herself, the scarred skin would tighten and strap down her muscles, trapping her mobility. Every dip into her bowl and movement to meet her mouth was more pain than she could describe with words. Thankfully she loved to sing opera, so instead of screaming or just giving up because of the fear of repeating the misery, she just let it rip and sung in her loudest operatic voice whatever came into her mind. Family members said it rang victoriously through the house. Her story is so inspiring to me. She was a singing overcomer and got creative instead of disabled.

Reminding each other of this kind of tenacity is needed because, too often, our human strength jumps ship when the waves get bumpy. But God's strength is endless, limitless, and new every day. Tapping into that supernatural endurance is much easier than striving on our own. We have the simple choice to receive it, to rest in it, and to be daily revived in it so we can run this good race and be a strong finisher!

I WILL CONFIDENTLY SAY:

I'M THAT GIRL OF UNRELENTING GRIT

I'M THAT GIRL WHO KNOWS WHAT'S WORTH FIGHTING FOR

I'M THAT GIRL WHO LASTS WELL BEYOND HUMAN LIMITS

I'M THAT GIRL WHO FINISHES WELL

I'M THAT GIRL WHO NEVER TURNS HER BACK ON TRUTH

I'm That Girl Who Moves for Life

From Serene . . .

The desire to move . . . to stretch . . . to search out and investigate all possible dimensions of movement is an instinctual ambition from before we were even liberated from the womb. Even before a pregnant mama detects those first tiny butterfly kicks, her little athlete has been kickboxing to the motivational beat of her heart.

The celebration of dance, the privilege to walk, the exploration of reach, the freedom to run and jump and leap . . . Wow, and yay for our brilliant bodies designed for all this.

We have 650 or so skeletal muscles in the human body. There are actually billions more smooth muscles that are part of the autonomic nervous system, responsible for squishing and squeezing stuff from one place to another. That's a lot to keep greased and running well. We don't want any of these awesome God-given parts to get all rusty and crusty from not taking good care of His prezzies (down under for presents). They're gifted to keep us agile and free.

What we don't use, we are gonna lose . . . we've all heard that right? But is there a way to keep a healthy attitude toward movement that doesn't land us in Sad Camp? You know what that camp is like . . . we drag ourselves into exercise because we know we *have* to, but really, it feels like a yucky, no fun part of our to-do list. And due to this sadness of Sad Camp . . . we usually give up on it because nobody wants to be sad for long. Or if not sad . . . then there are two other extremes . . . "burned out" from overdoing it or "dried up" from not doing it at all.

I'd like to nominate a better way to look at movement. I put forward "love of movement" for your consideration, and hopefully, by the end of this little light-hearted life changer, I'll get plenty of you saying "aye" for it with me. Maybe you don't feel like you love it now; those feelings will come later . . . for now, you'll have to just wear the identity until it feels true. For the sake of sustainable strength and vitality that lasts our entire journey on this earth, I think this love of movement mindset is worth searching out and wearing.

Before we get more into how to put on this love of movement, let's talk about why we need to love it. Some of this you know already, but reminder seshes are good. And some of it might be new to you.

All this modern talk of getting all "et up" and "over the hill" as we age is not Biblical, nor is it found in cultures of the world that keep actively moving and don't grow up and hit a point where they somehow feel excused from this vital part of life. It is actually possible to experience lasting health and fitness well into the most latter stages of life. Joshua 14:11 proves my point, *"As yet I am as strong this day as I was in the day that Moses sent me; just as my strength was then, so now is my strength for WAR, both for going out and for coming in."* Caleb was 85 when he said this! Getting stiff and starchy isn't inevitable.

He said *"strength for war"* because he wanted to take the high hill country that was his inheritance and promise from the Lord. The Anakites occupied the territory and were mighty men, descendants of giants. Their cities were large and fortified, and yet here is this 85-year-old man chomping at the bit for WAR! He wasn't leaving it to all the 18-year-olds with newly blooming biceps. He reckoned his tried and tested muscles were perfectly adequate to enter the fight and were powered by the overarching strength of the Lord. The story goes that Caleb was victorious and that Hebron has belonged to his descendants ever since.

> Maybe you don't feel like you *love* it now; those feelings will come later . . . for now, you'll have to just wear the *identity* until it feels true.

Studies show older adults who are physically active sustain a better quality of life and have a lower risk of dying. Regular exercise fights disease and drastically slows the rate of muscle depletion as you age. Research conducted in 2007 and published in an article entitled *Resistance Exercise Reverses Aging in Human Skeletal Muscles* used candidates who were an average of 70 years of age. These seniors engaged in resistance training and closed the strength gap between themselves and a group forty years younger by 36% in a mere 6 months study. Strength training turns back the clock . . . literally.

Muscle biopsies from this research revealed astonishing reversals of 179 genes associated with aging!!!!!! The mitochondria (the primary engine of energy production) is where this decline usually occurs with age. This study proved that when it comes to the mitochondria, strength training reversed nearly 40 years of aging! But exercise doesn't only protect the mitochondria, it also safeguards your DNA from the wear and tear of aging. Anaerobic training like our *BLAZE* exercises in the Trim Healthy Mama Workins (shameless plug for our 20-minute core healing and overall body fitness workout sessions) and strength training like the exercises in the *BRAVE* section, develop your fast-twitch muscle fibers which blast fat, reverse insulin resistance, and rev your metabolism primarily by acting on your telomeres.

What on earth are telomeres? They are darling precious things that cap the DNA chromosomes in your cells and protect them from damage. Think of them like the end caps on your shoelaces. Aging shortens your telomeres eventually. They become unraveled, leaving your cell's chromosomes vulnerable. People who exercise have been shown to have longer telomeres than their peers who are sedentary. A study on 2,401 pairs of twins aged 18 to 81 probing the questions of telomeres, exercise, and age found that participants that spent more than 3 hours per week enjoying vigorous movement and resistant training had longer telomeres than subjects 10 years younger!

Studying twins made sure these differences were not due to genes but solely due to the lifestyle factor of exercise. Diets, disease status, socioeconomic status, smoking, or nonsmoking . . . the whole thorough gamut was taken into consideration and carefully factored in for accurate results. It came down to this . . . when one twin exercised more than the other, they consistently had longer and more durable telomeres. In short, this means they became wired to live longer.

I say all this to encourage you that exercise is not just for the young or middle-aged. If you are 85 and reading this, get your telomeres and your mitochondria ready for a rejuvenating overhaul and for the adventure of stepping into a time machine set for a few decades earlier. If you are 18 and reading this, you will hope-fully be motivated to cultivate this healthy habit of being active that has such splen-did kickback your whole future life through. If you are 37, 48, or 56, yay! You can maintain what you've got or gain a bunch back, depending on what you put into your new or freshly encouraged habit. Personally, at 44, I'm revving myself up to move this incredibly designed body God gave me like the smart twin. I sure ain't going to be the dumb one . . . he-he!

Exercise escorts energy into your bloodstream and actually fuels you. That's right, exercise (not slug your guts out stuff), but jolly good movement can feel like a little meal. It takes glucose from the stores in your muscles and releases it to spread about your body. Sometimes I am sooo tired in the afternoon because I have just been sitting around. When I go out for a brisk walk, I feel energized and lose that "snacky, pecky, have to eat every 20 minutes before supper" feeling. I've heard people say exercise will make you hungrier. I have to disagree. Exercise will feed you! There's smart snacking . . . I'm all about that. But there's stupid snacking, and I've done my share of that, too. Adding exercise into our days can curb the snacks we think we need after our already sensible snack. What's not to "love" about extra energy and sane boundaries to our snacking life?

Now that we got some "why's" to love exercise out of the way, let's get back to how we can cultivate it. Love is patient and kind, the scriptures tell us. It is not brutal obsession. Enjoying the gift of movement and learning the art of body train-ing can be fun and exhilarating, but just like anything wonderful, it can also be perverted into enslavement and a ball and chain dirge existence.

I'm so thankful to have a wonderful love relationship with exercise now, but it wasn't always this way. Just as I had to learn some hard lessons with food extremism, I also had to learn with exercise that "drill sergeant" adherence and obsessing over the duty of perfection never bred life in me. If I didn't tick the exercise box on a particular day, I would feel like a failure and be emotionally miserable. This type of attitude made the joy of movement a "have to" instead of a "get to".

Love is full of gratitude. When we love our husbands properly, we wear a mind-set of thankfulness for who they are and how they bless us. We don't fall into nitpicking their not-so-great points. This applies to exercise too. I have learned over the years that if I want an active life to be sustainable, there has to be this gratitude involved. We get to move, girls! We love movement because we have been blessed with bodies primed for it. Movement completes us!

Now this doesn't mean that you have to "love" the feeling of burning muscles and being out of breath. It doesn't mean you have to feel feelings of actual love when sweat is running down your chest and you wonder why you are huffing and puffing when you could be still and sipping coffee instead. But love overarches all that. It may mean that the "love" part comes by "loving" your body into this habit of vitality or "loving" yourself by allowing rest days, and just crazy hectic days without "having to" exercise. The "love" may come by honoring your family by loving them enough to create this exercise habit, that will keep you around longer and more physically involved in their lives. No matter what, remember the grateful LOVE . . . the humble LOVE . . . the love of movement that makes babies antsy to go from scooting and crawling to walking and running. They're so elated to do so. Remember the privilege. Some folks can only dream of the freedom to be able to move their bodies and get their hearts pumping and massaging their cells to health.

> If I want an *active* life to be sustainable, there has to be this *gratitude* involved.

Another way to bring love to the heart of exercise is to do what you love. There are one or two caveats to this, but I'll get to them in a jiff. If you love to walk . . . walk. Walk outside when you can . . . walk inside to walking YouTube videos if you can't. If you love to swim . . . swim. Is it streaming workouts, old-fashioned DVD's or great outdoor hikes that beckon your leap? Is it dancing, even if you look like a loon, or sprint intervals or volleyball . . . or whatevaaaah? Just do it. Sorry to copy Nike, but they're right on that slogan. Do kettlebells or just grab your babies or grandbabies and swing them around any ol' how making them laugh like hyenas because of how "sillyfitfun" you are. It doesn't really matter as long as you find the exercise you love, and then practice this love. Keep your gratitude for being able to move and your budding love for it around in your thoughts. Send up a little prayer of thanks or two before you exercise . . . we do it before we eat . . . why not before we move? "*Thank you, Father, for the ability to move my limbs and get my heart pumping. I honor Your creation of my body by tending to it. May You bless and strengthen my heart and my muscles during this session . . . Amen.*" Can I get an "Amen," SISTAHS!!!!! WHO'S GOING TO START PRAYING THIS WITH ME???

> Keep your gratitude for being able to *move* and your budding love for it around in *your* thoughts.

Let's get to the first caveat . . . if you are a full-time hater of all forms of physical exertion, then you've got to fake the love till ya make the love. The other is that alongside this hopeful "love" of your choice of training, you might have to swallow a toad from time to time. What!!!!!??? I'll explain.

Just doing what you love without a toad from time to time might not give you the best bang for your buck. A little toad (code word for torture) occasionally thrown in the mix gives awesome rewards. Just remember, "a toad for a treat." My sister Pearl has a special love in her heart for all of the "Workins" (our workout training plan I mentioned earlier that heals your core while it gets you fit) except for the "Lungies in my Grungies" session out of the 8 sessions in total. She hates . . .

> You've got to *fake* the love till ya *make* the love.

nope . . . she loathes the Lungies. Does that mean she doesn't do them? Nope! She swallows the toad. She just holds her nose and shoves it down the hatch. The key is not to think about it too much. Once swallowed, that toad goes to work, making her body stronger and more resilient to other toads. God made toads, too . . . along with the prettier green frogs, He made turd brown toads. They have their place.

You see, what doesn't kill you makes you stronger . . . using all sorts of overly done phrases here, but this one absolutely fits. The whole point is to get out of your comfort zone from time to time and make your body stretch itself to a higher level. Don't get me wrong. I'm not talking long hard-core workout sessions that leave you lying on the floor like a dying cockroach. I am just saying, don't get boring and comfy and stay "same ole, same ole" when you can chuck a toad in the ring from time to time and progress into your unique form of awesome.

If you literally can't swallow a toad whole . . . cut him up a little bit and nibble as you can. Place him between a nice fluffy sandwich of pre-coffee and an after-hot steaming shower with your favorite song blaring, while you relax under the spout, all the while sipping your favorite protein-iced shake. Fabulous how you can dress up a toad. He's almost delightful now.

Keeping the "love" alive with exercise can also be encouraged by never getting into ruts and being adventurous enough to try different things. I'm not talking about the varying forms of exercise anymore; I am now addressing the ways in which you fit it into your busy life. Personally, I have a hard time getting the mojo to exercise in the afternoon. For decades, I always preferred working out mid to late morning. I thought it was my only sane time. But life has become soooo busy and cray-cray lately that fitting it into my lovely mid-morning zone makes me be a rusher and a hectic pusher. I always thought getting up early to exercise would be the most "spartanest" love-sabotaging thing I could ever do. But lately, it has been either get up early and exercise or do no exercise at all. I refuse to let my body rot, so up early I get and guess what? I have completely fallen in love with it.

As I mentioned, I used to think that the 10:00–10:30 am mark when breakfast was digested and there was a little break in the responsibilities of the morning was my only real doable exercise option. To be honest, though, with the warm tea just sipped and going soothingly down, I wasn't ever really in the mood to rev it up and do the clams and the squats. This recent early morning exercise try-out has been a huge game-changer.

I go to bed earlier so that I don't cut back on any healthy sleep, which is a winner because in doing this, I also slay the nighttime snacking monster. Our mom always told us, too, that the hours of sleep before midnight are the most refreshing and restorative. I set the alarm for 5:30 am, and when it rings, I just get up before I start to think. I get my cute black yoga pants on and head to my workout corner. First, I spend a few minutes having a heart-to-heart with my best friend Daddy God, then I suck on a teaspoon of manuka honey or swig a 1/4 cup of kombucha for an energy burst and then just press play. (I'm old school and still love DVD's.)

I have this strange and wonderful sense of stored up energy and clarity from placing nothing between sleep and the lovely toad, and strangely, everything that used to be hard is just a whole lot easier when I'm the only one up. The house is quiet, and I can really get in my zone. It's over before I realize (I rarely do more than 15–30 minutes, 20 minutes is about my jive), and then I treat myself to a scrumptious protein smoothie that I sip in my hot shower while listening to worship music. I am up early enough that I even get time to massage in some lotions and potions while still praising. There is so much love in the whole morning that by the time the household erupts, I am the love bug ready to hug all of them. This is a big difference from my crusty-eyed, bed head self that awoke to a big "to do" list and was already feeling behind.

Now, if this whole thing I just described to you still sounds like spit and vomit because I typed the numbers 5:30, then just rebuke the whole idea and resist the devil, and he will flee. If early mornings make a hater out of ya, then run away, please! Fast! Run! It is not for you at this time.

This joy of feeling fit and the journey along the way is something to dearly protect. Don't let my early morning exercise story shenanigans make you feel like you have to clone me. Find your own best time. Maybe it is in the afternoon. Maybe it is in the evening . . . and I say that not even really wanting to type it because I am not a huge endorser of late-night exercise. I don't encourage after-dinner workouts unless it is just walking (gentle walking is fantastic after dinner). Personally, I think intense workouts in the evening mess with the winding down of the day, and they do not protect your circadian rhythm, hormones, and body chemicals that promote sleep. But hey! Don't let me put a big "hate" on your nighttime sessions if that is "love" for you. The love is the healthiest part of it all. Try things out. I'm not your exercise boss . . . just your encourager . . . oh, and your warner!

Here's my big warning . . . over-exercising turns on cortisol and inhibits healthy weight loss, so don't get too encouraged to the point of obsession and injury. What does exercise obsession look like?

- When you wake up so early just to get your session in that you're missing adequate sleep.

- When you don't know how to enjoy rest days. You absolutely don't need to do more than 5 workout sessions a week (4 or 5 sessions is a nice balanced amount), although walking every day is fine if you love it.
- When you exercise intensely for over 30 to 45 minutes (unless it is natural outdoorsy hiking and walking . . . that's just great stuff that's always good for you).

If you're trapped in this unwise, unkind, and unhealthy over-exercise pattern, I want you to take my hand. I've been there, and I want to . . . need to . . . pull you out . . . come on . . . grab it . . . grab my hand! Let's get you out . . . out . . . out! I know it feels like this is your only way . . . you have to be cruel to yourself to be kind. But that's one phrase I'm using now that is not the truth. You have to be kind to yourself to be truly kind.

Having said this, if you are sitting here wondering if your 20 to 30-minute session a handful of times a week is too much . . . no worries, you are just "not being sedentary." While over-exercising devours a small group of people, it doesn't snare the majority of folk. The opposite is true. Most cultures are intrinsically more active than us Americans. (I'm still a Kiwi by birth, but I live here in the US and think of this as my home.)

This sustainable approach to movement that screams FREEDOM instead of prison is a truly precious privilege. I have chosen to create the love, protect the love and sustain the love, because strength, vitality, and healthy spunk are gifts extended to me. I have been gifted these 650 muscles and a beautiful life to move them throughout. It is truly a choice to open and celebrate or neglect the gift and let it rot.

> This sustainable *approach* to movement that screams FREEDOM instead of prison is a truly *precious* privilege.

I WILL CONFIDENTLY SAY:

I'M THAT GIRL WHO LOVES TO GET HER HEART RATE UP

I'M THAT GIRL WHO MOVES HER BODY TO
SET IT FREE (no rust buckets for bodies)

I'M THAT GIRL WHO PUTS "LOVE" INTO HER EXERCISE

I'M THAT GIRL WHO GIVES THE "EXERCISE SAD CAMP" A SHOVE

I'M THAT GIRL WHO REMEMBERS THE PRIVI-
LEGE AND JOY OF MOVING

I'M THAT GIRL WHO DOESN'T MIND AN OCCASIONAL TOAD

CHAPTER FORTY-THREE

I'm That Girl Who Values the Mundane

From Serene . . .

Big things are made up of a bunch of little things. It takes 206 bones to build up the frame of an adult human body. If just one of the littlest of these bones is out of joint or broken, you will surely know it. I don't know how many times I have injured a teensy little part of the farthest region of my body to be found demonstratively exclaiming, "I didn't know you needed your pinky toe to do everything . . . I can't walk or drive or even sit down on the loo properly with this little thing not working right."

The events in life that take our breath away with their magnificence and significance are all made possible by the everyday humdrum moments that cultivate the right environment for something marvelous. It's the constant nighttime peeing . . . I mean, each trip traversed in the dark over the LEGOs and dirty laundry you have been too morning sick to pick up is part of the miracle and journey to birthing a human from your belly. Each jab in the ribs, every episode of heartburn, and every hormonal tear shed is collected in the bottle of nine months that, when ripened and ready, will overflow into the wine of baby joy.

Even the Kingdom of Heaven is described in a parable as starting from something as small as the tiniest of seeds. This puny tidbit of a mustard seed was the precious beginning of something that, when fully grown, was the most grandiose of all trees, and the birds of the air nested in its magnificent branches.

We were all microscopic once. One of the reasons why I am unashamedly pro-life is that the fullness, design, creativity, potential, power, capability, essence, nature, being, soul, personality, and totality of a human life is packed into this seemingly insignificant speck. It's this extremely small beginning that God has so sovereignly and wisely designed to be the right of passage to usher life.

1 Corinthians 1:27 talks about God choosing what seems foolish to the world to confound the wise and what is weak to shame the things that are mighty. Verse 28 in the Holman Christian Standard Bible translation goes on to say, *"God has chosen what is insignificant and despised in the world—what is viewed as nothing—to bring to nothing what is viewed as something."* This glorious mystery is colossal and reaches far beyond the point I am making. It enfolds faith and even the quantum realm, which, as we've discussed elsewhere in this book, the scriptures were well aware of before it was science. But it is in this regard for the small beginnings, the seemingly pointless, the humble, the sometimes worthless and meaningless things in the eyes of worldly reason, that God wants us to recognize and appreciate.

All those diapers we mamas have changed mean something to God. The constant stack of dishes and the perpetual hungry bellies chirping at you all day and hanging off your skirts for another crumb . . . all significant to the God of the Universe. He calls this humble life powerful. Each and every pot scrubbed and toilet cleaned is an influential task in building up something great . . . your lasting family legacy. Humility is the way of our tremendous God. He chose to come from a speck too, and then to be birthed through an unassuming young woman and be laid in an animal trough.

> He *calls* this humble life *powerful.*

God chose little David, young and skinny, and refused his tall, strong, and handsome older brothers to be king. He used the simple little thing in young David's hand to defeat the giant. That silly little sling and a plain ol' stone.

When God commissioned Moses to lead His people out of slavery, He asked Moses what he had in his hand. Moses answered, "A staff." That stick was all that was needed. God can use the simple thing in your hand.

You can achieve the fullness of your purpose and all of God's promises for your life with what is already around you. You can bloom right where you are . . . with laundry, babies, grocery lists, and homeschooling if you're in such a powerful season. If you're in another one that has you out of the home more . . . every car ride to work can be filled with praise and thankfulness and power through dwelling on things lovely, pure, and positive as the scriptures urge us all to do. You can move mountains right from your so-called mundane setting.

Every nutritious meal you take time to make . . . never despise those mundane minutes puttering around in the kitchen, heating pans, chopping, and sprinkling. Each time you fill a plate with greens and healthy protein and natural fats or gentle carbs, and when you take those 30 little seconds to season it up and present it in a way that makes you feel blessed to have a mouth, nose, and eyes . . . these moments are to be highly esteemed. They may look menial, and perhaps you and I have looked down on them in the past, perhaps even despised them, but they add up to huge positive changes in our bodies, and their significance is beyond worth.

> . . . never despise those *mundane* minutes puttering around in the *kitchen,* heating pans, chopping, and sprinkling.

Every single little time you say "no" to sugar . . . just that one small decision adds up to untold benefits for your body and your mind.

Pearl and I grew up with our mom telling us a story of when she was early married. Mom was, and is, a very motivated, world shaker of a woman, and prior to getting married, had been very involved in missions and big ideas. Small projects and small-mindedness were not the stuff our mother got out of bed to get busy with. One day when she was feeding dozens of nappies (cloth diapers) through the old ringer washing machine for three babies under 17 months, she lost her cool. The twins and their older brother were crawling around her feet at the washing machine when the thing broke, and she slammed her fist down on the top of it, yelling out to God. She cried, "I'm sorry, Lord, for this life I'm living where I can't do anything great for You. I can't serve you anymore. All I do is wash nappies, and I'm stuck in this little home all day!"

It was there by the pile of poopy cloth nappies that God spoke to her in her heart. She began to understand that she had never done anything as grand as she was doing now among the soiled laundry and crawling humans. This moment by the washing machine changed the course of her life. It birthed her revelation and eventual nationwide ministry encouraging mothers in their powerful calling of raising children. She realized she was in her Father's perfect will, and one day a giant stately tree would grow from her small menial offering, and fruit . . . good and ripe and influential, would sprout for generations.

I have ever been changed from this story myself, and when another dinner needs to be served, and more little teeth need to be brushed, I remember the power and purpose in small steppingstones.

Rivers are crossed, and feet stand on the soil of new land, through the small progress made between one stone and the other. When it comes to quintessential potential, small is huge, and boring is spectacular. Baby steps cross miles eventually. We grew up with that famous verse in Zechariah 4:10 (NLT) that tells us, *"Do not despise these small beginnings . . ."* This is a truth that sets the trudging feet free to leap and dance.

> When another *dinner* needs to be served, and more little teeth need to be brushed, I remember the *power* and purpose in small steppingstones.

The humble, the simple, the small . . . God regards them all. Luke chapter 1 records Mary's song of praise. Verses 46 through 52 say, *"My soul magnifies the Lord, And my spirit has rejoiced in God my Savior. For He has regarded the lowly state of His maidservant; For behold, henceforth all generations will call me blessed. For He who is mighty has done great things for me, and holy is His name. He has shown strength with His arm; He has scattered the proud in the imagination of their hearts. He has put down the mighty from their thrones, and exalted the lowly."*

Research shows that even our health is exalted by humbling ourselves to enjoy mundane tasks. A new study published in the journal *Mindfulness,* reveals that chores can relieve stress, boost your immune system and have a positive impact on your mood. The lead researcher, Adam Hanley, was inspired to research the key to finding out how chores can become health boosters after he noticed his 91-year-old grandmother always enjoying washing dishes at big family gatherings, while he did not find joy in it at all.

He noted that attitude is the big game changer . . . allowing joy to flow in simple things. The repetitive action of daily chores with the right focus was linked with soothing the mind and body and rewiring it for creativity. Some of my best ideas or light bulb moments have come while scrubbing in the shower or washing dishes in the warm suds while staring mindlessly out of the window. It's that humble beginning that births greatness.

Small things and small beginnings have a potent influence. It takes just a tiny rudder to move a massive ship upon the sea. It's that little bit of yeast that raises the whole big lump of dough. It's just one set of loving arms that rocks a slumbering baby. Just one word can speak life and decree a victory. Just one simple little choice over and over . . . to love, to laugh, to mend, to enjoy, to worship, to truly live.

> The repetitive action of *daily* chores with the right focus was linked with soothing the mind and body and *rewiring* it for creativity.

I WILL CONFIDENTLY SAY:

I'M THAT GIRL WHO KNOWS THE POWER OF LITTLE STEPS

I'M THAT GIRL WHO DOESN'T MIND STARTING SMALL

I'M THAT GIRL WHO FINDS MY TIME IN THE KITCHEN RELAXING

I'M THAT GIRL WHO KNOWS HER TIME
SPENT AT HOME IS NOT INSIPID

I'M THAT GIRL WHO KNOWS HUMILITY IS HER HIGHEST GOAL

I'M THAT GIRL WHO'S LITTLE "NO'S" TO SUGAR
ADD UP TO HUGE ACHIEVEMENTS

I'M THAT GIRL WHO RECOGNIZES THE INSIG-
NIFICANT AS MAGNIFICENT

CHAPTER FORTY-FOUR

I'm That Girl Whose "Always Wants More" Is Not in Charge

From Pearl . . .

I'm a well-fed girl. I really am. I never skip meals . . . like ever . . . unless I'm fasting for spiritual reasons. And my meals? They are no little "diety" type of things, let me tell you. I eat big . . . smart big . . . not dumb big . . . but big. I'm a volume eater (which I look at as my superpower, not my curse) so I really fill my plate with tons of yummy veggies, and, of course, I also enjoy nice protein and either wonderful carbs or glorious fats. That's my Trim Healthy Way, and oh, how my body loves it so much!

So, no . . . I'm not deprived in any way. I also get to have a lovely snack every afternoon. I even get to eat dessert if I want a little something after dinner. I can bless myself with a wise choice of a bit of stevia-sweetened chocolate or another Trim Healthy treat like a nice light pudding . . . such a perfect way to end my meal! Sometimes I'll even eat cake (THM, sugar free, healthy cake) after my meal. Food deprived is certainly not what I am. I end the day blessedly and comfortably full.

But . . .

There's this voice in my head. You might be familiar with it. It says stuff like, "Pearl, go get you a little more something-something. Go keep the pleasure alive! You'll be so sad and bored if you stop eating now. You know that stopping eating is such a sad, sad, lonely, robbed feeling."

I consider this and think to myself, *But I just had dinner . . . my stomach is not empty. It feels quite right.*

But the voice keeps on, "What if you just had an extra little helping? Or perhaps go get you half of one of those muffins you made earlier today and had for your afternoon snack. Remember how delightful those were?"

The voice starts making sense. I mean . . . I do love eating! The voice senses an inroad and urges me on, "Go on . . . you know you don't want to stop. What . . . you're just going to sit there on the couch and do nothing? Where's the fun in that? When you're on the couch relaxing after your day, you need to eat."

Ugghh . . . sitting there not eating seems suddenly hideous when I envision it. So, I do the voice's bidding and eat half that muffin. And oh boy, the voice is right. It sure is enjoyable. There's bliss in every bite. But then it's over.

The voice says, "Go get the other half . . . Might as well finish it."

So, I do.

Then the voice says, "You're still peckish, aren't you? Poor you, having such a hungry evening, aren't you? You need a handful of nuts, me thinks. Go get a handful . . . you'll stop after that."

So I do.

Then the voice says . . . "Just another half handful of nuts perhaps . . . then you'll be truly satisfied."

So I do.

BUT I'M NOT!

I am not truly satisfied because this voice is lying to me. It is only feeding my mind hunger. This is not natural, healthy stomach hunger which can be filled up. This is mind hunger which always wants more.

> This is not *natural,* healthy stomach hunger which can be filled up. This is *mind* hunger which always wants more.

The only way I end up not eating more when I give in to this voice is to get a stomachache from constant nibbling and going back for another little bit or handful or piece of food experience. Or I end up rather disgusted with myself.

I had to finally learn to identify this lying voice because it is ever so sneaky. It makes all sorts of sense at the time, but I've come to realize that it's not a wise voice at all. It is filled with foolishness. It keeps me unsatisfied.

The awesome thing is, though . . . it is not in charge! Not if I decide it's not. I'm so thankful I now know it for what it is, and I'm learning to mute it. I'm so done with how frequently it makes me sorry for myself and not able to be content in the moment.

I've realized I'm actually that girl who *can* sit there on the couch in the evening to unwind after dinner and not feel robbed without putting food to my lips.

The scriptures tell me there is a time to plant and a time to reap, a time to laugh and a time to cry. Well, there is a time to eat and a time to take back the reigns and tell myself, *Kitchen's closed, Pearl! Sip on your tea and just be grateful. You are well-fed and perfectly fine without always longing for another food experience. If the voice gets too loud, go show it who is boss and brush your teeth or crochet something or snuggle with your husband. Put your faith into action and do something to defy it! But another bite of muffin . . . what a whopping lie that you need that. You're good as you are.*

> There is a *time* to eat and a time to take back the *reigns* and tell myself, *Kitchen's closed!*

Yep, I'm that girl who can tell that voice, *Nah . . . I'm good.* Then just shut it down.

I WILL CONFIDENTLY SAY:

I'M THAT GIRL WHO IS WELL FED

I'M THAT GIRL WHO IGNORES SNEAKY VOICES

I'M THAT GIRL WHO LOVES TO EAT BUT KNOWS HOW TO STOP

I'M THAT GIRL WHO CAN BE CONTENT WITHOUT NIBBLING

I'M THAT GIRL WHO IS A FOOD LOVER BUT NOT A FOOD ADDICT

I'M THAT GIRL WHO KNOWS HOW TO CLOSE A MEAL

CHAPTER FORTY-FIVE

I'm That Girl Who's Hot for Her Man

From Pearl . . .

Why not be hot for him? I mean, if you're married, you're hopefully doing the one thing that is (or should be) exclusive to marriage.

Wearing a mindset of "hotness for my husband" just helps things along and takes so much of the complication out of it all. Maybe I'm oversimplifying a complex subject . . . this married sex thing. There have been thousands of books written to help waning sex lives. Nothing wrong with them . . . probably a lot right . . . I've read some of them myself. They delve into sorting out junk from your past and his past . . . figuring out boundaries, and who gets to initiate or who gets to decline. Oh, the long list of things to work through in the married sex world. In the end, I just live by this simple motto, "I'm hot for my husband." I'm happier, saner, healthier, and yeah . . . not to boast but . . . smarter because of it (I'll back the smartness thing up soon).

I love not having to consult and analyze my current level of physical desire or lack of it. I'm not hot for him due to how perfect or imperfect he has been today as a husband. I'm not hot for him because he brought me flowers, or massaged my shoulders, or did dishes or said kind things to me. I'm not hot for him because the stars align, and somehow, I'm perfectly in the mood. I'm simply hot for him by mindset, and my body usually follows along.

I'm certainly not hot for him because it has been so easy to be that way. Don't get me wrong . . . my husband is super attractive in my mind with his country boy/strong silent type/cowboy-ish kinda ways. All those things and more are what attracted me to him in the first place, and they're still true close to 30 years later. But you think all those sensual neurotransmitters that were flying through my body at the beginning of our relationship have been there day in and day out for almost 28 years of marriage? Nope.

All the seasons of life have posed challenges to our marital intimacy . . . the babies in our bed stage . . . the teenagers in our home stage . . . the stress of hard financial times stage . . . illnesses we have both had to walk out of . . . decline in hormones we both have had to address. Our hotness for each other is from determination to stay hot for each other. We've had to talk some things out, too . . . still do sometimes . . . to ensure we both stay on the "hot for each other" page. Hotness can lapse without open communication.

All I'm saying is . . . long term hotness in marriage doesn't just happen . . . it is cultivated and then continually watered. Then its roots go deep. They become strong and not easily shaken. The winds come . . . you better believe they still come to my marriage . . . they try to blow the passion out. But when your roots go deep, you're not easily shaken.

> Long term *hotness* in marriage doesn't just happen . . . it is *cultivated* and then continually watered.

He's a good guy, my husband, not a perfect one. I don't want a perfect man, though, and who am I to talk about being perfect? I'm betting your man is decent, too. If not, you wouldn't still be married to him. So, I'm writing this coming from a "you probably have a good man" kinda angle. If your husband is currently involved in adultery or some other serious sexual issue . . . I think that calls for different advice than what I am bringing here, so you can just skip this little blurb and hopefully get some solid guidance elsewhere. But if your man is solid, then sister lend me your ear . . . he deserves your hotness just for the very fact that you're married to the guy!

I say this because many other relationships have love . . . familial love, parental love, friendship love . . . but they are not sexual. Marriage is that whole next intimate step . . . two becoming one, and that is definitely sexual. Sex sets marriage apart from every other relationship because it is based around this one intimate thing the others don't have. Married love can, of course, include friendship . . . awesome to be best friends with your spouse. I'm pro being my hub's bestie, but that AIN'T the fullness of marriage. Marriage starts out sexual, and unless a grave disease or an accident completely steals sexual function . . . it should stay sexual. If you're married . . . then be truly married. Don't play-act like you're married and just be roommates!

How's that for me getting on your case and in your face? I'm pretty fired up about this topic. But hear me well because I am not one of those judgy woeful voices saying, "Submit to thy marriage bed, oh ye doormat woman! It's your sad cross to bear, but ye must do it for thine husband." I am saying this intimacy is for you as much as it is for him . . . that's the awesome, Biblical way. The scriptures don't say, "Wives . . . service your man." They actually say . . . our bodies are one another's . . . both husband and wife share one another. At its beautiful core, married sex is a shared passion. But for something to be shared, you gotta be in on the gift.

Oh, how the accuser would love to steal the sex from us married girls . . . steal it and give it to the depiction of Hollywood or Netflix. You know . . . where sex is glamorized pretty much for new relationships only . . . usually for the unmarried . . . where hormones are high, clothes are torn off, consequences are abandoned, and the challenging stuff of "together life" hasn't been lived through yet. Nothing wrong with high hormones; personally, I like 'em, but the sex depicted on screen and idolized in our culture is not gold sex, me thinks. Gold sex is refined by fire. Sex is golden when it is fought for, nurtured, tended to, and valued as so very precious for marriage.

There are so many "why's" for keeping your married sex life tended to. I don't have room in this little chapter to list all the health benefits regular married sex

> Sex sets *marriage* apart from every other relationship because it is based around this one *intimate* thing the others don't have.

brings to your body and mind (and your husband's body and mind). I want to focus on the identity of being hot for your husband rather than the reasons to do so here. But those reasons? They are numerous and astounding. We did two "Foxy Mama" themed episodes (ep. 29 and ep. 32) for our Trim Healthy Podcast. You can go to our website to listen or listen on your fave podcast app. We also had a whole chapter on this topic in our first original book . . . the 34th chapter of Trim Healthy Mama. The most read chapter of that book, and for good reason. The studies are all cited there and referenced on the podcast, so I'm not going to list them all here. I'll just briefly give you the highlights, then get back to the identity of actually being hot rather than the reasons to be so.

Gold sex is refined by *fire*. Sex is golden when it is fought for, nurtured, tended to, and valued as so very *precious* for marriage.

Sex, in a committed relationship (marriage has the advantage here as uncommitted sex doesn't show all these same health benefits), averaging twice weekly does the following:

Greatly boosts your immune system by raising immunoglobulin levels (people who have regular, monogamous sex get sick far less)

Increases your HGH hormone for more youthful skin, hair, and muscle tone

Reduces your physiological age anywhere from 6 to 10 years

Raises your oxytocin levels, which fights depression and anxiety

Decreases your pain through a rise in endorphins (and oxytocin)

Keeps your breasts healthier

Protects and improves your brain function through neurogenesis (the creation of new neurons in the brain)

Improves incontinence

Provides you with health-boosting shots of zinc, vitamin C, and B12 (from your husband's semen into your highly absorbent vaginal walls)

Burns on average 200 calories

Improves your sleep

Powerfully fights depression

Lowers both blood pressure and heart attack risk

Boosts your libido through raising estrogen and testosterone (strange but true . . . most women who have more sex want more sex)

Helps and prevents vaginal dryness and thinning

Significantly lowers prostate cancer risk for your man

So, there you go . . . be healthier, happier, smarter, better hormonally balanced, and protect your marriage from the winds that want to blow it apart! But how . . . when you don't feel like it? You don't feel "hot", or "sexy", or "in the mood"? Sometimes you don't even know if you feel attracted to your guy anymore. What's a girl to do? And if I'm not telling you to grudgingly be that "good wife" who caves into sex just for her husband because it is the last thing on her mind . . . what am I actually telling you to do here?

I'm telling you to put on a mindset of hotness . . . an overarching identity to be that girl who is hot for her man.

Let me explain it with some examples. I love how the scriptures exhort older women to teach younger women on how to be good wives, etc. I'm referring to that Titus 2 scripture you've probably heard more than a few times. It's a goodie. Perhaps you haven't seen a marriage emulated that has kept hotness alive. I have . . . and observing marriages like this has helped me so much. I want to pass along some examples from my own family in case you don't have any in your own life. I want you to know long, hot marriages are there . . . alive and well. I also hope that my own marriage will be an inspiration to you.

Let me tell you about our Aunty L. My sisters and I talk a lot about her and her hilarious ways. We laugh about her words and actions because we can always rely on her to say something a little bit inappropriate and slightly naughty at family gatherings. Our Aunty is a Jesus lover and an extrovert. She loves to encourage all her many nephews and nieces with scriptures. Her love for God continually bubbles out of her. When you're with her, you know she truly cares. She loves to hear about our lives and gives us solid advice when it is needed. But the very next minute, she'll see her husband walk across the room and say something along the lines of, "Oh . . . we might have to leave this party early . . . I'm just all flustered up with desire." Actually . . . that's a pretty tame example . . . she gets a little worse.

Doesn't matter who's listening . . . she'll just blurt it out. We heard these kinds of things from her when we were young children, and she is still saying them all these decades later.

She's half-joking, of course . . . but only half. She never actually leaves early to fulfill her barely restrained desires lol . . . but she looks at her husband with true passion. He just laughs . . . he's used to it . . . but I think he secretly loves it.

When one of our other aunties or uncles (she's one of nine children) give her the eye roll or say something in response, like "C'mon, L . . . keep it clean," she just grins.

She replies in all innocence, "What? God made me this way! I'm a very special woman!"

All of us cousins who have to hear this sort of thing from an aunty squirm a little and never quite know how to react, but deep down . . . we love it, too. We *really* love it because she has kept her hotness alive through a simple resounding mindset to stay hot for her man.

Aunty L. is in her mid-seventies now. This flame she holds toward her husband has nothing to do with primed hormones or newly ignited love . . . they've been married for eons. She is decades past menopause. But she proudly wears her hotness as an identity. She's the "crazy, loveable, hot for her husband" aunty that we all want to visit whenever we go back Down Under. We wouldn't miss it!

My encouragement for you to be hot does not mean, of course, that you have to be like Aunty L and publicly declare it all the time . . . you can be as private as you want. I'm just showing you that hotness can still burn decade after decade if it is a decision. I feel blessed to have been able to observe so many long marriages in my family stay burning hot. My parents are still absolutely head over heels in love with one another and their parents before them were the same. I come from a long line of hot marriages. My mom is more private about her and dad's intimacy, but you bet they're still doing it! I know because she loves to tell the following story. As a newly married woman, she met with an elderly lady who was in her 80's. My mom asked her how old you have to be before sex dies out in marriage. This woman smiled at my mom and said, "Well, I'll let you know when I get there." My mom is 80 now, but she repeats this story as often as she can. She told me the other day, "I could just stare at Colin (my dad) all day long . . . he's so dreamy." Now, my dad might be a nice-looking 81-year-old, but nobody would call him dreamy . . . just my mom . . . and that's just because she has cultivated a mindset of dreaminess for him through year after year . . . it's her truth!

My sisters and I love to encourage one another to stay hot. But my sister Serene here that you're reading from? She actually doesn't need too much encouragement; she takes after my Aunty L . . . perhaps not quite as inappropriate, but I'm always telling her and her husband to get a room. They just laugh . . . their behavior is not over the top or unsuitable for children to watch . . . it's just there . . . sizzling. She's always hugging and kissing him and looking at him with honey-moon eyes. Seeing this frequently modeled in

> Hotness can still *burn* decade after decade if it is a *decision.*

my family keeps me going . . . it inspires me . . . it makes sure I never grow cold. I love reminding myself that I'm from a family of lovers . . . it's in my veins. If this is not your family history, you can be the first generation of long lovers.

I love this expression . . . "long lovers." The term "young lovers" is famous, but I think "long lovers" should get the prestige. Imagine cultivating this long-lived passion and setting this amazing example for your own family history. Your grandchildren and children will talk about you. They will look back and be inspired. More than anything in my life, I want my children and grandchildren to look back and say, "Wow . . . she really loved him, and it showed."

You see . . . it does show. If we are to wear this identity of hotness, it will look and sound like something. It doesn't have to be over the top . . . but what does a woman who is passionately in love look like . . . act like . . . talk like? She doesn't say, "I've lost my desire." That would be a lie. Maybe she doesn't actually "feel" desire at that moment, but an overall identity of hotness prevails over current feelings. Thoughts and feelings of lost desire need to be quickly "**put off**," as we discussed earlier in this book. They don't belong. So, for the sake of long term, sustainable hotness . . . can we all just stop consulting our feelings of desire or lack thereof please! That practice is not only irrelevant, it's harmful.

In earlier chapters, we talked about what is truth and what is a lie according to God's ultimate truth . . . His Word. You may not feel "righteous," but who cares because the scriptures say you have indeed been made righteous through Christ. So why the heck do you have to actually "feel" hot to be hot? You don't. Feelings come and go. Truth stays. But tip . . . the more that you faith-talk, think, and act like you're hot . . . the more it will become your actual reality.

A girl who is hot for her man smiles at him . . . she touches him. In private, she says hot stuff to him here and there, and she initiates sex sometimes. She doesn't think it is only his job to do the initiating. Over the years, he doesn't ever have to wonder whether her hotness for him is fading. Even when hormones physically decline during seasons of breastfeeding or menopause, he "knows" she has an overarching hotness for him that will prevail even if her body goes through some changes.

For the sake of long term, sustainable *hotness* . . . can we all just stop consulting our feelings of *desire* or lack thereof please!

I'm not saying every night needs to be actually hot . . . meaning you don't have to have daily sex, but I am saying you do have to have regular sex. Exceptions, of course, are post-baby seasons or illness. All couples are different with frequency, and I wondered for a long time just how "regular" a hot for each other couple should be? I'm nerdy like that. It came down to this for me . . . if studies show the health benefits start at twice weekly . . . I think that's a fair place to say what "regular" is and go upwards from there if you want. You're not an awful failure if some weeks aren't quite so "regular." Life happens. But my opinion . . . once or twice a month is not cutting it.

So, if you will, join me in this little assessment that I like to do on myself . . .

"Pearl (insert your own name), are you hot for your man?"

This question is not asking myself whether I feel desire at that moment. It is simply my reminder . . . my activator to walk back into the fullness of a "hot for husband" identity if I've drifted. Sometimes I catch myself falling into coolness, and this question ignites me to reaffirm my identity. *Yes . . . that's me . . . I'm Pearl, the hot for her man girl!* And I once again start talking, acting, and loving like the true me . . . the hot me. Coldness is a lie. I **put** it off! Sure, it may feel like the truth if I've been practicing cold habits, but as we've been harping through this whole book . . . we walk in the new, not the old! If hotness doesn't feel authentic because it doesn't match up with my recent thoughts and actions, well, too bad. I'm going for hot because I'm called to walk in it! It is God's new, far better identity for me . . . His desire for me to be a fully loving wife who will leave a legacy of love that future generations can look back on and aspire to.

Before ending, I need to address one last thing. Personally, I think there is a lot of junk circulating out there (especially in Christian circles) about the stereotype of husbands always being "ready to go" and wives constantly fighting them off by feigning a headache. Sure, there is usually someone in the marriage with a bit of a higher physical sex drive . . . this doesn't always mean it is the man. It often is . . . especially with younger men, but guys go through physically challenging seasons, too. Men slowly lose their hormones as they age and this is accelerated by things like Type 2 diabetes. This particular health issue is on the rise due to modern diet and it sadly affects the desire and function of many men.

But sometimes it is neither hormones nor health issues, it is just that men are all different as we women are. Some men are just wired in a way that they are not constantly primed to want to jump into bed. I've heard from so many women over the years with questions about why their man "isn't like most men" and doesn't want to do it every night. If your intimacy is lacking because your husband isn't very interested, my best advice is to open up a discussion. True, many guys don't want to talk about this topic if they feel it is somehow their fault, or if they feel inadequate. But there are ways to do this without indicating, "You're failing me in the bedroom."

Coldness is a lie. I put it off!

Opening up a discussion about ways to optimize your intimacy can feel excruciatingly awkward, and even scary at first . . . especially if it has been a non-topic for a long time. But God wants great things for your marriage. And you **can** do this because you do not walk in fear . . . you walk in *". . . power and of love and of a sound mind."* (2 Timothy 1:7)

There are bio-identical hormones and other therapies that can help. It is a good idea to find a health care professional who is knowledgable in these matters and ask them about optimizing hormones if they are low. Low dose daily tadalafil can help some men and the use of certain peptides such as PT 141 may help both men and women with both sexual function and desire (you can give that peptide an online search). A well versed practitioner in these matters is worth seeking out. These can sometimes be incredibly helpful (think of them like the "figs" Serene talked about on page 286). Eating right and exercise are foundational, too. But the greater goal here is not to have your man performing perfectly functioning sex like a young stallion on a daily basis. The goal is sexual intimacy with much patience and understanding between one another. Your sex life won't look like the Joneses . . . meaning if you hear Laura's husband wants it every night, but your husband is fine with much less . . . you haven't been robbed! God gave you your man, and with much openness and discussion and determination to stay hot for one another, you two can become the best loving couple you can uniquely be . . . for God . . . for each other . . . and for future generations!

> The goal is sexual *intimacy* with much patience and understanding *between* one another.

I WILL CONFIDENTLY SAY:

I'M THAT GIRL WHO UNDERSTANDS THE PRECIOUS-NESS AND AWESOMENESS OF MARRIED HOTNESS

I'M THAT GIRL WHO LOOKS, ACTS, AND THINKS HOTNESS TOWARD HER HUSBAND

I'M THAT GIRL WHO DECIDES TO KEEP HOTNESS AFLAME THROUGH ALL THE SEASONS OF LIFE

I'M THAT GIRL WHOSE HUSBAND DOESN'T HAVE TO WONDER IF SHE'S STILL HOT FOR HIM

I'M THAT GIRL WHO REPAIRS BROKEN HOTNESS

I'M THAT GIRL WHO OPENS UP CONVERSA-
TIONS IN ORDER TO RESTORE HOTNESS

I'M THAT GIRL WHO WILL LEAVE A LEGACY OF
LONG LOVE FOR FUTURE GENERATIONS

CHAPTER FORTY-SIX

I'm That Girl Who Loves All Her Bits & Pieces

From Serene . . .

When I was a young girl, I was always the tallest. Growing up Down Under, in New Zealand and Australia, I often heard from well-meaning adults who had no clue of how their words hit. "You're such a big girl, dearie, aren't you?"

"Big" . . . it stuck in my head.

At 13 years old, I hit my full height . . . a half-inch shy of six feet, without one wee curve to help broaden out the giraffe impression. It didn't help that my best friend from down the road was 4 feet something and as cute as a button.

But let's go back a few years to when I was just 7. My gangly, long chicken bone legs looked like stove pipes next to that same best friend's dainty ones as we sat and ate lunch every day at school. It didn't take too long before I felt like I should finish less and less of my sandwich with every passing day. I was just too big.

By eight years old, I had full-blown anorexia and patted my stomach firmly down flat as I passed every mirror. The image I saw reflecting back at me was ginormous. The world was surely revolted by such bigness. I kept track of every morsel I ate and repeated those amounts in my head with a strict tally checker.

The natural hunger that grew like a monster within me to furnish my rapid growth in height helped slay the habit of only pecking like a bird at food. I am thankful for that ferocious growth hunger but suffered burdensome shame for many hours after feeling fullness inside of my belly. That fullness made me feel like Shrek the Giant until hunger arrived again, and the cycle continued.

Funnily enough, my body dissatisfaction flipped as I grew into my teen years. All of my lovely, little, fun-sized friends had grown nice and curvy, and I realized I was still a stretched-out GUMBY creature. I realized that skinny wasn't the cool thing to crave anymore. My A-cups were terribly lacking, so I resorted to stuffing my bras. Now as I passed the mirror, instead of worrying about my stomach and caving it in, I would only see my inadequacy in the curves department. Once upon a time, I was the big ogre of the play yard, and then, with the wind of a new season, I sadly identified myself as a pirate's favorite treasure . . . a sunken chest.

Comparing body types and evaluating my worth and beauty on whether I matched up to what my generation viewed as "pretty" bred worms inside my soul. They ate my confidence, my contentment, and riddled my mind with maggots of self-loathing. Instead of being a happy little clay pot, I was a mouthy bit of earth that thought she knew better than the Master Potter who had made her. I couldn't see the splendor that my Creator had in mind because I was nitpicking every detail without standing back and seeing the beautiful picture from His lovely and wise viewpoint.

It is interesting how we women with certain body struggles cannot imagine another with a different discord suffering the same low self-esteem. I have known very slender women with deep emotional holes in their spirit because they feel they weren't blessed with enough voluptuous vavoom and enchanting feminine curves. I have known heavier women who've commented that all the tight and toned little wisps of women must be supremely happy. The truth is that the accuser will eat all of us for dinner as a sad soup dunked with burned toast if we let his whispers define us.

Present-day . . . well, it took me years to get here, but I refuse to live like a shaky reed whose confidence gets snapped by appointing myself or others judge of my body. The only judge of my worth and beauty is my Maker and Father, who finds delight in what He made and calls His work beautiful. His loving thoughts of me are more than the sand of the sea, and He sings over me with rejoicing. He loves me like a bride.

I no longer desire a different shape. Thankfully, all those wasted days of despising my body are behind me. My bone structure and genetic coding of lighter curves and straighter lines is fabulous to me now. I refuse to be repulsed by my thighs, hate my stomach, or wish for anything other than my B-cup breasts. Yeah, I eventually made it out of the A's, but my B's sure do not define my self-worth.

Of course, I believe in tending to this precious gift of my body. It only makes sense to eat well, to exercise, and to look after my skin and hair. I'm a bit of a makeup girl, too . . . of the non-toxic kind. My dad used to say, "If the ship needs painting, then paint it." He was never referring to his daughters needing makeup to be beautiful. It was more of a tease about us primping and preening and taking up all the space and time in the bathroom. But I enjoy applying a dazzle of glam on the bow and love to paint up my ship from time to time with healthy makeup products. This is just my own little makeup passion . . . you certainly don't need to put makeup on to shine your own beauty.

I am determined to love all of my female stages along my future, too. To keep up dad's ship metaphor . . . I refuse to let my anchor stay back on the island of 18. I'd only miss the grandeur and adventure of gracing the horizon of menopause and beyond with a seafaring brave heart.

> I refuse to live like a shaky *reed* whose confidence gets *snapped* by appointing myself or others judge of my body.

Being a Princess might be special for a time, but every Princess needs to celebrate entering Queendom one day, and every Queen should celebrate the graduation to Empress. The New World was always the coveted expedition and passage of purpose for every true sailor. It is instinctive . . . *"Turn the page!"* Augustine of Hippo wrote, *". . . those who do not travel read only one page."* We were designed to explore, carve out, and take dominion of new territory. *"To travel is to live,"* was so aptly penned by the classic children's author, Hans Christian Andersen.

I asked my mom one day as she was nearing her eighties if she would ever want to go back a few decades and reverse the clock. She almost fell off her seat from the drama with which she displayed her utter disgust at the idea of return. "Ugh, I would hate going back even one year," she said. "I have never been so confident

We were *designed* to explore, carve out, and take *dominion* of new territory.

As a 40-something-year-old now, I have *traveled* past the first few islands and am far *happier* here than back there.

in who I am and my purpose on this Earth. I have grown out of all those insecurities, and I am totally loving my season." I was completely sidled by her answer. I didn't expect it, but it has blessed my socks off ever since.

My mother (I suppose she is Pearlie's mummy, too) is a vibrant, redheaded (from birth, but now from henna LOL), flourishing eighty-year-old who sparks life and bestows grace into every room she enters. I want to go on a similar voyage to the one she has taken in days to come. I will sail with excitement and won't be dragging my feet with any "I'm old, stiff, and ugly" junk. As a 40-something-year-old now, I have traveled past the first few islands and am far happier here than back there. But I don't want to stay here in the land of middle age forever. I am excited about taking a trip as a Countess of Courage or a Duchess of New Dawns to distant lands of dignity!

I will embrace the beauty of the brushstroke of time. My Father has chosen it in His creative wisdom. My job is only to smile, laugh, and live alive more . . . and to frown, scowl, throw fits, and live dead less. This way, my story, read through the lines of my face, will be glorious.

I WILL CONFIDENTLY SAY:

I'M THAT GIRL WHO REFUSES TO DESPISE HER BODY

I'M THAT GIRL AT PEACE WITH HOW HER POTTER MADE HER

I'M THAT GIRL WHO KNOWS THERE ARE BILLIONS OF DIFFERENT "BEAUTIFULS"

I'M THAT GIRL WHO DOESN'T NEGLECT HER SHIP

I'M THAT GIRL WHO WILL FIND HER BODY'S NEW HORIZONS DAZZLINGLY GORGEOUS

CHAPTER FORTY-SEVEN

I'm That Girl Who Practices Her Comeback

From Pearl . . .

So . . . you fell off the wagon?

Or perhaps it wasn't a mere fall . . . perhaps you spectacularly tumbled to the ground, then the wagon ran over you a few times. I'm talking healthy eating face plants here, but this applies to any "fall from grace" part of your life. It definitely applies to your "I'm That Girl" journey. Maybe you'll start out with full gusto right after reading this book . . . you'll change your speech and direct your thoughts with awesome fervor. But what if time goes on and old speech and thought patterns somehow sneak back in? Hear me well . . . I want you to come back and read this when they do. I say, "when," because I'm just going by my own journey. And I've had plenty of "when's." So, *when* it happens . . . I have a word for you here, sister!

But back to food wisdom abandoned. Maybe you caved to the doughnuts or the fries, and one meal led to another . . . to another. Pretty soon, you're weeks into mindless eating. You feel you're so far from where you were . . . it's not even worth trying to catch back up to that wagon. It is long gone . . . might as well just grab another doughnut.

Have you blown it for good?

My hands are holding your face right now . . . a little bit too firmly . . . look into my eyes! That couldn't be further from the truth! You're simply going to practice your comeback. Comebacks are a natural part of your journey. And the more

359

you practice them, the better you get. There is absolutely no shame in a comeback. There is only a Heavenly Father waiting with open arms welcoming you back to your true identity. There are only backslaps and that-a-girls. There is only a welcome home party. And parties are fun, so if you get a lot of them, well, more power to you.

> There is absolutely *no* *shame* in a *comeback.*

When you return to wisdom . . . to the "new creature" you are called to be, it is always right, always perfect, and always the exact thing to do. Living outside your new identity is what's foreign now. Oh, reverting back to old ways might feel kinda easy and cozy and deceitfully familiar, but it's not your real nature. It's not the new you we talked about in the very first chapter of this book. You've met her now . . . all her power and potential. Practicing your comeback is just getting back to your God-breathed, truly natural self.

In the past, you may have fallen out of wise ways and thought, *"Well . . . here I am again . . . this is just the true me, I guess. I'm back here because this is where I always end up . . . why even kid myself?"*

Baloney to that, Simba!!!!

You are an empowered daughter of the King of Kings . . . that's your true identity. So, get yourself off the ground and out of the lie! Shake off the dust, straighten your shoulders, and go be the real you! Go do the real you! Go proclaim the real you!

I don't care how many times you forget who you really are . . . even if you gain back 20, 30, or 50 pounds . . . multiple times. The very moment you wake up out of the sugar fog and wonder how you got there, you shove the shame and just PRACTICE YOUR COMEBACK!!!

Analogy coming your way . . . like Superman, get yourself to the nearest phone booth and do the quick changearoo into your "victorious" outfit. It's a simple, quick switch of identity from the old back to the new. Superman is far more comfortable walking around in his cape and boots than in anything else. The more time you spend wearing your new identity get-up, the more it will truly feel you. These switcharoo mindset comebacks can get faster and faster the more you practice them. Eventually, you'll be wearing your royalty garb far more than you will your old, out-of-fashion stuff. It will be the true familiar.

But let me be all get-out-honest for a minute as we say goodbye to our time together here in this book and hello to your own "I'm That Girl" journey. Even in the last few years, while writing this book, I've had multiple times of falling back into negative speaking and thinking. I've abandoned God's truth for my life. I've doubted, and I've failed. There have been days when I've felt like a hypocrite typing any words to you because I knew I wasn't perfectly "I'm That Girl-ing" in my own life. I'd hear the accuser's whispers, "Look at you . . . writing a book for other women while you're still full of fear . . . you just told your husband you're stressed . . . What a hypocrite! What a loser!"

Get yourself _off_ the ground and _out_ of the lie!

But you know what? He didn't win. Too bad for the accuser because I just kept practicing my comeback. I ignored his accusations and ran back into my Father's arms. I ran back to His Word, which tells me I have been made more than a conqueror. It tells me I haven't been given a spirit of fear. It tells me to rest in His wisdom. I realize old nature Pearl likes to try to speak from the grave sometimes. She's the one saying, "I'm stressed." She's the one doubting and fretting. So, I just turn her to mute and step back into the royal clothes of my new identity. I am clothed with faith, clothed with belief, clothed with love. I don't have to try for them . . . I only have to walk in them. They are gifted to me. Ahhhh . . . the peace and the certainty.

If you find yourself back in the brambles of unhealthy eating or if you find yourself back to thoughts and words of stress, despondency, fear or anger and you feel like a complete failure . . . a complete fake of an "I'm That Girler" . . . no, sister . . . you are not. Neither am I. Let's just put our rightful nature right back on . . . let's do it together . . . again and again, if we have to. There are no limits to our comebacks. They are free, and they are fantastic. They are God-designed and God-approved. Our amazing Heavenly Father actually originated the comeback; it is His mercies that are new every morning the scriptures tell us.

Just thinking about that makes me want to weep . . . how good is He???!!!! How unworthy we are in and of ourselves, yet He has made us worthy of each and every comeback and multitudes to come if we need them! I'm having me some church here right now! And if truth be told, I'm actually tearing up a little as I sit here at my kitchen table and type these words to you. It's probably because this is the end of this big ol' 47-chapter book that was supposed to take 3 months but took us well over 3 years. Feels like Serene and I have been talking to you almost everyday for these last few years and now we're leaving you to fly on your own after all this time. It's a little hard to let you go honestly.

Let's just put our rightful *nature* right back on . . . let's do it *together* . . . again and again, if we have to.

Don't get me wrong with the "weeping" thing though. I'm not patting my forehead with a special spiritual white hanky and letting black mascara dramatically run down my face here. But I am feeling His Spirit and there is dabbing at misty eyes going on. I'm feeling nudged to pray for you. It's about to go down so I hope you don't mind.

Father . . . amazing Father who pours Your love and good gifts all over us . . . thank You for Your life changing Words of truth. I ask that they leap from these pages and settle into the one reading them. May Your "newness" sink deeply into her mind and body and she'll know she is made for it. Help her open herself to be filled with all the wisdom, grit and victory that is the mind of Christ. Thank You for Your gift of peace . . . may she unwrap it. May it surround her and her family even in the storm . . . may she experience it and walk in it when it makes no earthly sense. Father, you see her needs, her trials, her daily challenges . . . I speak victory, healing and deliverance in the name of Your Son who defeated the accuser and his lies at the cross. I stand with my sister who is reading these words right now and together we remind You of Your Words. You told us to do this and You said they will not come back empty. So, here we are Father, we're standing, we're reminding . . . we are loving You back with every fiber of our beings. Finally, Father, may she never feel unworthy or too far gone for a comeback. May she be that girl who takes every single one you give her!

A to the men! That's it. I don't think God cares about long prayers. I think He likes 'em brief, so we don't get carried away with ourselves. But that's just me and my thoughts. Not trying to make a religion out of that.

Serene and I will be practicing our comebacks with you . . . and of course, our wild, crazy sister Vange too. She'll be the first to tell you none of us have arrived, we all still mess up . . . often. But together . . . let's be the girls who constantly run back to our wise, Good Shepherd. Let's constantly return to His green pastures. For as His sheep, we hear His voice, and His voice is loving. It is welcoming. It is forgiving. It tells us to return. Then when we mess up, to return again. It lovingly assures us we *are* His new creatures . . . no matter how we feel or how often we haven't measured up. *"Old things have passed away; behold, all things have become new."* (2 Corinthians 5:7)

I WILL CONFIDENTLY SAY:

I'M THAT GIRL WHO SHOVES THE SHAME

I'M THAT GIRL WHO NEVER LIMITS HER COMEBACKS

I'M THAT GIRL WHO PROMPTLY PUTS HER CAPE AND BOOTS BACK ON

I'M THAT GIRL WHO MUTES HER OLD NATURE

I'M THAT GIRL WHO SPEAKS, THINKS, WALKS, MOVES AND EATS IN THE NEW

My Own Declarations

My Own Declarations

My Own Declarations

Continued
Scriptures

"I Am" Verses and Declarations
(continued from page 8)

Genesis 17:1, *"I am Almighty God; walk before Me and be blameless."*

So, I'm that girl who has God "ALMIGHTY" backing her up and leading her forward.

Isaiah 46:9 (NLT), *"Remember the things I have done in the past. For I alone am God! I am God, and there is none like me."*

So, I'm that Girl who remembers the blessings of the Lord and stands in awe of His goodness towards me.

John 11:25, *"Jesus said to her, 'I am the resurrection and the life. He who believes in Me, though he may die, he shall live'."*

So, I'm that Girl who has eternal life . . . and that victory starts now.

John 10:11, *"I am the good shepherd. The good shepherd gives His life for the sheep."*

So, I'm that Girl who is so LOVED that she had someone lay down their life for her. That someone is my Shepherd, who after saving me . . . he leads me . . . and I do not want for anything.

Exodus 34:6 (NLT), *". . . Yahweh! The Lord! The God of compassion and mercy! I am slow to anger and filled with unfailing love and faithfulness."*

So, I'm that Girl who is loved by UNFAILING LOVE and FAITHFULNESS. My God is compassionate towards me as I am toward others.

John 8:58, *"Jesus said to them 'Most assuredly, I say to you, before Abraham was, I AM'."*

So, I'm that Girl whose God was always there . . . the Alpha . . . the Author . . . the Creator.

John 8:12, *"Then Jesus spoke to them again, saying, 'I am the light of the world. He who follows Me shall not walk in darkness, but have the light of life'."*

So, I'm that Girl who no longer walks in darkness but walks "IN" the "light of the world."

Genesis 26:24, *". . . 'I am the God of your father Abraham; do not fear, for I am with you. I will bless you and multiply your descendants . . .'"*

So, I'm that Girl who has been set free from the chains of fear and whose God is with me and longs to bless me and my family.

Exodus 15:26, *". . . 'I am the Lord who heals you'."* Exodus 15:26

So, I'm that Girl who is whole through Christ and claims her promise of healing.

Exodus 20:2, ***"I am the Lord your God, who rescued you from the land of Egypt, the place of your slavery."***

So, I'm that Girl who is no longer chained to the bondage of my old nature with all its old problems. I've been rescued into NEW LIFE!

Exodus 6:2 (NLT), *"And God said to Moses, "I am Yahweh—'the Lord'."*

So, I'm that Girl whose God is Yahweh . . . which can be translated "I AM" and stands for His absolute existence and that He always was and always will be. This name reveals the entirety of His character and carries rich and vivid meaning to my soul.

Exodus 22:27 (NLT), *". . . **I am merciful.**" Exodus 22:27 (NLT)*

So, I'm that Girl who shows great mercy.

Leviticus 18:5 (NLT), *"If you obey my decrees and my regulations, you will find life through them. I am the Lord."*

So, I'm that Girl who obeys the voice of my Lord the "I AM" and has found LIFE in doing so.

Psalm 46:10, "Be still, and know that **I am** God; I will be exalted among the nations, I will be exalted in the earth!"

So, I'm that Girl, even in the midst of the chaos and busyness of life, finds soul rest through the knowledge that my God is the great I Am.

Jeremiah 23:23-24 (Aramaic Bible in Plain English), *"**I am** God who is from the nearness, says the LORD JEHOVAH, and **I am** not God who is from a distance. If a man will hide in secret places, am I not seeing him, says the LORD JEHOVAH? Behold, Heaven and Earth are filled by me says LORD JEHOVAH of Hosts!"*

So, I'm that Girl whose God is near. He doesn't leave me lonely. I am never hidden from the eyes of my Savior.

Ezekiel 12:25, *"For **I am** the LORD. I speak, and the word which I speak will come to pass . . ."*

So, I'm that Girl whose God keeps His Word and I can take all His promises to the bank.

Malachi 3:6, *"For **I am** the LORD, I do not change . . ."*

So, I'm that Girl who can rest in her unchanging God. I know the Word that says, *"Every good and perfect gift is from above, coming down from the Father of lights, who does not change like shifting shadows."* James 1:17

Mark 14:62, *"Jesus said, 'I am. And you will see the Son of Man sitting at the right hand of the Power, and coming with the clouds of heaven'."*

So, I'm that Girl whose Redeemer is sitting at the right hand of the Father and is coming for me, so we can have eternal life together.

John 4:26 (NCV), *"Then Jesus said, "I am he [the Messiah]—I, the one talking to you."*

So, I'm that Girl who dwells in Jesus. He is the Messiah, which means "the Anointed One." He is the anointed Christ. My Savior and Deliverer and He talks with me.

John 6:48 (CEV), *"I am the bread that gives life!"*

So, I'm that Girl who partakes of this LIFE. I have eaten of the Word and savored John 6:35 (CSB), *"'I am the bread of life,' Jesus told them. 'No one who comes to me will ever be hungry, and no one who believes in me will ever be thirsty again'."*

Isaiah 43:11-12 (NLT), *". . . 'I AM the Lord, and there is no other Savior. First I predicted your rescue, then I saved you and proclaimed it to the world. No foreign god has ever done this. You are witnesses that I am the only God,' says the Lord."*

So, I'm that Girl who is truly saved and rescued. The joy and freedom this births within me is a witness that my God is the only Savior.

Isaiah 43:13 (NLT), *"From eternity to eternity I am God. No one can snatch anyone out of my hand. No one can undo what I have done."*

So, I'm that Girl whose redemption can never be undone without me letting go. My God will never let go! His embrace is my lullaby and the melody of my day.

Isaiah 44:24 (NLT), *"This is what the Lord says—your Redeemer and Creator: 'I am the Lord, who made all things. I alone stretched out the heavens. Who was with me when I made the earth?'"*

So, I'm that Girl who is loved by her Creator. If my God stretched out the heavens then He is powerfully able on my behalf.

Isaiah 43:12, *". . . 'Therefore you are My witnesses,' Says the LORD, 'that I am God'."*

So, I'm that Girl who knows the One True God and who seeks to put Him first, above all other distractions.

John 10:9, *"I am the door. If anyone enters by Me, he will be saved, and will go in and out and find pasture."*

So, I'm that Girl who has entered through the only door to be saved. I do not want for I have found my sustaining green pasture.

John 15:1, *"I am the true vine, and My Father is the vinedresser."*

So, I'm that Girl who is grafted into the vine. I bear good fruit. I believe the Word that says in John 15:5 (ESV), *"I am the vine; you are the branches. Whoever abides in me and I in him, he it is that bears much fruit, for apart from me you can do nothing."*

John 14:6, *"Jesus said to him, 'I am the way, the truth, and the life. No one comes to the Father except through Me'."*

So, I'm that Girl who lives in "The Way." I look no further for the truth. I have found true transformation and LIFE through Jesus.

Isaiah 42:8, *"I am the LORD, that is My name; And My glory I will not give to another, Nor My praise to carved images."*

So, I'm that Girl whose Lord is far above carved idols. His name is the one to which sickness, addiction, depression and every other power must bow.

Exodus 3:14 (ESV), *"'God said to Moses, 'I am who I am.' And he said, 'Say this to the people of Israel, 'I am has sent me to you'."*

So, I'm that Girl whose God reveals Himself as "I AM" . . . He exists! He is the fullness of "I AM," complete love . . . complete abundance. He was sent to save me.

I'm That Girl Who Deletes Fear Verses
(continued from page 230)

Psalm 46:1-3, *". . . God is our refuge and strength, A very present help in trouble. Therefore we will not fear, Even though the earth be removed, And though the mountains be carried into the midst of the sea; Though its waters roar and be troubled, Though the mountains shake with its swelling. Selah."*

Genesis 50:21 (ESV), *"So do not fear; I will provide for you and your little ones," Thus he comforted them and spoke kindly to them."*

Matthew 6:34, *"Therefore do not worry about tomorrow, for tomorrow will worry about its own things. Sufficient for the day is its own trouble."*

Deuteronomy 3:22, *"You must not fear them, for the LORD your God Himself fights for you."*

Psalm 27:3 (ESV), *"Though an army encamp against me, my heart shall not fear; though war arise against me, yet I will be confident."*

I'm That Girl Who Defies Anxiety Verses
(continued from page 234)

Psalm 37:11, *"But the meek shall inherit the earth, and shall delight themselves in the abundance of peace."*

Job 25:2 (CEB), *"Supreme power and awe belong to God; he establishes peace on His heights."*

Psalm 119:165, *"Great Peace have those who love Your law, And nothing causes them to stumble."*

Galatians 5:22, *"But the fruit of the Spirit is love, joy, peace . . ."*

Mark 4:39, *"Then He arose and rebuked the wind, and said to the sea, Peace, be still! And the wind ceased and there was a great calm."*

Luke 1:78-79, *"Through the tender mercy of our God, with which the Dayspring from on high has visited us. To give light to those who sit in darkness and the shadow of death, to guide our feet into the way of peace."*

Romans 8:6 (ESV), *"For to set the mind on the flesh is death, but to set the mind on the Spirit is life and peace."*

Isaiah 55:12, *"For you shall go out with joy, And be led out with peace; the mountains and the hills shall break forth into singing before you, and all the trees of the field shall clap their hands."*

Matthew 6:25-27, *"Therefore I say to you, do not worry about your life, what you will eat or what you will drink; nor about your body, what you will put on. Is not life more than food and the body more than clothing? Look at the birds of the air, for they neither sow nor reap nor gather into barns; yet your heavenly Father feeds them. Are you not of more value than they? Which of you by worrying can add one cubit to his stature."*

Luke 24:38, *"And He said to them, "Why are you troubled? And why do doubts arise in your hearts?"*

Psalm 94:19, *"In the multitude of my anxieties within me, Your comforts delight my soul."*

I'm That Girl Who Sheds Depression Verses
(continued from page 238)

Philippians 4:8, *"Finally, brethren, whatever things are true, whatever things are noble, whatever things are just, whatever things are pure, whatever things are lovely, whatever things are of good report, if there is any virtue and if there is anything praiseworthy—meditate on these things."*

Romans 12:2, *"And do not be conformed to this world, but be transformed by the renewing of your mind, that you may prove what is that good and acceptable and perfect will of God."*

Matthew 11:28-30, *"Come to Me, all you who labor and are heavy laden, and I will give you rest. Take My yoke upon you and learn from Me, for I am gentle and lowly in heart, and you will find rest for your souls. For My yoke is easy and My burden is light."*

Jeremiah 29:11, *"For I know the plans that I have for you,' declares the LORD, 'plans for prosperity and not for disaster, to give you a future and a hope."*

John 10:10 (NIV), *"The thief comes only to steal and kill and destroy; I have come that they may have life, and have it to the full."*

Isaiah 40:31, *"But those who wait on the LORD Shall renew their strength; They shall mount up with wings like eagles, They shall run and not be weary, They shall walk and not faint."*

John 10:10, *"The thief does not come except to steal, and to kill, and to destroy. I have come that they may have life, and that they may have it more abundantly."*

Psalm 9:9 (NIV), *"The Lord is a refuge for the oppressed, a stronghold in times of trouble."*

Psalm 23:4 (NIV), *"Even though I walk through the darkest valley, I will fear no evil, for you are with me; your rod and your staff, they comfort me."*

Psalm 30:5, *"... Weeping may endure for a night, But joy comes in the morning."*

Job 25:2 (CEB), *"Supreme power and awe belong to God; he establishes peace on his heights."*

Philippians 4:4, *"Rejoice in the Lord always; again I will say, Rejoice."*

I'm That Girl Who Banishes Bad Moods Verses
(continued from page 242)

We have a ton of extra scriptures for this topic because the Word of God is brimming with encouragement to upgrade our thinking. A renewed mind, determined to think on a higher plane, aligned with Christ, is the key to joy. It opens the door to an overcoming life. Moods and funks are a result of thoughts left to run amuck. A mind amuck is the accuser's greatest tactic. Most of our battles can be won in the mind.

Matthew 12:33, *"Either make the tree good and its fruit good, or else make the tree bad and its fruit bad; for a tree is known by its fruit."*

Proverbs 23:18 (CEB), *"Then you will have a future, and your hope won't be cut off."*

Nahum 1:7, *"The Lord is good, A stronghold in the day of trouble; And He knows those who trust in Him."*

Proverbs 14:30, *"A sound heart is life to the body, But envy is rottenness to the bones."*

Galatians 5:24, *"And those who are Christ's have crucified the flesh with its passions and desires."*

Proverbs 18:2, *"A fool has no delight in understanding, But in expressing his own heart."*

Philippians 4:7, *"And the peace of God, which surpasses all understanding, will guard your hearts and minds through Christ Jesus."*

Proverbs 16:32, *"He who is slow to anger is better than the mighty, And he who rules his spirit than he who takes a city."*

2 Timothy 1:14, *"That good thing which was committed to you, keep by the Holy Spirit who dwells in us."*

2 Peter 1:2, *"Grace and peace be multiplied to you in the knowledge of God and of Jesus our Lord."*

Philippians 1:10, *"That you may approve the things that are excellent, that you may be sincere and without offense till the day of Christ."*

Matthew 9:4, *"But Jesus, knowing their thoughts, said, "Why do you think evil in your hearts?"*

2 Corinthians 10:5, *". . . casting down arguments and every high thing that exalts itself against the knowledge of God, bringing every thought into captivity to the obedience of Christ."*

Psalm 26:2, *"Examine me, O Lord, and prove me; Try my mind and my heart."*

1 John 1:6 (NIV), *"If we claim to have fellowship with him and yet walk in the darkness, we lie and do not live out the truth."*

Philippians 4:8 (NIV), *"Finally, brothers and sisters, whatever is true, whatever is noble, whatever is right, whatever is pure, whatever is lovely, whatever is admirable—if anything is excellent or praiseworthy—think about such things."*

1 Corinthians 16:13 (NIV), *"Be on your guard; stand firm in the faith; be courageous; be strong."*

Proverbs 10:25, *"When the whirlwind passes by, the wicked is no more, But the righteous has an everlasting foundation."*

1 Corinthians 15:58 (NIV), *"Therefore, my dear brothers and sisters, stand firm. Let nothing move you . . ."*

Jude 1:24 (KJV), *"Now unto him that is able to keep you from falling, and to present you faultless before the presence of his glory with exceeding joy,"*

Hebrews 6:19, *"This hope we have as an **anchor of the soul**, both **sure and steadfast**, and which enters the Presence behind the veil."*

Colossians 2:5-7, *"For though I am absent in the flesh, yet I am with you in spirit, rejoicing to see your good order and the steadfastness of your faith in Christ. As you have therefore received Christ Jesus the Lord, so walk in Him, rooted and built up in Him and established in the faith, as you have been taught, abounding in it with thanksgiving."*

Isaiah 50:7, *"For the Lord God will help Me; Therefore I will not be disgraced; Therefore I have set My face like a flint, And I know that I will not be ashamed."*

Job 27:6, *"My righteousness I hold fast, and will not let it go; My heart shall not reproach me as long as I live."*

Job 23:11, *"My foot has held fast to His steps; I have kept His way and not turned aside."*

Isaiah 26:3, *"You will keep him in perfect peace, Whose mind is stayed on You, Because he trusts in You."*

Ephesians 3:17, *"That Christ may dwell in your hearts through faith; that you, being rooted and grounded in love."*

Hebrews 3:14, *"For we have become partakers of Christ if we hold the beginning of our confidence steadfast to the end."*

1 Peter 5:10, *"But may the God of all grace, who called us to His eternal glory by Christ Jesus, after you have suffered a while, perfect, establish, strengthen, and settle you."*

Ephesians 4:14 (ASV), *"That we may be no longer children, tossed to and fro and carried about with every wind of doctrine, by the sleight of men, in craftiness, after the wiles of error."*

Hebrews 10:39 (ASV), *"But we are not of them that shrink back unto perdition; but of them that have faith unto the saving of the soul."*

Psalm 125:1, *"Those who trust in the Lord Are like Mount Zion, Which cannot be moved, but abides forever."*

Psalm 73:28, *"But it is good for me to draw near to God; I have put my trust in the Lord God, That I may declare all Your works."*

Philippians 2:16, *"Holding fast the word of life, so that I may rejoice in the day of Christ that I have not run in vain or labored in vain."*

Proverbs 3:1-2, *"My son, do not forget my law, But let your heart keep my commands; For length of days and long life And peace they will add to you."*

2 Corinthians 13:11, *"Finally, brethren, farewell. Become complete. Be of good comfort, be of one mind, live in peace; and the God of love and peace will be with you."*

Colossians 3:1-2, *"If then you were raised with Christ, seek those things which are above, where Christ is, sitting at the right hand of God. Set your mind on things above, not on things on the earth."*

Psalm 143:10, *"Teach me to do Your will, For You are my God; Your Spirit is good. Lead me in the land of uprightness."*

Philippians 4:9, *"The things which you learned and received and heard and saw in me, these do, and the God of peace will be with you."*

John 15:4 (NIV), *"Remain in me, as I also remain in you. No branch can bear fruit by itself; it must remain in the vine. Neither can you bear fruit unless you remain in me."*

Romans 12:21, *"Do not be overcome by evil, but overcome evil with good."*

Proverbs 4:14, *"Do not enter the path of the wicked, And do not walk in the way of evil."*

Psalm 34:14, *"Depart from evil and do good; Seek peace and pursue it."*

Romans 12:2, *"And do not be conformed to this world, but be transformed by the renewing of your mind, that you may prove what is that good and acceptable and perfect will of God."*

Romans 12:12, *"Rejoicing in hope, patient in tribulation, continuing stead-fastly in prayer."*

Matthew 16:23, *"But He turned and said to Peter, "Get behind Me, Satan! You are an offense to Me, for you are not mindful of the things of God, but the things of men."*

1 Corinthians 13:11, *"When I was a child, I spoke as a child, I understood as a child, I thought as a child; but when I became a man, I put away childish things."*

Colossians 1:21, *"And you, who once were alienated and enemies in your mind by wicked works, yet now He has reconciled."*

Jeremiah 4:14, *"O Jerusalem, wash your heart from wickedness, That you may be saved. How long shall your evil thoughts lodge within you?"*

Proverbs 4:27, *"Do not turn to the right or the left; Remove your foot from evil."*

Psalm 1:2, *"But his delight is in the law of the Lord, And in His law he medi-tates day and night."*

Isaiah 55:8-9, *"For My thoughts are not your thoughts, Nor are your ways My ways," says the Lord. "For as the heavens are higher than the earth, So are My ways higher than your ways, And My thoughts than your thoughts."*

I'm That Girl Who Grabs Joy Verses
(continued from page 246)

Again, lots of leftover verses here that we couldn't fit into the earlier chapter. The words "joy", "joyful", or "rejoice" appear 430 times in the English Standard Version of the Bible. Happiness can be found only ten times. Joy is a spiritual gift and defies circumstances. It is the consequence of the indwelling of the Holy Spirit within us. In the Bible it often refers to the joy "of the Lord". It is not our own joy that we can muster up, but the joy that is of God and from God. Joy cannot be plucked out or stolen. We can only lose it when we let our sight slip from our Father and all that He is for us.

Isaiah 61:10, *"I will greatly rejoice in the LORD, My soul shall be joyful in my God; For He has clothed me with the garments of salvation, He has covered me with the robe of righteousness, As a bridegroom decks himself with ornaments, And as a bride adorns herself with her jewels."*

1 Chronicles 16:27 (NIV), *"Splendor and majesty are before him; strength and JOY are in his dwelling place."*

Psalm 126:5-6, *"Those who sow in tears shall harvest with joyful shouting. He who continually goes forth weeping, Bearing seed for sowing, Shall doubtless come again with rejoicing, Bringing his sheaves with him."*

Zephaniah 3:17, *"The LORD your God in your midst, The Mighty One, will save; He will rejoice over you with gladness, He will quiet you with His love, He will rejoice over you with singing."*

Habakkuk 3:17-19 (NIV), *"Though the fig tree does not bud and there are no grapes on the vines, though the olive crop fails and the fields produce no food, though there are no sheep in the pen and no cattle in the stalls, yet I will rejoice in the Lord, I will be joyful in God my Savior. The sovereign LORD is my strength; he makes my feet like the feet of a deer, he enables me to tread on the heights . . ."*

Galatians 5:22, *"But the fruit of the Spirit is love, joy, peace, patience, kindness, goodness, faithfulness."*

Romans 14:17, *"For the kingdom of God is not eating and drinking, but righteousness and peace and joy in the Holy Spirit."*

Psalm 118:24, *"This is the day which the LORD has made; Let's rejoice and be glad in it."*

Psalm 5:11, *"But let all those rejoice who put their trust in You; Let them ever shout for joy, because You defend them; Let those also who love Your name Be joyful in You."*

Psalm 70:4, *"Let all those who seek You rejoice and be glad in You; And let those who love Your salvation say continually, "Let God be magnified!"."*

I'm That Girl Who Only
Looks Back to Give Thanks Verses
(continued from page 250)

John 10:10, *"The thief does not come except to steal, and to kill, and to destroy. I have come that they may HAVE LIFE, and that they may have it more abundantly."*

Revelation 21:4-5, *"And God will wipe away every tear from their eyes; there shall be no more death, nor sorrow, nor crying. There shall be no more pain, for the former things have passed away. Then He who sat on the throne said, 'Behold, I MAKE ALL THINGS NEW.' And He said to me, 'Write, for these words are true and faithful'."*

Colossians 3:9-10, *"Do not lie to one another, since you have put off the old man with his deeds, and have put on the NEW man who is renewed in knowledge according to the image of Him who created him."*

Romans 12:2, *"And do not be conformed to this world, but be TRANSFORMED by the RENEWING of your mind, that you may prove what is that good and acceptable and perfect will of God."*

John 3:3, *"Jesus answered and said to him, "Most assuredly, I say to you, unless one is BORN AGAIN, he cannot see the Kingdom of God."*

Hebrews 12:1-2, *"Therefore we also, since we are surrounded by so great a cloud of witnesses, let us lay aside every weight, and the sin which so easily ensnares us, and let US RUN with endurance the race that is SET BEFORE US, looking into Jesus, the author and finisher of our faith, who for the joy that was set before Him endured the cross, despising the shame, and He sat down at the right hand of the throne of God."*

Lamentations 3:22-23, *"Through the LORD's mercies we are not consumed, Because His compassions fail not. They ARE NEW EVERY MORNING; Great is Your faithfulness."*

Acts 3:19, *"Repent therefore and be converted, that your sin's may be **blotted out**, so that times of REFRESHING may come from the presence of the Lord."*

2 Peter 3:13 (NIV), *"But in keeping with His promise we are looking forward to a **new** heaven and a **new** earth where righteousness dwells."*

Philippians 4:8, *"Finally, brethren, whatever things are true, whatever things are noble, whatever things are just, whatever things are pure, whatever things are* lovely, whatever things are of good report, if there is any virtue and if there is any-thing praiseworthy—meditate on these things."

Galatians 6:15, *"For in Christ Jesus neither circumcision nor uncircumcision avails anything, but a NEW creation."*

Romans 6:14, *"For sin shall NOT HAVE DOMINION OVER YOU, for you are not under law but under grace."*

Titus 3:5, *"Not by works of righteousness which we have done, but according to His mercy He save us, through the washing of REGENERATION and RENEW-ING of the Holy Spirit."*

Colossians 3:3, *"For you died, and your life is hidden with Christ in God."*

Galatians 2:20, *"I have been crucified with Christ; it is no longer I who live, but Christ lives in me; and the life which I NOW LIVE in the flesh I live by faith in the Son of God, who loved me and gave Himself for me."*

Romans 13:12-13, *"The night is far spent, the day is at hand. Therefore let us cast off the works of darkness, and let us PUT ON THE ARMOR OF LIGHT. Let us walk properly, AS IN THE DAY . . ."*

Romans 6:6, *"Knowing this, that our old man was crucified with Him, that the body of sin might be done away with, that we should no longer be slaves of sin."*

Romans 6:2, *". . . How shall we who DIED to sin LIVE ANY LONGER IN IT."*

Psalm 51:10, *"CREATE in me a clean heart, O God, And RENEW a steadfast spirit within me."*

Psalm 40:3, *"He has put a NEW song in my mouth—Praise to our God; Many will see it and fear, And will trust in the Lord."*

Ezekiel 18:30-32, *". . . Cast away from you all the transgressions which you have committed, and get yourselves a NEW heart and a new spirit. For why should you die, O house of Israel? For I have no pleasure in the death of one who dies,' says the Lord God. 'Therefore TURN and LIVE!'."*

Lamentations 3:22-23, *"The steadfast love of the LORD never ceases; his mer-cies never come to an end; They are NEW EVERY MORNING; great is Your faithfulness."*

2 Corinthians 4:16, *"Therefore we do not lose heart. Even though our outward man is perishing, yet the inward man is being renewed day by day."*

Jeremiah 29:11(ESV), *"For I know the plans I have for you, declares the LORD, plans for welfare and not for evil, to give you a FUTURE and a HOPE."*

Ecclesiastes 3:11, *"He has made everything beautiful in its time. Also He has put eternity in their hearts, except that no one can find out the work that God does from beginning to end."*

Proverbs 3:5-6 (ESV), *"Trust in the LORD with all your heart, and do not lean on your own understanding. In all your ways acknowledge Him, and he will make STRAIGHT YOUR PATHS."*

1 Peter 1:3 (ESV), *"Blessed be the God and Father of our Lord Jesus Christ! According to His great mercy, he has caused us to be BORN AGAIN to a LIVING hope through the resurrection of Jesus Christ from the dead."*

Luke 1:78 (ESV), *"Because of the tender mercy of our God, whereby the sunrise shall visit us from on high."*

Isaiah 65:17, *"For behold, I create new heavens and a new earth; And the former shall not be remembered or come to mind."*

I'm That Girl Who
Walks in Healing Verses
(continued from page 254)

Matthew 4: 23-24 (NIV), *"Jesus went throughout Galilee, teaching in their synagogues, proclaiming the good news of the kingdom, and healing every disease and sickness among the people. News about him spread all over Syria, and the people brought to him all who were ill with various diseases, those suffering severe pain, the demon-possessed, those having seizures, and the paralyzed; and he healed them."*

Matthew 14:14, *"And when Jesus went out He saw a great multitude; and He was moved with compassion for them, and healed their sick."*

Luke 6:19, *"And the whole multitude sought to touch Him, for power went out from Him and healed them all."*

Matthew 10:1 (NIV), *"Jesus called his twelve disciples to him and gave them authority to drive out impure spirits and to heal every disease and sickness."*

Matthew 10:8, *"Heal the sick, cleanse the lepers, raise the dead, cast out demons. Freely you have received, freely give."*

Luke 4:18, *"The Spirit of the Lord is upon me, because He has anointed me to preach the gospel to the poor; He has sent me to heal the brokenhearted, to proclaim liberty to the captives and recovery of sight to the blind, to set at liberty those who are oppressed."*

Acts 4:30-31(NIV), *"Stretch out your hand to heal and perform signs and wonders through the name of your holy servant Jesus." After they prayed, the place where they were meeting was shaken. And they were all filled with the Holy Spirit and spoke the word of God boldly."*

John 14:12, *"Most assuredly, I say to you, he who believes in Me, the works that I do shall he do also; and greater works than these shall he do; because I go unto my Father."*

Malachi 4:2 (NLT), *"But for you who fear My name, The Sun of righteousness will rise with healing in His wings. And you will go free, leaping with joy like calves led out to pasture."*

Proverbs 17:22, *"A merry heart does good, like medicine, but a broken spirit dries the bones."*

James 5:16, *"Confess your trespasses to one another, and pray for one another, that you may be healed. The effective, fervent prayer of a righteous man avails much."*

1 Peter 2:24, *"Who Himself bore our sins in His own body on the tree, that we, having died to sins, might live for righteousness—by whose stripes you were healed."*

Luke 13:10-13, *"Now He was teaching in one of the synagogues on the Sabbath. And behold, there was a woman who had a spirit of infirmity eighteen years, and was bent over and could in no way raise herself up. But when Jesus saw her, He called her to Him and said to her, 'Woman, you are loosed from your infirmity.' And He laid his hands on her, and immediately she was made straight, and glorified God."*

Psalm 146:8, *"The Lord opens the eyes of the blind; The Lord raises those who are bowed down; The Lord loves the righteous."*

Luke 10:9, *"And heal the sick there, and say to them, 'the kingdom of God has come near to you'."*

Exodus 15:26, *"If you diligently heed the voice of the Lord your God and do what is right in His sight, give ear to His commandments and keep all His statutes, I will put none of the diseases on you which I have brought on the Egyptians. For I am he Lord who heals you."*

Exodus 23:25, *"So you shall serve the LORD your God, and He will bless your bread and your water. And I will take sickness away from the midst of you."*

Jeremiah 30:17, *"But I will restore you to health and heal your wounds, declares the LORD . . ."*

Isaiah 57:18-19 (NIV), *"I have seen their ways, but I will heal them; I will guide them and restore comfort to Israel's mourners, creating praise on their lips. Peace, peace, to those far and near,"* says the Lord. *"And I will heal them."*

Isaiah 58:8, *"Then your light shall break forth like the morning, your healing shall spring forth speedily, and your righteousness shall go before you; The glory of the LORD shall be your rear guard."*

Psalm 30:2, *"O LORD my God, I cried out to You, And You healed me."*

I'm That Girl Who Gets
Her Hopes Up Verses
(continued from page 258)

Colossians 1:23, *"If indeed you continue in the faith, grounded and steadfast, and are not moved away from the hope of the gospel which you heard, which was preached to every creature under heaven, of which I, Paul, became a minister."*

Colossians 1:27, *"To them God willed to make known what are the riches of the glory of this mystery among the Gentiles: which is Christ in you, the hope of glory."*

Psalm 42:11, *"Why are you cast down, O my soul? And why are you disquieted within me? Hope in God; For I shall yet praise Him, The help of my countenance and my God."*

Proverbs 13:12, *"Hope deferred makes the heart sick, But when the desire comes, it is a tree of life."*

Lamentations 3:24, *"The Lord is my portion,"* says my soul, *"Therefore I hope in Him!"*

Romans 5:3-4, *"And not only that, but we also glory in tribulations, knowing that tribulation produces perseverance; and perseverance, character; and character, hope."*

Romans 5:5, *"Now hope does not disappoint, because the love of God has been poured out in our hearts by the Holy Spirit who was given to us."*

Jeremiah 29:11, *"For I know the thoughts that I think toward you, says the Lord, thoughts of peace and not of evil, to give you a future and a hope."*

Hebrews 10:23, *"Let us hold fast the confession of our hope without wavering, for He who promised is faithful."*

Psalm 119:114, *"You are my hiding place and my shield; I hope in Your word."*

Psalm 31:24, *"Be of good courage, And He shall strengthen your heart, All you who hope in the Lord."*

Psalm 130:5, *"I wait for the Lord, my soul waits, And in His word I do hope."*

Psalm 130:7, *"O Israel, hope in the Lord; For with the Lord there is mercy, And with Him is abundant redemption."*

Hebrews 3:6, *"But Christ as a Son over His own house, whose house we are if we hold fast the confidence and the rejoicing of the hope firm to the end."*

Psalm 33:18, *"Behold, the eye of the Lord is on those who fear Him, On those who hope in His mercy."*

Psalm 33:22, *"Let Your mercy, O Lord, be upon us, Just as we hope in You."*

1 Peter 3:15 (NIV), *"But in your hearts revere Christ as Lord. Always be prepared to give an answer to everyone who asks you to give the reason for the hope that you have. But do this gentleness and respect."*

1 Corinthians 13:6-7 (NIV), *"Love does not delight in evil but rejoices with the truth. It always protects, always trusts, always hopes, always perseveres."*

Jeremiah 17:7, *"Blessed is the man who trusts in the Lord, And whose hope is the Lord."*

Hebrews 11:11, *"By faith Sarah herself also received strength to conceive seed, and she bore a child when she was past the age, because she judged Him faithful who had promised."*

Romans 15:4, *"For whatever things were written before were written for our learning, that we through the patience and comfort of the Scriptures might have hope."*

Romans 12:12, *"Rejoicing in hope, patient in tribulation, continuing steadfastly in prayer."*

Psalm 39:7, *"And now, Lord, what do I wait for? My hope is in You."*

1 Corinthians 13:13, *"And now abide faith, hope, love, these three; but the greatest of these is love."*

Proverbs 24:14, *"So shall the knowledge of wisdom be to your soul; If you have found it, there is a prospect, And your hope will not be cut off."*

Titus 3:7, *"That having been justified by His grace we should become heirs according to the hope of eternal life."*

Hebrews 6:19, *"This hope we have as an anchor of the soul, both sure and steadfast, and which enters the Presence behind the veil."*

1 Thessalonians 5:8, *"But let us who are of the day be sober, putting on the breastplate of faith and love, and as a helmet the hope of salvation."*

Titus 2:13, *"Looking for the blessed hope and glorious appearing of our great God and Savior Jesus Christ."*

Titus 1:2, *"In hope of eternal life which God, who cannot lie, promised before time began."*

1 John 3:3, *"And everyone who has this hope in Him purifies himself, just as He is pure."*

1 Peter 1:13, *"Therefore gird up the loins of your mind, be sober, and rest your hope fully upon the grace that is to be brought to you at the revelation of Jesus Christ."*

Psalm 146:5, *"Happy is he who has the God of Jacob for his help, Whose hope is in the Lord his God."*

Psalm 62:5, *"My soul, wait silently for God alone, For my expectation is from Him."*

1 Thessalonians 4:13, *"But I do not want you to be ignorant, brethren, concerning those who have fallen asleep, lest you sorrow as others who have no hope."*

Philippians 3:13-14, *"Brethren, I do not count myself to have apprehended; but one thing I do, forgetting those things which are behind and reaching forward to those things which are ahead, I press toward the goal for the prize of the upward call of God in Christ Jesus."*

Romans 4:18, *"Who, contrary to hope, in hope believed, so that he became the father of many nations, according to what was spoken, 'So shall your descendants be'."*

Proverbs 10:28, *"The hope of the righteous will be gladness, But the expectation of the wicked will perish."*

Zechariah 9:12, *"Return to the stronghold, You prisoners of hope. Even today I declare That I will restore double to you."*

Job 13:15, *"Though He slay me, yet will I trust Him. Even so, I will defend my own ways before Him."*

Numbers 23:19, *"God is not a man, that He should lie, Nor a son of man, that He should repent. Has He said, and will He not do? Or has He spoken, and will He not make it good."*

Psalm 78:7, *"That they may set their hope in God, And not forget the works of God, But keep His commandments."*

Hebrews 6:11, *"And we desire that each one of you show the same diligence to the full assurance of hope until the end."*

1 John 5:14-15, *"Now this is the confidence that we have in Him, that if we ask anything according to His will, He hears us. And if we know that He hears us, whatever we ask, we know that we have the petitions that we have asked of Him."*

I'm That Girl Who Heals Her Home Verses
(continued from page 262)

2 Chronicles 7:15-16, *"Now My eyes will be open and My ears attentive to prayer made in this place. For now I have chosen and sanctified this house, that My name may be there forever; and My eyes and My heart will be there perpetually."*

Nehemiah 4:14 (NIV), *". . . Remember the Lord, who is great and awesome, and fight for your brothers, your sons and your daughters, your wives and your homes."*

Ephesians 2:20-22, *"Having been built on the foundation of the apostles and prophets, Jesus Christ Himself being the chief corner stone, in whom the whole building, being fitted together, grows into a holy temple in the Lord, in whom you also are being built together for a dwelling place of God in the Spirit."*

1 Corinthians 3:9, *"For we are God's fellow workers; you are God's field, you are God's building."*

Matthew 12:25, *"But Jesus knew their thoughts, and said to them: Every kingdom divided against itself is brought to desolation, and every city or house divided against itself will not stand."*

Hebrews 3:4, *"For every house is built by someone, but He who built all things is God."*

Psalm 127:1, *"Unless the Lord builds the house, They labor in vain who build it; Unless the Lord guards the city, The watchman stays awake in vain."*

Isaiah 32:18 (NIV), *"My people will live in peaceful dwelling places, in secure homes, in undisturbed places of rest."*

Proverbs 10:11 (NIV), *"The mouth of the righteous is a fountain of life . . ."*

2 Samuel 7:29, *"Now therefore, let it please You to bless the house of Your servant, that it may continue forever before You; for You, O Lord God, have spoken it, and with Your blessing let the house of Your servant be blessed forever."*

Deuteronomy 6:5-7, *"You shall love the Lord your God with all your heart, with all your soul, and with all your strength. And these words which I command you today shall be in your heart. You shall teach them diligently to your children, and shall talk of them when you sit in your house, when you walk by the way, when you lie down, and when you rise up."*

1 Thessalonians 5:11, *"Therefore comfort each other and edify one another, just as you also are doing."*

Hebrews 3:13, *"But exhort one another daily, while it is called 'Today,' lest any of you be hardened through the deceitfulness of sin."*

Ephesians 4:32, *"And be kind to one another, tenderhearted, forgiving one another, just as God in Christ forgave you."*

Isaiah 41:6, *"Everyone helped his neighbor, And said to his brother, 'Be of good courage!'."*

2 Corinthians 1:4, *"Who comforts us in all our tribulation, that we may be able to comfort those who are in any trouble, with the comfort with which we ourselves are comforted by God."*

Hebrews 10:24, *"And let us consider one another in order to stir up love and good works."*

1 Thessalonians 3:12, *"And may the Lord make you increase and abound in love to one another and to all . . ."*

Romans 12:10, *"Be kindly affectionate to one another with brotherly love, in honor giving preference to one another."*

James 5:9, *"Do not grumble against one another, brethren, lest you be condemned. Behold, the Judge is standing at the door!"*

1 Peter 4:8, *"And above all things have fervent love for one another, for love will cover a multitude of sins."*

1 Peter 4:10, *"As each one has received a gift, minister it to one another, as good stewards of the manifold grace of God."*

Ephesians 5:19 (ASV), *"Speaking one to another in psalms and hymns and spiritual songs, singing and making melody with your heart to the Lord."*

1 Thessalonians 5:14, *"Now we exhort you, brethren, warn those who are unruly, comfort the fainthearted, uphold the weak, be patient with all."*

John 13:14, *"If I then, your Lord and Teacher, have washed your feet, you also ought to wash one another's feet."*

Romans 12:10, *"Be kindly affectionate to one another with brotherly love, in honor giving preference to one another."*

Galatians 5:13, *"For you, brethren, have been called to liberty; only do not use liberty as an opportunity for the flesh, but through love serve one another."*

Philippians 2:3, *"Let nothing be done through selfish ambition or conceit, but in lowliness of mind let each esteem others better than himself."*

Colossians 3:13, *"Bearing with one another, and forgiving one another, if anyone has a complaint against another; even as Christ forgave you, so you also must do."*

I'm That Girl Who Has Chosen Faith Verses
(continued from page 266)

Hebrews 11:1, *"Now faith is the substance of things hoped for, the evidence of things not seen."*

John 14:12, *"Most assuredly, I say to you, he who believes in Me, the works that I do he will do also; and greater works than these he will do, because I go to My Father."*

Romans 10:10, *"For with the heart one believes unto righteousness, and with the mouth confession is made unto salvation."*

Luke 1:37, *"For with God nothing will be impossible."*

Mark 11:22-24, *"So Jesus answered and said to them, "Have faith in God. For assuredly, I say to you, whoever says to this mountain, 'Be removed and be cast into the sea,' and does not doubt in his heart, but believes that those things he says will be done, he will have whatever he says. Therefore I say to you, whatever things you ask when you pray, believe that you receive them, and you will have them."*

Matthew 17:20, *". . . for assuredly, I say to you, if you have faith as a mustard seed, you will say to this mountain, 'Move from here to there,' and it will move; and nothing will be impossible for you . . ."*

Matthew 21:22, *"And whatever things you ask in prayer, believing, you will receive."*

Romans 10:17, *"So then faith comes by hearing, and hearing by the word of God."*

Ephesians 2:8, *"For by grace you have been saved through faith, and that not of yourselves; it is the gift of God."*

Romans 1:17, *"For in it the righteousness of God is revealed from faith to faith; as it is written, The just shall live by faith."*

James 1:5-8, *"If any of you lacks wisdom, let him ask of God, who gives to all liberally and without reproach, and it will be given to him. But let him ask in faith, with no doubting, for he who doubts is like a wave of the sea driven and tossed by the wind. For let not that man suppose that he will receive anything from the Lord; he is a double-minded man, unstable in all his ways."*

Philippians 4:13, *"I can do all things through Christ who strengthens me."*

Psalm 86:11, *"Teach me Your way, O Lord; I will walk in Your truth; Unite my heart to fear Your name."*

1 Timothy 6:12, *"Fight the good fight of faith, lay hold on eternal life, to which you were also called and have confessed the good confession in the presence of many witnesses."*

Galatians 2:20 (NIV), *"I have been crucified with Christ and I no longer live, but Christ lives in me. The life I now live in the body, I live by faith in the Son of God, who loved me and gave himself for me."*

Luke 17:5, *"The apostles said to the Lord, ‹Increase our faith!›."*

Ephesians 3:16-17 (NIV), *"I pray that out of his glorious riches he may strengthen you with power through his Spirit in your inner being, so that Christ may dwell in your hearts through faith. And I pray that you, being rooted and established in love."*

James 1:3, *"Knowing that the testing of your faith produces patience."*

1 Peter 1:8-9 (NIV), *"Though you have not seen him, you love him; and even though you do not see him now, you believe in him and are filled with an inexpressible and glorious joy, for you are receiving the end result of your faith, the salvation of your souls."*

1 John 5:4, *"For whatever is born of God overcomes the world. And this is the victory that has overcome the world—our faith."*

1 Timothy 6:12, *"Fight the good fight of faith, lay hold on eternal life, to which you were also called and have confessed the good confession in the presence of many witnesses."*

Galatians 3:26-27 (NIV), *"So in Christ Jesus you are all children of God through faith, for all of you who were baptized into Christ have clothed yourselves with Christ."*

James 5:14-15, *"Is anyone among you sick? Let him call for the elders of the church, and let them pray over him, anointing him with oil in the name of the Lord. And the prayer of faith will save the sick, and the Lord will raise him up. And if he has committed sins, he will be forgiven."*

Mark 16:16, *"He who believes and is baptized will be saved; but he who does not believe will be condemned."*

James 2:17 (NIV), *"In the same way, faith by itself, if it is not accompanied by action, is dead."*

Hebrews 12:2 (NIV), *"Fixing our eyes on Jesus, the pioneer and perfecter of faith. For the joy set before him he endured the cross, scorning its shame, and sat down at the right hand of the throne of God."*

John 7:38 (NIV), *"Whoever believes in me, as Scripture has said, rivers of living water will flow from within them."*

John 6:29, *"Jesus answered and said to them, 'This is the work of God, that you believe in Him whom He sent'."*

2 Thessalonians 1:3 (NIV), *"We ought always to thank God for you, brothers and sisters, and rightly so, because your faith is growing more and more, and the love all of you have for one another is increasing."*

Romans 10:9 (NIV), *"If you declare with your mouth, 'Jesus is Lord,' and believe in your heart that God raised him from the dead, you will be saved."*

Luke 8:50, *"But when Jesus heard it, He answered him, saying, 'Do not be afraid; only believe, and she will be made well'."*

1 John 5:5 (NIV), *"Who is it that overcomes the world? Only the one who believes that Jesus is the Son of God."*

Galatians 3:22 (NIV), *"But Scripture has locked up everything under the control of sin, so that what was promised, being given through faith in Jesus Christ, might be given to those who believe."*

Romans 1:16, *"For I am not ashamed of the gospel, for it is the power of God for salvation to everyone who believes . . ."*

Romans 5:1, *"Therefore, having been justified by faith, we have peace with God through our Lord Jesus Christ."*

Habakkuk 2:4 (NIV), *"'See, the enemy is puffed up; his desires are not upright—but the righteous person will live by his faithfulness'."*

Mark 10:52, *"Then Jesus said to him, 'Go your way; your faith has made you well.' And immediately he received his sight and followed Jesus on the road."*

Galatians 5:6, *"For in Christ Jesus neither circumcision nor uncircumcision avails anything, but faith working through love."*

Mark 1:15 (NIV), *"'The time has come,' he said. The kingdom of God has come near. Repent and believe the good news!'"*

Visit **www.trimhealthymama.com** for all archived episodes of the Trim Healthy Podcast, the free THM Food Analyzer App, cooking videos with Serene and Pearl, the store with other books by the authors and ALL the Trim Healthy things! There you can also find locations for the first two Blue Butterfly Cafes and future locations to come.

Coming 2022

Trim Healthy Wisdom

By Pearl Barrett

Your guide through challenging hormonal
seasons and tough weight stalls